Lecture Notes of the Institute for Computer Sciences, Social Informatics and Telecommunications Engineering   **345**

More information about this series at http://www.springer.com/series/8197

Luca Foschini · Mohamed El Kamili (Eds.)

Ad Hoc Networks

12th EAI International Conference, ADHOCNETS 2020
Paris, France, November 17, 2020
Proceedings

 Springer

Editors
Luca Foschini (ORCID)
DISI
University of Bologna
Bologna, Italy

Mohamed El Kamili (ORCID)
Higher School of Technology
Hassan II University of Casablanca
Casablanca, Morocco

ISSN 1867-8211 ISSN 1867-822X (electronic)
Lecture Notes of the Institute for Computer Sciences, Social Informatics
and Telecommunications Engineering
ISBN 978-3-030-67368-0 ISBN 978-3-030-67369-7 (eBook)
https://doi.org/10.1007/978-3-030-67369-7

This Springer imprint is published by the registered company Springer Nature Switzerland AG
The registered company address is: Gewerbestrasse 11, 6330 Cham, Switzerland

Preface

We are delighted to introduce the proceedings of the 12th edition of the European Alliance for Innovation (EAI) International Conference on Ad Hoc Networks (AdHocNets 2020). The aim of the annual AdHocNets conference is to provide a forum that brings together researchers and engineers from academia, government laboratories as well as industry to meet, network, exchange ideas and present their recent research work, and discuss future directions on all aspects of ad hoc networks.

An ad hoc network is a wireless system in which mobile or static nodes are connected using wireless links and cooperate to self-organize into a network without the requirement for any infrastructure such as access points or base stations. In recent years, ad hoc networks have been attracting increased attention from the research and engineering communities. The distributed and multi-hop nature of ad hoc networking as well as the highly dynamic topology of an ad hoc network due to node mobility has introduced many formidable challenges such as scalability, quality of service, reliability and security, and energy-constrained operations for the network. Ad hoc networking covers a variety of network paradigms including mobile ad hoc networks (MANETs), wireless sensor networks (WSNs), vehicular ad hoc networks (VANETs), airborne networks, underwater networks, underground networks, personal area networks, and home networks, etc. It promises a wide range of applications in civilian, commercial, and military areas.

The technical program of AdHocNets 2020 consisted of 16 full papers. Aside from the high-quality technical paper presentations, the technical program also featured two keynote speeches, a tutorial talk, and a technical workshop. The two keynote speakers were Prof. Shiwen Mao, from Auburn University, Auburn, AL, USA and Prof. Cheng Li, Head of the Department of Electrical and Computer Engineering, Memorial University of Newfoundland, St. John's, Canada. Dr. Sahar Hoteit, an associate professor at Université Paris Saclay-CentraleSupélec, presented the tutorial talk. The workshop organized were the Cooperative vehicular networking (CVNET) is widely acknowledged as a key enabler of the next generation of Intelligent Transportation Systems (ITS), known as Cooperative-ITS. The CVNET workshop was intended to cover all aspects of vehicular communication technologies and cooperative V2X systems. It aimed to bring together engineers and scientists from both academia and industry to exchange ideas and foster discussion about the main challenges facing the deployment of C-ITS.

Coordination with the steering chairs, Imrich Chlamtac, Shiwen Mao, and Jun Zheng was essential for the success of the conference. We sincerely appreciate their constant support and guidance. It was also a great pleasure to work with such an excellent organizing committee team for their hard work in organizing and supporting the conference. In particular, the Technical Program Committee, led by our TPC Co-Chairs, Dr. Moayad Aloqaily, Dr. Abdellatif Kobbane, and Dr. Feng Yan who completed the peer-review process of technical papers and made a high-quality technical program. We are also grateful to Conference General Chair, Professor Jalel Ben-Othman, for his support and to all the authors who submitted their papers to the AdHocNets 2020 conference and workshops.

We strongly believe that the AdHocNets conference provides a good forum for all researchers, developers, and practitioners to discuss all scientific and technological aspects that are relevant to ad hoc networks. We also expect that future AdHocNets conferences will be as successful and stimulating, as indicated by the contributions presented in this volume.

Mohamed El Kamili
Luca Foschini

Conference Organization

Steering Committee

Imrich Chlamtac	Bruno Kessler Professor, University of Trento, Italy
Shiwen Mao	Auburn University, USA
Jun Zheng	Southeast University, China

Organizing Committee

General Chair

Jalel Ben-Othman — Université Paris-Saclay, France

TPC Chair and Co-chairs

Abdellatif Kobbane	ENSIAS, Mohammed V University of Rabat, Morocco
Feng Yan	Southeast University, China
Moayad Aloqaily	Al Ain University, Abu Dhabi, UAE

Local Chair

Sahar Hoteit — Université Paris-Saclay, France

Workshops Chair

Ismail Berrada — Mohammed VI Polytechnic University, Morocco

Publicity and Social Media Chairs

Hyunbum Kim	Incheon National University, South Korea
Khalil Ibrahimi	Ibn Tofail University, Morocco
M. Satheesh Kumar	National Engineering College, India
Safa Otoum	University of Ottawa, Canada

Publications Chairs

Luca Foschini	University of Bologna, Italy
Mohamed El Kamili	Higher School of Technology, Hassan II University of Casablanca, Morocco

Web Chairs

Ouns Bouachir	Zayed University, Dubai, UAE
Amine Abouaomar	ENSIAS, Mohammed V University of Rabat, Morocco

Tutorials Chair

Lynda Mokdad   University of Paris-Est, France

Technical Program Committee

Omar Ait Oualhaj	Qatar University, Qatar
Tarik Moufakir	ETS, University of Quebec, Canada
Mohammad Bany Taha	University of Quebec, Canada
Yaser Jararweh	Duquesne University, USA
Rasheed Hussain	Innopolis University, Russia
Issam Jabri	Al Yamamah University, KSA
Abdelrahman Elfaki	University of Tabuk, KSA
Leyan Zhangswu	Australia
Ismaeel Al Ridhawi	KCST, Kuwait
Abdalraheem Alsmadi	Jordan University of Science and Technology, Jordan
Mohammad Alsmirat	Jordan University of Science and Technology, Jordan
Venkatraman Balasubramanian	Arizona State University, USA
Abderrahime Filali	Université de Sherbrooke, Canada
Vahideh Hayyolalam	Koç University, Turkey
Bouchaib Assila	ENSIAS, Mohammed V University of Rabat, Morocco
Mohamed El Kamili	Higher School of Technology, Hassan II University of Casablanca, Morocco
Safae Lhazmir	ENSIAS, Mohammed V University of Rabat, Morocco
Essaid Sabir	ENSEM, Hassan II University of Casablanca, Morocco
Haya Elayan	Altibbi, Jordan
Arun Samuel	National Engineering College, India
Suthendran Kannan	Kalasalingam Academy of Research and Education, India
Ashu Sharma	Mindtree, India
Zakaria Alomari	ÉTS, University of Quebec, Canada
Taqwa Hariguna	Universitas Amikom Purwokerto, Indonesia
Mariame Amine	ENSIAS, Mohammed V University of Rabat, Morocco
Bohong Xiang	Southeast University, China
Yaping Zhu	Tongji University, China
Abderrahime Filali	Université de Sherbrooke, Canada
Geng Chen	Shandong University of Science and Technology, China
Zhaoming Ding	Southeast University, China
Yassine Ben-aboud	International University of Rabat, Morocco
Amine Abouaomar	ENSIAS, Mohammed V University of Rabat, Morocco
Haythem Bany Salameh	Al Ain University, UAE
Umarani P.	Vellore Institute of Technology, India
Prithivirajan Velraju	CMR Engineering College, India
Andree E. Widjaja	Universitas Pelita Harapan, Italy

Wang Cong	Southeast University, China
Zhixu Cheng	Southeast University, China
Jun Wu	Hangzhou Dianzi University, China
Imen Jemili	University of Carthage, Tunisia
Toufik Ahmed	CNRS LaBRI Lab, France
Amina Adadi	Sidi Mohammed Ben Abdellah University, Morocco
Rachid Oucheikh	Sidi Mohammed Ben Abdellah University, Morocco
Nisrine Dad	Sidi Mohammed Ben Abdellah University, Morocco
Afaf Bouhoute	Sidi Mohammed Ben Abdellah University, Morocco
Kaoutar Sefrioui Boujemaa	FSDM, University Sidi Mohamed Ben Abdellah, Morocco

Contents

Ad Hoc Networks

An IoT-Based Non-invasive Diabetics Monitoring System
for Crucial Conditions 3
   Hermon Yehdego, Safa Otoum, and Omar Alfandi

Model-Based and Machine Learning Approaches for Designing Caching
and Routing Algorithms.................................... 16
   Adita Kulkarni and Anand Seetharam

New Results on Q-Routing Protocol for Wireless Networks 29
   Alexis Bitaillou, Benoît Parrein, and Guillaume Andrieux

Vehicle Software Update over ICN Architectures 44
   Ali Elgammal, Mena Safwat, Wael Badawy, Eslam G. AbdAllah,
   Marianne A. Azer, and Changcheng Huang

Joint Mobility-Aware UAV Placement and Routing in Multi-Hop UAV
Relaying Systems 55
   Anousheh Gholami, Nariman Torkzaban, John S. Baras,
   and Chrysa Papagianni

Analysis and Performance of Topology Inference in Mobile
Ad Hoc Networks....................................... 70
   J. David Brown, Mazda Salmanian, and Tricia J. Willink

A Stochastic Traffic Model for Congestion Detection
in Multi-lane Highways................................... 87
   El Joubari Oumaima, Ben Othman Jalel, and Vèque Véronique

Flexibility of Decentralized Energy Restoration in WSNs.............. 100
   Osama I. Aloqaily

Carrot and Stick: Incentivizing Cooperation Between Nodes in Multihop
Wireless Ad Hoc Networks 116
   Karol Rydzewski

Cost-Effective Controller Placement Problem for Software Defined
Multihop Wireless Networks 130
   Afsane Zahmatkesh, Thomas Kunz, and Chung-Horng Lung

Efficient Backbone Routing in Hierarchical MANETs 147
   Thomas Kunz

Transmission Power-Control Certificate Omission in Vehicular
Ad Hoc Networks... 164
Emmanuel Charleson Dapaah, Parisa Memarmoshrefi,
and Dieter Hogrefe

CVNET'2020: The 1st International Workshop on Cooperative Vehicular NETworking

Analyzing Driving Behavior: Towards Dynamic Driver Profiling 179
Anas Ouardini, Imane El Ouazzany Ech-chahedy, Afaf Bouhoute,
Ismail Berrada, and Mohamed El Kamili

Energy Efficient Adaptive GPS Sampling Using Accelerometer Data....... 191
Saad Ezzini and Ismail Berrada

Deep Anomaly Detector Based on Spatio-Temporal Clustering
for Connected Autonomous Vehicles............................ 201
Rachid Oucheikh, Mouhsene Fri, Fayçal Fedouaki, and Mustapha Hain

Cacao, a CAN-Bus Simulation Platform for Secured
Vehicular Communication 213
Olivier Cros, Alexandre Thiroux, and Gabriel Chênevert

Author Index 225

Ad Hoc Networks

An IoT-Based Non-invasive Diabetics Monitoring System for Crucial Conditions

Hermon Yehdego, Safa Otoum$^{(\boxtimes)}$, and Omar Alfandi

College of Technological Innovation (CTI), Zayed University,
Dubai, UAE
{m80007275,Safa.Otoum,Omar.AlFandi}@zu.ac.ae

Abstract. Diabetes is among the major chronic disease around the world since the Glucose level could change drastically and lead to critical conditions reaching to death sometimes. To avoid this, diabetes patient are always advised to track their glucose level at least three times a day. Fingertip pricking - as the traditional method for glucose level tracking - leads patients to be distress and it might infect the skin. In some cases, tracking the glucose level might be a hard job especially if the patient is a child. In this manuscript, we present an optimum solution to this drawback by adopting the Wireless Sensor Network (WSN)-based non-invasive strategies. Near-Infrared (NIR) -as an optical method of the non-invasive technique - has been adopted to help diabetic patients in continuously monitoring their blood without pain. The proposed solution will alert the patients' parents or guardians of their situation when they about to reach critical conditions specially at night by sending alarms and notifications by Short Messages (SMS) along with the patients current location to up to three people.

Keywords: Wireless Sensor Network (WSN) · Healthcare application · Diabetes · Non-Invasive · Blood glucose · Near Infrared Spectroscopy (NIRS) · IR sensor

1 Introduction

Diabetes is one of the major chronic diseases which could lead to different complication and risk to human life [1]. Even though diabetes is not as fatal as other chronic diseases, it could cause a person with a major complex disease like heart disease, stroke, kidney failure and blindness. Diabetes happen when the body either produce insufficient insulin or produce the insulin effectively. For this, the glucose level becomes abnormally high and as a result the patient has to take extra insulin by injection to reduce the glucose level. To control and balance glucose levels in the blood, diabetic patients have to manage their glucose levels throughout the day. Most diabetic patients forced to use the obtrusive technique (prick their finger) at least three times a day to know their glucose level which it always make the patient to be distress and also cause infection of the skin

© ICST Institute for Computer Sciences, Social Informatics and Telecommunications Engineering 2021
Published by Springer Nature Switzerland AG 2021. All Rights Reserved
L. Foschini and M. El Kamili (Eds.): ADHOCNETS 2020, LNICST 345, pp. 3–15, 2021.
https://doi.org/10.1007/978-3-030-67369-7_1

in the pricked area of the body. Thus, this paper has replaced this method by a non-obtrusive methods that could be comfortable to measure blood glucose levels. As blood is not needed in a non obtrusive method, the patient does not need to cut their finger every time they want to know their sugar level. It helps a diabetic patient to detect their glucose level, without any pain, distress and being infected with other diseases.

Knowing the hardship of diabetic life living with needles, different people have been trying to replace the obtrusive method with a different kind of non-obtrusive technology i.e. Polarization change, Raman Spectroscopy, Fluorescent spectroscopy, Near-infrared spectroscopy (NIRS), Mid-infrared spectroscopy, Bio-impedance spectroscopy, spit as analytic liquid and warm discharge spectroscopy [2]. Those non-obtrusive technologies replace blood with spit, sweat, skin, eye, fingertip, ear cartilage and others for glucose level detection. In this paper non-obtrusive prototype utilizing NIRS methodology is proposed. NIRS methodology is one of the most painless and comfortable non-invasive blood glucose measuring technology than the others.

Most non-invasive blood glucose detecting technology has to be implemented inside the skin and some of them are made as lenses to put in the eyes. Even though they replace the painful finger pricking method of glucose measuring, the patients don't get comfortable to use them every day. Therefore, as Near-Infrared (NIR) use of intensive light to penetrate the skin and detect glucose level, it will be the most pain-free and promising method of glucose measurement. NIR can penetrate through the skin and detect the glucose level when its range is between 650–1350 nm [3]. It has been used as a sensor that reads the glucose level, by applying them in the thinner part of the body i.e. fingertip, forearm, earlobe etc. NIR gives accurate glucose reading when it applies to the boneless part of our body. NIRS methodology detects the glucose level by placing NIR transmitter radiation of 950 nm from one side of the finger. The other side of the finger places NIR receiver (photo-diode) radiation of 900 nm to receive the attenuated light. The change in the intensity of NIR light received BY the photo-detector after passing through the finger used to detect the amount of glucose level in a person. NIR method have also more advantages in sensitivity, complexity, power consumption, cost, and accuracy than the other non-obtrusive glucose detection methodology.

In this manuscript, we used NIR as a biosensor to detect the glucose level in a diabetic patient. As NIR is pain-free and doesn't cause skin infection, a diabetic patients will be able to wear this device 24/7 h a day in their wrist as watches. The device will be able to detect the glucose level of a person every 30 min or could configure it as a preference when to send the glucose reading. As this device send the glucose reading every 30 min, the patient can detect his glucose before he reaches Hypoglycemia (when blood sugar drops below 4 mmol/L) and Hyperglycemia (when blood sugar is above 11.0 mmol/L two hours after a meal). This device is mostly useful for pediatric age patients because they don't understand when their sugar level starts to drop or go high. Thus, this device will alert the parent by setting the alarm to go off when their child reaches

Hypoglycemia or Hyperglycemia, especially at night. Also, this device will help the parents or guardians to monitor the glucose level of their child remotely when he is away from them. It will start to alert them by sending SMS attaching with the current location of their child if the sugar level of their child starts to drop while he away.

The organization of this manuscript is as follows: Sect. 2 outlines the related works in the area. Section 3 presents the used techniques in this paper as well as the proposed approach and Sect. 4 analyzes the performance evaluation of the proposed approach. Finally, we present the conclusion in Sect. 5.

2 Related Works

There is a long history of using sensors in healthcare and medical applications [4–8] and [9]. Sensors can provide patients and their healthcare providers better understanding into the health states that are crucial to detect and diagnose. Recently, we have seen huge innovations in health information technology [10, 11]. The authors in [12] reviewed these technologies in term of health sensing, healthcare data analytics, and the use of cloud computing.

The work in [5] proposed the EPMS which is a WSN-based healthcare monitoring application for epilepsy patients which focused on decreasing the response time for the sudden seizures, protect patients against possible severe consequences and help them become comfortable with the monitoring process. The authors in [13] presented the design and development of a sensor-based system to detect blood glucose non-invasively using NIR radiation using spectroscopic refection analysis. The authors in [14] and [15] implemented noninvasive blood glucose monitoring device using NIR light which is based on optical transmission and radiation respectively. The work in [16] proposed the IR sensor to detect blood glucose level. In [17], the work proposed a detection system for the glucose level by using infrared light (NIR). In [17], as in [18], the authors proposed mechanisms for detecting glucose level by using infrared light (NIR). In their work they used urine samples instead of blood. The works in [19–21] and [22] adopted the notification properties. In [19], the authors proposed a home fire alarm system that notify the home owners about the fire detection, while in [22], the authors proposed an automatic vehicle accident detection and message sending.

To the best of our knowledge, an IoT-based diabetes detection system that use IR sensors, notify the patients guardians and send the current location of the patients still an open research issue.

3 Proposed Solution

3.1 Proposed Approach

There are a lot of non-obtrusive technologies built in order to get over the pain and distress that patients get from the pricking finger method of detecting the glucose level. NIRS techniques are the most pain free and can detect the glucose without harming the skin. In this manuscript, we use the NIRS method to build a bio-sensor for glucose measuring where the sensor clip is made of NIR LED with 950 nm wavelength in one side of the finger, which penetrate through tissue and attenuates the light signal. The attenuates signal will be received by the photo-diode with 900 nm wavelength in the opposite side of the finger clip, the attenuates light will then converted to voltage after received by the photo-diodes.

The variation in voltage received by photo-diodes will be received as a result for the glucose concentration in the blood which attenuate the transmitted light. The voltage will be filtered and amplified where the amplified signal will then be changed to analog signal and to digital signal by the micro-controller, in order to be read by the electronic devices. When the result of the glucose level display on the LCD, the micro-controller will differentiate it according to the amount of glucose. When the result is in normal level, it will just show the result with no notifications.

Once the results reach certain amount, the buzzer will turn on and the GSM will send SMS message attaching location by the GPS module to the person mobile phone. Figure 1 represents the proposed model.

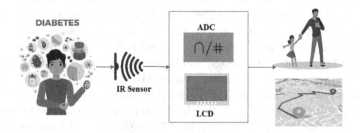

Fig. 1. IoT-based diabetic patient monitoring system

Figure 2 shows the overview of this project, when the fingertip sample pass between the NIR LED and photo-diode the system will detect the glucose value. It then determine how to react according to the glucose level result. Whether to send an alert message to the registered numbers or not.

Table 1. Notations used in tested methods

Notation	Description
I	Light Intensity
I_0	Incident light intensity
L	Optical path length
μ_{eff}	Effective attenuation coefficient

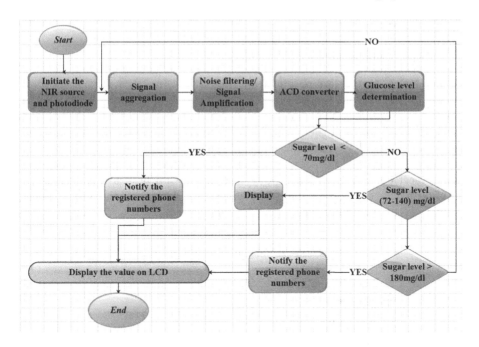

Fig. 2. The flowchart of the proposed IoT-based diabetics monitoring system

This manuscript worked based on the absorbance of light through different objects. As Beer-Lambert Law is based on absorbance measurement [23], this low plays a big role in this manuscript. Beer-Lambert Law state that absorbance of light through any solution is in proportion with the concentration of the solution and the length path traveled by the light ray [23]. In this project, we try to pass the light through fingertip. When light pass through fingertip it can be observed and scattered by tissue. The amount of glucose level in blood will affect the amount of light either observed or scattered in the tissue. Light attenuation theory [24] describe as represented in Eq. 1:

$$I = I_0 * \epsilon - \mu_{eff} * L \qquad (1)$$

where I, I_0 , and L refer to light intensity, incident light intensity, and optical path length inside the tissue respectively. The Attenuation of light inside the tissue depends on the μ coefficient which refer to the effective attenuation coefficient (μ_{eff}) is given as presented in Eq. 2:

$$\mu_{eff} = [3 * \mu_s(\mu_s + \mu'_s)]^{\frac{1}{2}} \qquad (2)$$

Therefore, this equation can tell us based on the scattered light, the glucose concentration in blood.

4   Performance Evaluation

4.1   Simulation Settings

The simulation settings are presented in Table 2.

This project use one sensor which is the IR Sensor - to measure the glucose level in blood by infrared radiation. The patient have to put his fingertip not farther than 0.1 cm from the sensor in order to read the exact measurement of glucose level. The device will take 5 s to display the result on the LCD as well as 7 s to send the SMS attaching with current location of the patient when the reading meet critical condition. The buzzer noise could be heard in a range of 500 X 500 m. The communication range between the device and the SMS message sending, cover every range inside local communication.

Table 2. Simulation settings

Simulation inputs	Input value
Number of sensors	1
Displaying result on LCD	5 s
Range of sensor	0.1 cm
Simulation time	5 s
Sending SMS and location	7 s
Range of communication	Everywhere (Etisalat range)
Communication range	0.1 cm
Operational area	200 m x 200 m
Routing protocol	DSR
Showing result	Every 30 min
Packet size	250 bytes

4.2   Tested Scenarios

A sample of 30 diabetic patients have been considered in the test. First we test the glucose reading of the patients by the glucometer (pricking fingertip) method and collect the readings. The proposed model has been used to test the voltage reading of the patients' sugar level. The glucose reading of the patients have be predicted by the proposed system. Table 3 presents the collected readings.

By considering the data in Table 3, we use the polynomial regression method in MS Excel to track whether there is correlation between the voltage reading and glucose reading or not as shown in Fig. 3.

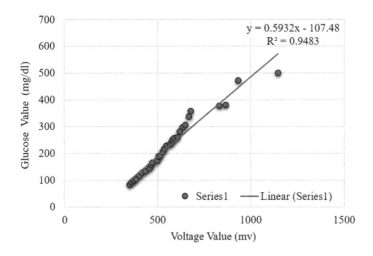

Fig. 3. Correlation between voltage and glucose readings

All the data collected from the voltage reading in non-invasive method and glucose reading in invasive method shows that there is a correlation between them, as shown in the regression analysis in Fig. 3. This study help us to predict the glucose concentration by using the polynomial regression analysis and equation applied in the data-set. Thus, the voltage reading received by the photodiode when the fingertip placed will be sent to the micro-controller to be calculated as glucose reading. When the micro-controller receive analog voltage, it will calculate and display it as glucose reading in the LCD.

The relation between the glucose concentration results come from the invasive and non-invasive as shown in Fig. 4.

Table 4 presents the glucose reading between the invasive and non-invasive method.

In this project, we have done three testing method to find out the more accurate one.

1. **First Scenario**

   A person in normal condition which is between 4.0 to 5.4 mmol/L (72 to 99 mg/dL) when fasting up to 7.8 mmol/L (140 mg/dL) 2 hours after eating. When the person put his finger on the sensor, after 5 s the system will display the result in the LCD. No further action will be taken by the system, when a person is in this condition.

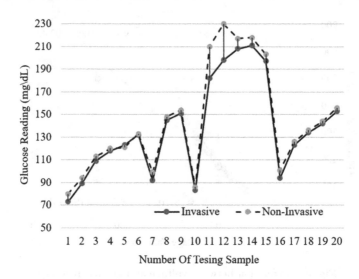

Fig. 4. The relation between the glucose concentration results received from the invasive and non-invasive

2. **Second Scenario**

   Hyperglycemia when a person above 180 to 200 mg per deciliter (mg/dL), or 10 to 11 millimoles per liter (mmol/L). When the system display the glucose level in LCD, after 3 s the alarm will be on. It will continue making noise for about 1 min. Also, immediately after 4 s of the alarm on, the SMS attaching with the current location will be send to the registered numbers of the responsible persons.

3. **Third Scenario**

   Hypoglycemia when a person reach a level below 3.9 mmol/L (70 mg/dL). When the person put his finger on the sensor, after 5 s the system will display the result in the LCD. After this, the system will take the same action that taken with the second scenario.

4.3   Results Analysis

For the invasive method to measure the glucose level we use the glucometer. And for the non-invasive method of detecting glucose level the person have to place his finger tip on the sensor. We perform for about 20 times, in both the invasive and non-invasive method of detecting.

Figure 5 presents the Bar graph chart that compare the accuracy of the glucose detected by the proposed non-invasive system with the value detected by using the invasive method.

To know in which scenario the system give the more accurate value, we try several times with three of them. When a person is in normal condition, the system give the most accurate value. As shown in the chart, we take the average value from all the sample values. For the normal condition, we got average value

115 mg/dL in non-invasive and 112 mg/dL in invasive method. Which the difference between the average values are +3, most accurate value from the other two. Also, as shown in the graph, for hyperglycemia condition we got average value 245 mg/dL in non-invasive and 213 mg/dL in invasive. Which the difference between the two average value is +32, less accurate of all. For the hypoglycemia the average value difference is 92 mg/dL for non-invasive and 85 mg/dL in invasive, which the difference is +7. Thus, in hyperglycemia and hypoglycemia the system difference was a bit greater. Therefore, the system give most accurate value when the person is in normal condition.

Table 3. Voltage and glucose readings using the invasive method

No	Voltage reading	Glucose reading	No	Voltage reading	Glucose reading	No	Voltage reading	Glucose reading
1	350	83	11	499	172	21	608	261
2	361	92	12	506	189	22	619	282
3	372	99	13	514	190	23	634	297
4	384	105	14	528	205	24	649	305
5	401	116	15	536	216	25	668	337
6	416	128	16	549	228	26	679	359
7	435	134	17	568	234	27	833	377
8	457	145	18	577	244	28	868	381
9	466	157	19	583	251	29	934	472
10	472	166	20	591	257	30	1146	501

Table 4. Invasive and Non-Invasive methods comparison

No	Invasive method	Non-invasive method	No	Invasive method	Non-invasive method
1	73	80	11	182	210
2	89	94	12	198	230
3	109	112	13	208	217
4	118	120	14	211	218
5	123	121	15	197	203
6	133	133	16	94	101
7	92	99	17	123	126
8	145	146	18	134	136
9	151	153	19	142	144
10	85	88	20	153	156

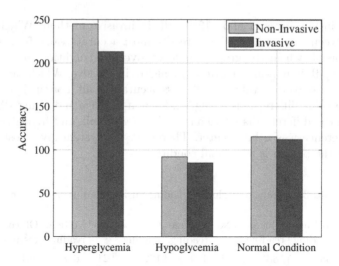

Fig. 5. Accuracy comparison of glucose detected by the proposed non-invasive system with the value detected by using the invasive method

Figure 6 Shows the developed non-invasive sensing module used for testing. When a person place his finger on the sensor, the result will come as voltage reading in Arduino Uno. When the value is displayed on the LCD, it will show as glucose reading.

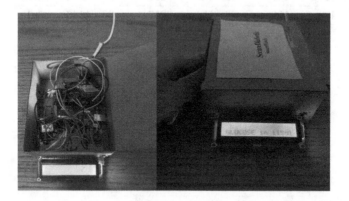

Fig. 6. Developed module

Figure 7 shows an example in which when a person place his finger on the sensor, the LCD is showing that the glucose level is 76 mg/dl which means that the glucose level of this person is about to reach Hypoglycemia (when a person glucose level reach below 3.9 mmol/L (70 mg/dL). Thus, the device will alert the parents by making noise along with sending alert SMS messages attaching the patient current location to the registered number. The same caution messages will be sent when the person reach hyperglycemia.

Fig. 7. The module work

5   Conclusion

Diabetic is a simple chronic disease if we know how to manage our glucose level. This manuscript will help diabetic patients, particularly the paediatric age patients, to monitor their glucose level continuously and alert their guardian in critical condition. Most diabetic patients use the traditional technique (pricking finger) to know their glucose level which is painful, stressful and uncomfortable. In this paper the non-invasive method using IR sensor which is pain- free technique has been proposed for continuous glucose monitoring in which the ray emitted by the IR LED has pass through the skin and observe the glucose level by the photo-diode. The glucose level will then be displayed on the LCD as well as it send alert messages when the glucose level meet hypo or hyperglycemia. Finally, SMS by GSM Module along with GPS location will then be sent to the responsible person, when the glucose level reach a certain level. The manuscript prove that the usage of the proposed non-invasive mechanism performs with the highest accuracy along with the shortest response time.

Acknowledgment. This research was partially supported by ZU STG046 grant. We thank **Dr. Huthaifa Otoum** from Jarash Governmental Hospital, Jordan, who provided insight medical revision and comments that greatly improved the manuscript.

References

1. W.H. Organization.: Diabetes (2019). https://www.who.int/news-room/fact-sheets/detail/diabetes
2. Balan, V., et al.: Vibrational spectroscopy fingerprinting in medicine: from molecular to clinical practice (2019)
3. Boatemaa, M.A., Doss, S.: Non-invasive glucose estimation based on near infrared laser diode spectroscopy. Asian J. Biomed. Pharm. Sci. **7**, 22–27 (2017)
4. Öberg, P.Å., Togawa, T., Spelman, F.A.: Sensors in Medicine and Health Care. Wiley Online Library, Hoboken (2004)
5. Otoum, S., Ahmed, M., Mouftah, H.T.: Sensor medium access control (SMAC)-based epilepsy patients monitoring system. In: 2015 IEEE 28th Canadian Conference on Electrical and Computer Engineering (CCECE), pp. 1109–1114 (2015)
6. Oueida, S., Kotb, Y., Aloqaily, M., Jararweh, Y., Baker, T.: An edge computing based smart healthcare framework for resource management. Sensors **18**(12), 4307 (2018)
7. Oueida, S., Aloqaily, M., Ionescu, S.: A smart healthcare reward model for resource allocation in smart city. Multimed. Tools Appl. **78**(17), 24 573–24 594 (2019)
8. Otoum, S., Kantarci, B., Mouftah, H.: Adaptively supervised and intrusion-aware data aggregation for wireless sensor clusters in critical infrastructures. In: IEEE International Conference on Communications (ICC), pp. 1–6 (2018)
9. Otoum, Y., Liu, D., Nayak, A.: DI-IDS: a deep learning-based intrusion detection framework for securing IOT. Trans. Emerg. Telecommun. Technol. **n/a**(n/a), e3803, e3803 ett.3803. https://onlinelibrary.wiley.com/doi/abs/10.1002/ett.3803
10. Elayan, H., Shubair, R.M., Kiourti, A.: Wireless sensors for medical applications: current status and future challenges. In: 2017 11th European Conference on Antennas and Propagation (EUCAP), pp. 2478–2482 (2017)
11. Verma, V.K., Gupta, P., Jha, A.V., Barbhuiya, P.N.: Recent trends in wireless sensors for medical applications. In: International Conference on Communication and Signal Processing (ICCSP), vol. 2017, pp. 1588–1592 (2017)
12. Yang, J.-J., et al.: Emerging information technologies for enhanced healthcare. Comput. Ind. **69**, 3–11 (2015). special Issue: Information Technologies for Enhanced Healthcare. http://www.sciencedirect.com/science/article/pii/S0166361515000226
13. Parihar, M., Lawand, K., Patil, S.: Design and development of infrared led based non invasive glucometer, April 2014
14. Sarkar, K., Ahmad, D., Singha, S., Ahmad, M.: Design and implementation of a noninvasive blood glucose monitoring device, vol. 12, pp. 1–5 (2018)
15. Narayanan, S., Sivagnanam, R., Smrithisri, V.K., Bai, T.: Smartphone based non-invasive glucose monitoring, pp. 119–123 (2019)
16. Prawiroredjo, K., Julian, E., Tjahjadi, G.: Infrared-based glucose level measurement, February 2019
17. Lawand, K., Parihar, M., Patil, S.N.: Design and development of infrared led based non invasive blood glucometer. In: Annual IEEE India Conference (INDICON), pp. 1–6 (2015)
18. Wardana, H., Indahwati, E., Fitriyah, L.: Measurement of non-invasive blood glucose level based sensor color tcs3200 and Arduino. In: IOP Conference Series: Materials Science and Engineering, vol. 336, p. 012019, April 2018
19. Mahzan, N.N., Enzai, N.I.M., Zin, N.M., Noh, K.S.S.K.M.: Design of an Arduino-based home fire alarm system with GSM module. J. Phys. Conf. Ser. 1019, 012079 (2018). https://doi.org/10.1088

20. Prabha, C., Sunitha, R., Anitha, R.: Automatic vehicle accident detection and messaging system using GSM and GPS modem. Int. J. Adv. Res. Electr. Electron. Instrum. Eng. **3**, 10 723–10 727 (2014)
21. Srabanti, S., et al.: A proposed system for automatic vehicle monitoring and accident detection in Bangladesh, February 2018
22. Fizzah, B., Munam, A.S., Carsten, M., Islam, S.U.: A novel internet of things-enabled accident detection and reporting system for smart city environments. Sensors **19** (2019). https://doi.org/10.3390/s19092071
23. Allen, E.J., Sabines-Chesterking, J., Birchall, P.M., McMillan, A., Joshi, S.K., Matthews, J.C.F.: Quantum sensing of absorbance and the beer-lambert law. In: 2019 Conference on Lasers and Electro-Optics Europe European Quantum Electronics Conference (CLEO/Europe-EQEC), p. 1 (2019)
24. Ressom, H., et al.: Neural network based light attenuation model for monitoring Seagrass health. In: 2004 IEEE International Joint Conference on Neural Networks (IEEE Cat. No.04CH37541), vol. 3, pp. 2489–2493 (2004)

Model-Based and Machine Learning Approaches for Designing Caching and Routing Algorithms

Adita Kulkarni[1(✉)] and Anand Seetharam[2]

[1] Department of Computing Sciences, SUNY Brockport, Brockport, USA
akulkarni@brockport.edu
[2] Department of Computer Science, SUNY Binghamton, Binghamton, USA
aseethar@binghamton.edu

Abstract. In this paper, we compare and contrast model-based and machine learning approaches for designing caching and routing strategies to improve cache network performance (e.g., delay, hit rate). We first outline the key principles used in the design of model-based strategies and discuss the analytical results and bounds obtained for these approaches. By conducting experiments on real-world traces and networks, we identify the interplay between content popularity skewness and request stream correlation as an important factor affecting cache performance. With respect to routing, we show that the main factors impacting performance are alternate path routing and content search. We then discuss the applicability of multiple machine learning models, specifically reinforcement learning, deep learning, transfer learning and probabilistic graphical models for the caching and routing problem.

Keywords: Caching · Routing

1 Introduction

Over the last decade, cache networking research (e.g., information-centric networking) has gathered significant momentum and its benefits are likely to impact a variety of future communication systems including 5G networks, clouds and IoT systems [6,13]. One of the salient features of cache networks is improving user performance by serving content from in-network caches rather than the content custodians (origin servers). To this end, a number of caching and routing strategies have been proposed over the last decade that effectively leverage in-network caching to improve performance.

Therefore, in this paper, we outline the key principles used in the design of these protocols and quantitatively demonstrate how these principles aid in improving performance. Based on prior work, we identify three main approaches for developing caching and routing protocols—*i)* Design optimized cache management strategies assuming that requests for content are routed according to

© ICST Institute for Computer Sciences, Social Informatics and Telecommunications Engineering 2021
Published by Springer Nature Switzerland AG 2021. All Rights Reserved
L. Foschini and M. El Kamili (Eds.): ADHOCNETS 2020, LNICST 345, pp. 16–28, 2021.
https://doi.org/10.1007/978-3-030-67369-7_2

the network's underlying routing strategy. *ii)* Design optimized routing strategies assuming that the network adopts some native cache management strategy. *iii)* Design strategies that jointly optimize for caching and routing. We then present research on the analysis of caching and routing protocols that complement and aid the understanding of the design factors required for developing new protocols. In particular, we present an overview of recent analytical research that seek to answer questions related to optimality, performance guarantees and attempt to determine the actual performance of particular protocols in specific settings.

We conduct experiments using multiple real-world networks and traces and show that the interplay between content popularity skewness and request stream correlation is an important factor affecting cache performance. We also demonstrate that augmenting shortest path routing with factors such as alternate path routing and content search can significantly improve performance.

We next present an overview of machine learning approaches that have been used to address the caching and routing problem. We discuss the potential benefits of multiple different classes of machine learning algorithms, in particular reinforcement learning, deep learning, deep reinforcement learning, transfer learning, and probabilistic graphical models to solve the caching and routing problem. We conclude by discussing the various challenges that need to be overcome to allow the seamless adoption of machine learning models to solve these problems.

The goal of this paper is to provide an overview of state-of-the-art research in cache networks in a succinct manner, to draw attention to key contributions in the field, to highlight the various model-based and machine learning approaches that can be used to solve the caching and routing problem and to stimulate further discussion.

2   Key Design Principles of Routing and Caching

In this section, we provide an overview of the main design considerations while developing new caching and routing protocols. We first outline the principles behind designing caching protocols, followed by routing and conclude by discussing joint caching and routing. Table 1 provides an overview of some of the recently proposed caching and routing algorithms. Due to lack of space, we are unable to cite each paper individually. Most citations can be found within [13].

2.1   Caching

When adopting a cache management strategy, the network has two options— static caching/content placement or dynamic caching. We first describe static and dynamic caching and then highlight the differences between them.

Static Caching. If static caching is adopted, the network decides the set of content to be placed at the different network nodes so as to optimize performance. The set of content to be placed at the various network nodes is determined a priori, primarily based on the content popularity and then these pieces of content are cached at network nodes. As network caches do not change their cached content, in static caching, requests for cached content result in hits while requests for all other content result in misses. While for the single cache case, the optimal static caching strategy is caching the most popular content, for an interconnected network comprising of multiple nodes, determining the set of content to cache, particularly at core network nodes is considerably harder. As upstream caches only receive the miss request stream from downstream caches, this miss stream dictates the content placement at these nodes. Though determining the optimal set of content to cache in a general network is still largely unsolved, Banerjee et al. propose a greedy solution to this problem [2].

Dynamic Caching. In dynamic caching, the content of network caches can potentially change as new content passes through them. Dynamic caching strategies thus have two important decisions to make, one is cache eviction and the other is cache insertion.

Cache Eviction: If a node decides to cache a particular content, the cache eviction policy decides what content to evict from the cache. Popular cache eviction policies are the Least Recently Used (LRU) and First In First Out (FIFO) policies.

Cache Insertion: The other important aspect of dynamic caching is cache insertion that aims to improve performance by increasing the network content diversity as well as by pushing popular content closer to the user. The simple Leave Copy Everywhere (LCE) policy results in a piece of content being cached at all nodes on the return path from the custodian. To increase network content diversity, two widely adopted metrics are—*i)* network centrality that uses the centrality of nodes to determine what content to cache, and *ii)* a probabilistic approach that takes factors such as content popularity, node connectivity and whether other nodes on the path have cached the same content into account to determine if a content should be inserted into a cache. Cache Less for More (CL4M) and ProbCache are two popular strategies that rely on network centrality and adopt a probabilistic approach, respectively.

Joint Cache Insertion and Eviction: A variety of policies have also been proposed in literature that attempt to address the cache insertion and eviction aspects together. For example, a number of different variants of LRU (e.g., p-LRU, k-LRU [7]) have also been proposed that address the cache insertion aspect assuming that the eviction policy is LRU. In p-LRU, a piece of content is inserted into a cache based on some probability p, while the k-LRU policy exploits a chain of $(k-1)$ virtual caches to filter content. Before a request arrives at the physical cache that stores the actual content, it passes through a chain of $(k-1)$ virtual caches that are in front of it. These virtual caches only store object pointers and perform caching operations on them. A content or a pointer can only be stored in the cache at level i if it obtains a hit at level $(i-1)$.

Table 1. A comparison of caching and routing algorithms

Protocol name	Type	Machine learning based approach	Summary of contributions
Greedy Caching [4]	Static Caching	No	Exploits content popularity and miss stream from downstream nodes to make caching decisions in a general network
Femto Caching	Static Caching	No	Exploits content popularity to make caching decisions in a heterogeneous cellular network with performance guarantees
Least Recently Used (LRU)	Dynamic Caching (Cache Eviction)	No	Evicts the content that has not been accessed for the longest time duration
Leave Copy Everywhere (LCE)	Dynamic Caching (Cache Insertion)	No	Cache a copy of the content on all en route caches
Leave Copy Down (LCD)	Dynamic Caching (Cache Insertion)	No	Cache a copy of the content at the node that is one hop downstream from the cache hit
Cache Less for More (CL4M)	Dynamic Caching (Cache Insertion)	No	Cache content based on network centrality
PopCache	Dynamic Caching (Cache Insertion)	No	Cache content based on popularity
ProbCache	Dynamic Caching (Cache Insertion)	No	Probabilistically cache content at a node
Hybrid Caching [10]	Combines Static and Dynamic Caching	No	Divide caches into static and dynamic components based on a utility function
Hash-Routing	Routing	No	Route requests based on hash tables
Breadcrumbs	Routing	No	Uses pointers (breadcrumbs) to keep track of content, follow pointers to obtain content
CTR [3]	Routing	No	Uses characteristic time of a content in a cache to route requests
Optimal Caching [5]	Joint Routing and Caching	No	Determine the optimal set of content to be cached and the routing strategy adopted by each node by taking network congestion into account
DeepCache [12]	Dynamic Caching	Yes	Deep LSTM based encoder-decoder model to predict the request stream, smart caching policy based on these predictions
Q-Caching	Dynamic Caching	Yes	Uses Q-learning based approach to determine what content to cache

Static vs. Dynamic Caching. A natural question that arises is what are the advantages of adopting one type of caching strategy (i.e., static or dynamic) over the other? To answer this question, it is important to understand how static caching and dynamic caching attempt to serve requests. Static caching strategies take advantage of the long tail of the content popularity distribution (i.e., small number of content receive majority of the requests) and cache popular content within the network, while dynamic caching leverages the correlation in the request stream. Therefore, the performance of static and dynamic caching strategies is dominated by the interplay of the skewness of the popularity distribution and the request stream correlation. Another important question that arises is how to adapt static caching to real-world scenarios where content popularity varies over time? In such scenarios, the approach adopted by static caching is to estimate content popularity over a certain time window and to cache content based on it. This process is repeated periodically to help static caching capture temporal variations in popularity.

2.2 Routing

Having studied the main principles adopted for designing caching strategies, in this section, we focus on routing. A key idea to effectively utilize in-network caches is to seek alternate paths for obtaining content in addition to the shortest path. In this context, the simplest approach is to adopt standard multi-path routing. A smarter approach is to perform bookkeeping in the form of keeping breadcrumbs (i.e., pointers) at users and intermediate routers in order to keep track of the node(s) from where a particular content is recently obtained. By following the trail of these breadcrumbs, a node can potentially obtain content faster than shortest path routing. Content search, particularly in mobile networks is another key principle that is used in conjunction with shortest path routing to improve performance [1]. It exploits the fact that the requested content may be cached nearby and thus readily available at neighboring nodes.

2.3 Joint Caching and Routing

Instead of focusing solely on caching or routing, recent research has also tried to jointly optimize caching and routing [5]. While solving the joint problem, majority of existing approaches attempt to find the optimal content placement and routing and do not approach the problem from the dynamic caching perspective. Based on previous research, we next outline the basic steps generally adopted by the research community to solve the joint caching and routing problem.

- The usual methodology adopted is to cast the joint content placement and routing problem as an optimization one subject to constraints such as the caching capacity at various nodes and the connectivity among the different nodes.
- The main objective functions considered in prior work are delay and hit rate with some recent research also focusing on general utility functions [5].

– Prior research has also demonstrated that most of these formulations turn out to be computationally hard (i.e., NP-hard) [5]. One of the main factors contributing to the hardness is the fact that finding the optimal content placement results in a combinatorial explosion.
– A natural next step is to formulate approximation algorithms that are computationally efficient and provide performance guarantees. Most of these problem formulations are integer linear programs, thus making them amiable to approximation algorithms. A commonly adopted technique is to demonstrate that the objective function is submodular and that the constraints follow a matroid. This subsequently entails that there exists a greedy solution that provides a $(1 - 1/e)$ approximation guarantee. Additionally, researchers have also proposed heuristic solutions that provide good performance in practice.
– The proposed approximation and heuristic solutions are generally centralized in nature which necessitates that the problem be solved in a central server and the results be distributed to network nodes. To address this concern, several efficient distributed solutions have also been proposed recently. A widely adopted technique is to design a gradient descent/ascent approach that asymptotically converges to the same solution as obtained by the centralized approach.

2.4   Analysis of Caching and Routing

While understanding the key factors governing performance is necessary to develop novel caching and routing strategies, analysis is essential to quantify the performance of algorithms in particular network settings and understanding the scenarios where one strategy is likely to outperform another. Additionally, analytical bounds and expressions can also be used to design better caching and routing strategies and can aid network management and maintenance.

Caching. A significant amount of effort has been invested in understanding the performance, in particular the network hit rate for different cache insertion and eviction policies. Table 2 succinctly describes the research in determining the hit rate of network caches. In one of the seminal papers, Che et al. derive approximations for the hit rate of LRU caches. This approximation, popularly known as Che's approximation has been shown to be applicable for general content popularity distributions. In recent years, this approximation has been extended to non-stationary requests and to general networks comprising of multiple nodes. Garretto et al. [7] derive expressions for the hit rate for multiple caching insertion and eviction policies such as LRU, p-LRU, k-LRU, FIFO, LFU and RANDOM, and LCE, Leave Copy Down (LCD) and Leave Copy Probabilistically (LCP) respectively. Simulation and trace-based evaluation show that the analytical and simulation results match closely. This study also demonstrates the superiority of the k-LRU policy in comparison to other strategies. Alongside, research effort has also been devoted to analyze the performance of Time To Live (TTL) based caches because in general it is easier to derive exact expressions for uncorrelated and correlated request streams.

Table 2. Analytical approaches for determining cache hit rate

Approach	Summary of contributions
Che et al.'s Approximation	Determines the hit rate of LRU caches
Rizk et al.'s Approximation [16]	Determines the hit rate at LRU caches in cache hierarchies described by a directed acyclic graph
a-Net [17]	Iterative algorithm to determine the hit rate of a network of LRU caches
Garretto et al. 's Approximation [7]	Extends Che's approximation to determine the hit rate of FIFO and RANDOM cache eviction policies. Also determines expressions for LCE, LCD and LCP cache insertion policies
Approximation of TTL caches	Determine how to set the parameters of TTL caches to mimic the behavior of other policies such as FIFO and LRU

In [14, 15] the authors analytically study the fundamental limits of caching in wireless networks. For example, the authors in [15] obtain upper bounds on capacity and achievable capacity lower bounds in wireless cache networks. Similarly, in [14], the authors investigate the capacity scaling laws in cache-enabled wireless networks considering the skewness of the Zipfian popularity distribution. They demonstrate that the capacity at individual nodes increases monotonically with the number of nodes for skewed popularity distributions. These scaling laws are invaluable and help us appreciate the maximum benefits of caching. Similarly, the authors investigate a general cache network modeled using queuing theory and determine how to place objects in caches to attain a desired objective [11].

Routing. Theoretical analysis has also been conducted to determine the extent to which content search and scoped flooding is beneficial. Analysis and experiments show that the optimal flooding radius is small (less than 3 hops). This means that flooding requests beyond the immediate neighborhood of a requester is likely to incur significant overhead while providing minimal performance improvement. The benefits of opportunistic routing, an important routing paradigm designed for wireless networks that exploits the broadcast nature of the wireless medium to select the best relay to forward a request toward the custodian has been analyzed in [8]. The authors design Markovian models to analyze the performance of opportunistic request routing in wireless cache networks in the presence of multi-path fading. Based on their results, the authors conclude that the benefits of in-network caching are more pronounced when the probability of successful packet transmission is low. This result suggests that caching is likely to have more benefits in a wireless network with lossy links.

Popular implementation of the ICN architecture such as Content-centric Networks (CCN) and Named Data Networks (NDN) perform aggregation of requests for same content (popularly known as Interest aggregation) through the use of a data structure called Pending Interest Table (PIT) to improve routing performance. A recent study investigates and quantifies the benefits that PITs provide under realistic conditions. This preliminary investigation suggests that only a small fraction of requests may benefit from request aggregation with the benefits being closely tied to the network cache budget.

3 Experimental Results

In this section, we experimentally demonstrate the performance benefits of the key principles discussed in the previous section in the design of caching and routing strategies. To demonstrate how the interplay of content popularity skewness and correlation impact the performance of caching strategies, we conduct experiments on multiple real-world topologies (e.g., GARR, WIDE, GEANT), synthetic and real-world request stream traces (e.g., YouTube, Wikipedia) and multiple cache insertion policies (LCE, CL4M and ProbCache). We present representative results for the GARR topology and the YouTube trace to avoid cluttering the paper with multiple similar figures. The GARR topology comprises of 61 nodes and 21 users. The YouTube request stream trace used here was collected over a campus network at the University of Massachusetts Amherst. In this particular trace, the long-term content popularity is low whereas the overall correlation among requests is high, which means that requests for the same content tend to occur in bursts. We assume that all content is of unit size and vary the cache size as a parameter in our experiments.

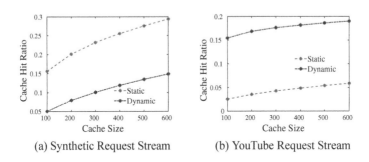

(a) Synthetic Request Stream   (b) YouTube Request Stream

Fig. 1. Performance of static and dynamic caching

To study the impact of request stream on the performance of static and dynamic caching, let us consider Figs. 1a and 1b. In Fig. 1a, we assume that content popularity is distributed according to a Zipfian distribution with skewness parameter $\alpha = 0.7$ and requests for content are generated following an independent request stream model, while Fig. 1b is generated for the YouTube trace. The static caching policy adopted in the figures is Greedy Caching [2], while the dynamic cache insertion and eviction policies are Leave Copy Everywhere (LCE) and LRU respectively. We observe from Fig. 1a that static caching outperforms dynamic caching while the opposite is true in Fig. 1b. This is because as Fig. 1a is generated considering an identically and independently distributed request stream, the correlation is 0 and hence, static caching outperforms dynamic caching. In comparison, as the overall correlation in the request stream increases, as is the case in the YouTube trace, dynamic caching outperforms static caching (Fig. 1b).

We next turn our attention to dynamic caching policies and study the impact of cache insertion policies on content diversity, which in turn affects performance. We define content diversity as the total number of unique content in the network. Figure 2a shows the content diversity for LCE, CL4M and ProbCache for various cache sizes for the GARR topology for the YouTube trace. We observe from Fig. 2a that the content diversity for CL4M and ProbCache is considerably higher in comparison to LCE. This content diversity also translates to improved performance (e.g., hit rate), with both ProbCache and CL4M outperforming LCE [2].

From the above discussion, it is evident that static and dynamic caching attempt to exploit different aspects of the request stream to improve performance. Hence, recent work has explored the benefits of hybrid caching that combines the best aspects of static and dynamic caching [10]. The key idea is to split a cache into two parts—a static part that statically caches content based on popularity and a dynamic part that leverages content popularity. Of course, determining the optimal split is an important researched question that is still being investigated.

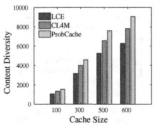
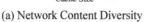
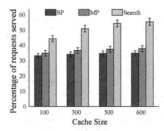

(a) Network Content Diversity   (b) Performance Impact of Multipath Routing and Content Search

Fig. 2. Comparing performance of caching and routing strategies

We next study the positive performance impact of ideas such as multi-path routing and content search (Fig. 2b). As paths to content custodians are always available in a static network, we consider a real-world mobile network comprising of pedestrian users to demonstrate their benefits. To this end, we consider the Stockholm pedestrian mobility trace that contains simulation traces of pedestrians walking in a part of downtown Stockholm, covering an area of 5872 sq. m. For our experiments, we consider 300,000 location entries consisting of 587 pedestrians. As mobility can result in frequent path breakages, Fig. 2b shows the percentage of requests served for various cache sizes if we adopt either multi-path or content search to execute on top of shortest path routing. We observe from the figure that both multi-path (denoted by MP) and content search aid in serving a greater number of requests. We observe that using shortest path (denoted by SP) and content search together serves significantly more number of requests than multi-path forwarding. The reason for the limited performance improvement in multi-path routing is that both paths in multi-path routing are calculated based on the prior network state and thus when the shortest path breaks due to node mobility, the alternate path to the custodian is also likely to be broken. In comparison, large number of requests can be served by content search because node mobility helps in exploiting content diversity by searching new neighbors.

4   Machine Learning Approaches for Caching and Routing

In this paper, so far we have focused on design principles and analysis of caching and routing strategies. In this section, we first investigate the benefits of adopting machine learning techniques to solve the caching and routing problem and then list some of the challenges that need to be overcome to allow the seamless adoption of machine learning for these problems.

4.1   Possible Machine Learning Models

The performance of caching strategies can be improved if one can accurately predict changes in content popularity and determine what content is likely to be requested in future. Learning web request streams and using them to improve the performance of HTTP caches has been well investigated in the early part of this century. Models such as n-gram models, Markov models and Markov trees developed in the context of HTTP caches can also be adopted in cache networks with certain modifications.

Reinforcement Learning: The necessity to make joint caching and routing decisions to improve performance makes this problem an ideal candidate for adopting reinforcement learning methods. To this end, a reinforcement learning method called Q-caching has been proposed that builds on standard Q-routing to make joint caching and routing decisions. Q-caching increases network content diversity, reduces the load at custodians and content download times for client. Similarly, in a recent work, the authors propose a reinforcement learning approach that uses model-free acceleration for online cache replacement by taking predicted content popularity, cache hits and replacement costs into account.

Deep Learning: Deep learning models have also been proposed to predict future content popularity variations by taking the spatial-temporal features of popularity into account. For example, a recently proposed approach DeepCache [12] uses a deep LSTM based encoder-decoder model to predict the changes in content popularity. The authors then design a caching policy, which takes predicted content popularity information into account to make smart caching decisions. Similarly, in other recent work, lightweight cache insertion and eviction schemes that take these deep learning predictions in consideration have also been proposed.

Deep Reinforcement Learning: In recent years, multiple deep reinforcement learning approaches (e.g., asynchronous advantage actor-critic (A3C), deep deterministic policy gradient (DDPG), Deep Q Networks (DQN), Trust Region Policy Optimization (TRPO)) have been designed that have been shown to provide good performance in multiple different domains. Most of the above-mentioned approaches are based on deep actor-critic architectures, a recent architectural improvement to reinforcement learning. Actor-critic architectures are also the easiest to adapt to an online training setting. For example, the asynchronous nature of A3C helps in designing parallel and distributed implementations of the algorithm that allow for greater exploration of the state space, resulting in good test performance on previously unseen data. Similarly, the presence of off-policy updates in DDPG allow for a wide exploration of the state space. DDPG also has provisions to learn from a large amount of past data and uncorrelated transitions from the replay buffer.

Transfer Learning and Bandit Models: Along with reinforcement learning, transfer learning and bandit models are also good candidates for determining changes in content popularity and making joint caching and routing decisions. The main idea behind transfer learning is to leverage the knowledge gained in one domain and apply it to related but 'new' domain. In this regard, content popularity estimation and in turn caching performance can potentially be improved by taking into account information such as a user's location and social networking connections. To apply bandit models to cache networks, we can assume the agent to have only partial knowledge of the network. Based on this current knowledge, the agent takes actions to maximize its accumulated reward while acquiring new knowledge.

Probabilistic Graphical Models: Probabilistic graphical models (both discriminative and generative) are also good candidates for predicting content popularity variations [9]. Moreover, the low computational requirements of graphical models during the training phase also make them a more attractive option than deep learning models. While discriminative models (e.g., conditional random fields (CRFs)) only learn the conditional dependencies in the output variables (future predictions) given the input variables (past data) at training time, generative models (e.g., Markov random fields (MRFs), hidden Markov models (HMMs)) learn the joint dependencies in the entire data. While at a cursory glance, generative models may appear to be superior than discriminative models as they jointly model the dependencies in the entire data, prior work has demonstrated that discriminative models often achieve superior prediction performance as they are tuned to maximize performance by learning structured outputs. In comparison, generative models capture the inherent dependencies in the data, help in accurately generating the data, and thus enable us to better understand the underlying network characteristics.

4.2 Challenges

One of the biggest hurdles in adopting machine learning models, in particular deep models is the high computational resource requirement necessary for training these models. This computational overhead makes it harder to train the models in an online manner. Apart from the computational overhead, another well-known issue with deep learning models is their lack of interpretability. Due to the complex inter-connection of cells in a neural network architecture as well as the large number of hidden layers, it is often very difficult to explain the predictive performance of deep learning models. Another important issue that has been largely overlooked in prior research is the applicability of a trained model for a variety of different settings. In majority of prior work, even though the models are trained and tested on different data, both the train and test data are usually collected in a similar setting. In our preliminary investigation, we have found that a model trained in one setting may not necessarily perform well in a new setting. The main reason is that the sequences and data seen by the model at test time may not be similar to the ones seen at training time, thus leading to poor performance at test time. A fundamental question that arises in this regard is—how to design training datasets so that one can obtain overall good performance even in previously unseen network settings?

5 Conclusion

In this paper, we highlighted the key principles adopted in the design of model-based caching and routing strategies to improve performance in cache networks. We then discussed the applicability of machine learning models, in particular deep learning, reinforcement learning, transfer learning and probabilistic graphical models for this problem.

References

1. Banerjee, A., Banerjee, B., Seetharam, A., Tellambura, C.: Content search and routing under custodian unavailability in information-centric networks. Comput. Netw. **141**, 92–101 (2018)
2. Banerjee, B., Kulkarni, A., Seetharam, A.: Greedy caching: an optimized content placement strategy for information-centric networks. Comput. Netw. **140**, 78–91 (2018)
3. Banerjee, B., Seetharam, A., Mukherjee, A., Naskar, M.K.: Characteristic time routing in information-centric networks. Comput. Netw. **113**, 148–158 (2017)
4. Banerjee, B., Seetharam, A., Tellambura, C.: Greedy caching: a latency-aware caching strategy for information-centric networks. In: 2017 International Conference on Networking. IFIP (2017)

5. Dehghan, M., et al.: On the complexity of optimal request routing and content caching in heterogeneous cache networks. IEEE/ACM Trans. Network. (TON) **25**(3), 1635–1648 (2017)
6. Din, I.U., Hassan, S., Khan, M.K., Guizani, M., Ghazali, O., Habbal, A.: Caching in information-centric networking: strategies, challenges, and future research directions. IEEE Commun. Surv. Tutor. **20**(2), 1443–1474 (2018)
7. Garetto, M., Leonardi, E., Martina, V.: A unified approach to the performance analysis of caching systems. ACM Trans. Model. Perform. Eval. Comput. Syst. **1**(3), 12 (2016)
8. Herath, J.D., Seetharam, A.: Analyzing opportunistic request routing in wireless cache networks. In: 2018 IEEE International Conference on Communications (ICC), pp. 1–6. IEEE (2018)
9. Koller, D., Friedman, N.: Probabilistic Graphical Models: Principles and Techniques. MIT Press (2009)
10. Kulkarni, A., Seetharam, A.: Exploiting correlations in request streams: a case for hybrid caching in cache networks. In: 2018 IEEE 43rd Conference on Local Computer Networks (LCN), pp. 562–570. IEEE (2018)
11. Milad Mahdian, A.M., Ioannidis, S., Yeh, E.: Kelly cache networks. In: 2019 IEEE International Conference on Computer Communications (INFOCOM). IEEE (2019)
12. Narayanan, A., Verma, S., Ramadan, E., Babaie, P., Zhang, Z.L.: DeepCache: a deep learning based framework for content caching. In: Proceedings of the 2018 Workshop on Network Meets AI & ML, pp. 48–53. ACM (2018)
13. Paschos, G.S., Iosifidis, G., Tao, M., Towsley, D., Caire, G.: The role of caching in future communication systems and networks. IEEE J. Sel. Areas Commun. **36**(6), 1111–1125 (2018)
14. Qiu, L., Cao, G.: Popularity-aware caching increases the capacity of wireless networks. In: IEEE INFOCOM 2017 - IEEE Conference on Computer Communications, pp. 1–9 (2017)
15. Qiu, L., Cao, G.: Cache increases the capacity of wireless networks. In: IEEE INFOCOM 2016 - The 35th Annual IEEE International Conference on Computer Communications, pp. 1–9. IEEE (2016)
16. Rizk, A., Zink, M., Sitaraman, R.: Model-based design and analysis of cache hierarchies. In: 2017 International Conference on Networking. IFIP (2017)
17. Rosensweig, E.: On the analysis and management of cache networks (2012)

New Results on Q-Routing Protocol for Wireless Networks

Alexis Bitaillou[1(✉)], Benoît Parrein[1], and Guillaume Andrieux[2]

[1] University of Nantes, LS2N, Polytech Nantes, Nantes, France
`alexis.bitaillou@univ-nantes.fr`
[2] University of Nantes, IETR, IUT La Roche-sur-Yon, La Roche-sur-Yon, France

Abstract. In the 90s, Q-routing assisted by reinforcement learning was introduced by Boyan and Littman with interesting results in terms of quality of service. Some recent works continue to promote the idea through improvement of the algorithm or specialized extensions. In this paper, we propose a simple modification to workaround the greedy behaviour of Q-routing by considering epoch notion. In comparison with the original Q-routing and the standard OLSRv2 under Qualnet simulator, we show that our extension provides an interesting improvement in terms of packet delivery ratio on the original irregular grid of Boyan and Littman with wireless links.

Keywords: Ad-hoc networks · Q-routing · Wireless networks · Qualnet simulator

1 Introduction

In the 90s, two new approaches appears to solve routing problem: *i)* bio-inspired algorithm and *ii)* reinforcement learning based algorithm. Q-routing [2] is one of the reinforcement learning based routing algorithm appeared. In their paper, Q-routing shown promising results. On their personal simulator, Q-routing offers a better average end-to-end delay than the Bellman-Ford protocol in high load condition. In fact, in congestion state, the Q-routing proposes alternative route based on the end-to-end delay while Bellman-Ford protocol is focused on the shortest path in terms of hops count. Those results have many potential applications especially for mesh and mobile ad-hoc networks (MANET). From their original work, many derived works has been proposed. A part of those are improvements of the algorithms such as AQFE [9]. Most of them are evaluated on home-made simulator. But, there are also specializations of Q-routing for specific applications such as mobility or cognitive radio.

In this paper, we demonstrate how a short congestion can potentially degrade performance of Q-routing. So, we propose to integrate to Q-routing an epoch-inspired mechanism. Epoch mechanism is a method from machine learning to

---

Supported by the COWIN project from the RFI Wise and Atlantic 2020, Région Pays de la Loire.
L. Foschini and M. El Kamili (Eds.): ADHOCNETS 2020, LNICST 345, pp. 29–43, 2021.
https://doi.org/10.1007/978-3-030-67369-7_3

prevent some side effects of greedy behaviour such as local optimum problem. We evaluate our modified Q-routing with epochs on several scenarios on ad-hoc wireless networks. We compare it to the original Q-routing and nuOLSRv2, an implementation of OLSRv2 [3]. Our results show that our modification improved slightly the performance of Q-routing. It offers better performance than nuOL-SRv2 in most our scenarios.

The organization of the paper is the following. In Sect. 2, we summarize some previous works about Q-routing. In Sect. 3, we detail the implementation of our distributed Q-routing protocol. Section 4 defines the experimental setup. Section 5 provides results in terms of QoS and a discussion as well. The last section concludes the work and draws some perspectives.

2   Related Work

In this section, we see in more details Q-routing algorithms and other related works.

2.1   Q-Routing

Watkins and Dayan [12] created a reinforcement learning algorithm called Q-learning in 1994. Two years later, Boyan and Littman [2] proposed to integrate Q-learning in routing algorithm. They named their algorithm Q-routing in reference to Q-Learning. In this algorithm, each node x looks for the lowest Q-value, defined using the Q function. The estimated delivery time from node x to node d by node y is noted: $Q_x(d, y)$. They define Q-value of function Q as:

$$\Delta Q_x(d, y) = \eta(q + s + t - Q_x(d, y)) \tag{1}$$

where η is the learning rate (usually 0.5 in [2]) q the unit of time spent in node x's queue, s the unit of time spent during the transmission between x and y and t as

$$t = \min_{z \in \text{neighbour of } y} Q_y(d, z). \tag{2}$$

In this case, the effective delivery time is the reward R and defined as: $R = q + s + t$. At the beginning, the Q-values are initialized with the value 0. Q-routing has a greedy strategy, so the first choice is very important. In order to make the first choice equitably, an exploration phase is needed to discover all the choices. During this phase, the Q-value is not updated.

Several networks topologies are tested in their work including an 6×6 irregular grid. The authors argue that only local information is used to proceed. The presented results of [2] concern only the 66 irregular grid. Q-routing is compared to Bellman-Ford's shortest path algorithm. In their works, Q-routing is not always able to find the shortest path under low network load. Nevertheless, the latency is similar to the shortest path in low load condition. Q-routing clearly outperforms the shortest path in high load condition (even if the high load condition is not well-defined in [2]). However, when the traffic load decreases, Q-routing keeps the high load policy. The original approach is thus not adapted to dynamic changes.

2.2 Q^2-Routing

The original Q-routing considers only the latency. Q-routing will select a low latency route even if the path loss more packets. Recently, Hendriks et al. [7] proposed an extension of Q-routing considering also the packet delivery ratio and the jitter. Their algorithm is called Q^2-routing. They adapted the Q function to include these QoS metrics:

$$Q_x(d, y) = (C_d \times C_j \times C_l)((1 - \alpha)Q_x(d, y) + \alpha r) \qquad (3)$$

where C are coefficient depending on the traffic QoS requirement, α is the learning rate and r is $q + s + t$ in (1).

In their paper, they evaluated Q^2-routing on a topology composed of 3 paths on ns-3. It compared to an implementation of the original Q-routing and AODV [5]. Packets loss and delay appeared during the simulation on different paths in order to test Q^2-routing features. According to their results, Q^2-routing outperforms AODV and Q-routing in most of the test cases in terms of PDR, average delivery time and jitter. However, their scenario is designed to advantage Q^2-routing as the simulation event can only detect by Q^2-routing and some of them by Q-routing.

2.3 AQ-Routing

Q-routing is a greedy algorithm. The mobility can easily degrade the performances. Serhani et al. [11] proposed an extension for Q-routing in order to improve performances in mobility scenario. They named their extension Adaptive Q-routing (AQ-routing). AQ-routing takes several concepts from OLSR [4] such as HELLO packets but also ETX metric [6]. Unlike the original Q-routing, AQ-routing doesn't use latency as routing metric. It uses a metric based on link stability:

$$Q_{metric_{ij}} = \alpha_{ij} \cdot \varphi(MF_j) + (1 - \alpha_{ij}) \cdot \lambda ETX_{ij} \qquad (4)$$

where MF is the Mobility Factor, α the learning rate, $\varphi(MF_j)$ is defined as: $\varphi(MF_j) = \frac{a}{1-e^{\frac{-MF_j}{b}}}$. In their paper, they compared AQ-routing to OLSR (standard and with ETX metric version) on ns-3. On static test case, AQ-routing offers the best PDR but the worst average delivery time. On mobility test case, AQ-routing provides a stable average delivery time and the best PDR. Start to $4\,\mathrm{m/s}$, the average delivery time is better with AQ-routing than with OLSR ETX. To obtain this performance, Serhani et al. have increased the complexity of Q-routing especially the computation of the reward.

2.4 Other Extensions and Derived Works

There are many other extension and derived works of Q-routing. For example, Kavalerov et al. [8] have improved Q-routing "Full Echo" with Adaptive Q-routing Full Echo (AQFE) and Adaptive Q-routing Random Echo (AQRE).

AQFE improved the stability Q-routing Full Echo by adding a second dynamic learning rate. AQFE outperforms Q-routing on the original test cases of Boyan and Littman [2]. After the learning phase, AQFE can become unstable under some conditions. In order to reduce this instability, AQRE doesn't send update to all neighbours but to a set randomly chosen. Finally, they proposed Adaptive Q-routing with Random Echo and Route Memory (AQRERM) [9], an improved version of AQRE. However, AQFE and its derived have only been tested on home-made simulator. So, other quality of service metrics such as PDR are not evaluated.

Besides improvements, specialized extensions have been made. For example, Paul *et al.* [10] created an extension of Q-routing for cognitive radio. Zhang and Ye [13] made a Q-routing optimized for optical networks-on-chips.

3 Q-Routing Implementation Details

In this section, we describe our implementation of Q-routing fully distributed and deployable on wired and wireless networks.

3.1 Implementation Overview

We do not implement Q-routing from scratch, but our implementation is based on the Bellman-Ford basic implementation of Qualnet simulator. This basic implementation is bare-bones, there is no auxiliary function as we can have in OLSR [4] for example. We redefine the maximum route length (16 hops), the timeout delay (120 s), the maximum number of routes per packet (32 routes per packets), and the periodic update delay (10 s). Nodes have access to local information only. Additionally, we add the parameter η from Eq. (1) and the exploration phase duration. The routing table has been replaced by the function Q inspired of Eq. (1). The two next subsections describe how we totally distributed our implementation of the Q-routing protocol.

3.2 Latency Measurement and Header Format

Q-routing aims to minimize the average delivery time. The Q function uses the duration of the transmission and the duration in-queue. To measure these times, we extend the header of the routing packet. The header of the routing packet contains a timestamp. Thanks to this information, the receiver can estimate the delay. The delay is sent back during the next update. This method has a little network overhead but needs two assumptions to work correctly. The latency is computed by the difference between the timestamp in the header and the moment when the packet is received according the local clock. So, the clock of the nodes needs to be synchronized to compute this difference. As the reward uses the latency in micro-second, the synchronization need optimally to be of the order of the micro-second. In fact, the synchronization can be less precise, but the difference between the clocks has to smaller than the lowest latency. This is the first assumption. This mechanism can be replaced by using the "echo" function of ICMP.

The second assumption concerns the number of queues. Nodes need to have only one queue. If a node has more than one queue, the measure of duration in-queue will depend on the number of queues, the quantity and the priority of packets in the queues and finally the scheduler. So, in order to not depend on these parameters, the measure of the duration in-queue is more accurate when nodes have only one queue.

3.3   Route Update Mechanism

As nodes have only access to local information only, our protocol needs a mechanism to update their routing table. We propose to reuse the routing management to propagate routes. There are two types of update: periodic and triggered. During a periodic update, all nodes broadcast all their routes to their 1-hop neighbourhood. Periodic updates occur every 10 s. As broadcast a new route will be too slow with periodic updates, there is triggered and asynchronous update. To broadcast a new with periodic updates only, it needs in the worst case 10 s per hop. For example, on a topology in line of 6 nodes, the new route will broadcast from an end to the other in 50 s in the worst case. Triggered update happens when a new route is available, or a route has been modified. A triggered update is not sent if a periodic update will be sent in less than 150 ms.

We define a route as triplet value: destination, mask and next hop. We complete the structure by adding a timestamp, the value of the t from (1) and the current latency. The timestamp comes from the last timestamp of the routing packet of the destination. A new route is accepted if the distance is less than 16 hops. As we explained, the routing packets are timestamped. The timestamp is also integrated to data structure of the original route and acts as sequence number. A route update is always accepted if the timestamp of the update is newer than the current timestamp. If the timestamp of the update is equal to the current timestamp, the update is only accepted if it minimizes the Q-value of Eq. (1).

3.4   Epoch Mechanism

In order to limit the greedy behaviour of Q-routing, we propose to add epoch-inspired mechanism. Epoch mechanism is a concept from machine learning in order to reset reward periodically and workaround the problem of local optimum. We define arbitrary the duration of the epoch to 300 s. At the end of the epoch, Q-routing creates a new empty Q-table. Q-routing starts an exploration phase, in which the new Q-table is filled. During this phase, the current Q-table works normally. At the end of the learning phase, the new Q-table replaces the current Q-table. This mechanism helps also to purge stale routes.

4   Experimental Set-Up

In this section, we describe the complete experimentation set-up and the results of our simulation. Our experimental plan concerns two wireless topologies: one simple with two main paths and the adaptation of 66 grid of Boyan and Littman [2]. The Table 3 sums up the different parameters. We benchmark three routing protocols: our implementation of Q-routing, our Q-routing with epoch mechanism and nuOLSRv2 (OLSRv2 [3] Niigata University implementation). OLSRv2 is the successor of OLSR, it is standardized routing protocol specialized in mobile ad-hoc networks (MANETs). We use Scalable Qualnet 8.2 as network simulator. 30 seeds are used for each combination of parameters.

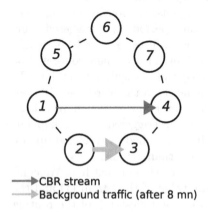

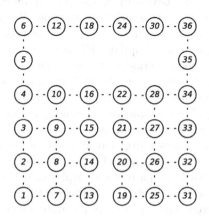

Fig. 1. Our wireless toy example. Numbers correspond to the node ID.

Fig. 2. Adapted wireless irregular grid. Numbers correspond to the node ID.

4.1   Q-Routing and Its Greedy Behaviour, a Toy Example

Before evaluating Q-routing and Q-routing epoch on a complex topology, we evaluate them on a simple test case as depicted on Fig. 1. Our test CBR is between node 1 and node 4 which are the source and the destination respectively. In this simple network, large background traffic appears on the shortest path between node 2 and node 3. In order to have two distinct paths, we move path away each other. The CBR source starts sending at 60 s and stop 60 s before the end of the simulation. The interval between two messages is 10 ms. To be sure that the routes are stables when background traffic appears, it starts after 8 min of simulation.

Scenario 1: One Second Congestion. For the first test, the background traffic appears at 8 min and stopped just a second after. The background traffic throughput is 5120 kb/s. The objective is to demonstrate the disadvantage of the greedy behaviour of Q-routing. In order to observe the clear change of the average hop count, the simulations run over 30 min. We benchmark Q-routing and our Q-routing epoch.

Scenario 2: Alternative Path. The goal is simply to verify that our Q-routing implementation prefers the longer path (through node 5) as soon as congestion occurs. The background traffic start at 8 min and stop one minutes before the end of the simulation. The simulation time is 15 min because it is enough for this simple test case. We benchmark Q-routing, our Q-routing epoch and nuOLSRv2.

4.2   Adapted Wireless Irregular Grid

In [1], we used the irregular 6×6 grid in [2]. But, when we replaced basically the wired link by wireless link, the irregular grid becomes a regular grid. We changed the location of some nodes. The topology is composed of two grids 4 nodes by 3 linked by two paths. Four nodes have been removed compared to the wired grid to keep the irregularity property. The Fig. 2 illustrates this topology in a logical and compact form. For example, the node 9 can only communicate with nodes 3, 10 and 8. We benchmark Q-routing, our Q-routing epoch and nuOLSRv2.

Scenario 3: Located Congestion. In this case, there are 4 CBR streams on the adapted irregular wireless grid. The CBR streams start one minute after the beginning and stop one minute before the end of the simulation. All the CBR streams have the same throughput. The location of the CBR streams is detailed in Table 1. This test case shares the same idea of the tests on the toy example. The goal is to verify that Q-routing can balance CBR streams between two paths. The simulation time is 15 min.

Table 1. CBR streams location on the wireless grid (scenario 3)

Source (Node ID)	Destination (Node ID)
35	5
4	34
9	27
26	8

Scenario 4: Diffused Traffic. In this case, there are 15 CBR streams on the adapted irregular wireless grid. The location of those CBR streams has been defined randomly. Their starting time and their stop time have been defined randomly but the CBR streams must start after one minute. All CBR streams

have the same throughput. The settings of the CBR streams are defined once and don't change between the simulations. The location of the CBR streams is detailed in Table 2. The goal is to evaluate Q-routing and Q-routing epoch on the adapted wireless grid with non-constant traffic. The simulation time is 30 min.

Table 2. CBR streams location on the wireless grid (scenario 4)

Source (Node ID)	Destination (Node ID)	Start (s)	End (s)
19	12	62	721
28	9	175	537
31	35	217	1262
28	22	371	665
2	5	463	1088
14	15	632	951
25	6	832	1714
7	15	1006	1653
26	8	1168	1212
30	9	1241	1713
3	32	1303	1569
21	4	1592	1683
6	32	1613	1715
21	14	1661	1755
20	7	1705	1762

5   Results

In this section, we present the results of the experimentation. We focus on three metrics: the average end-to-end delay (or average delivery time), the packet delivery rate (PDR) and the jitter. All those metrics are measured at the application layer (layer 7). Disordered messages are dropped by the receiver. Only the messages received and accepted contribute to the average delivery time and the jitter. The throughput of the CBR streams is expressed at the application layer.

5.1   Toy Example

Scenario 1: One Second Congestion. For this first test case, we benchmark Q-routing and our modified Q-routing with epoch. We focus on the average hop count for the CBR stream. The Fig. 3 shows the box plot of the average hop

Table 3. Simulation parameters

Feature	Parameter	Value
Network	Link	Wireless IEEE 802.11a 9 Mb/s link
		IEEE 802.11e link layer
	Topologies	Ring and irregular grid
Node	Number of queues	1 FIFO queue
	Mobility	No
CBR	Message size	512 bytes
	Start	1 min (scenario 2 and 3)
	End	1 min before the end (case 2 and 3)
Simulation	Seed	30 different seeds
	Duration	15 min (scenario 2 and 3)
		30 min (scenario 1 and 4)
Q-routing	Exploration	15 s (scenario 1 and 2)
		45 s (scenario 3 and 4)
	η	0.9

count for Q-routing over the time. Start to the congestion, the average delivery time increases. Q-routing uses the longer alternative path and stills use it after the congestion up to the end of the simulation. According to the Fig. 4, Q-routing epoch uses also the longer alternative path, but unlike Q-routing, it finally returns on the shortest path. This little test case shows the advantage of the epoch-inspired mechanism. It makes Q-routing less sensitive to very short congestion. The reactivity of Q-routing could be increased by decreasing the epoch duration.

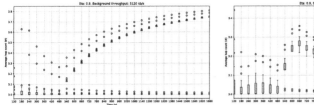
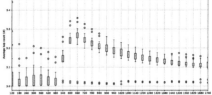

Fig. 3. Average hop count for Q-routing (scenario 1).

Fig. 4. Average hop count for our Q-routing with epochs (scenario 1).

Scenario 2: Alternative Path. On this second test, we benchmark Q-routing and our modified Q-routing epoch and nuOLSRv2. We focus on the packet delivery ratio (PDR), the average delivery time and the jitter. The background traffic doesn't contribute to the average delivery time, the PDR and jitter. The Fig. 5 shows the packet delivery ratio in function of the background traffic for Q-routing, Q-routing epoch and nuOLSRv2. According to our results, Q-routing and nuOLSRv2 have the same performance up to 3.5 Mb/s. Q-routing with "epochs" is less stable, the standard deviation is higher. nuOLSRv2 and Q-routing with "epoch" have a singularity between 4.5 Mb/s and 4.8 Mb/s. From 4 Mb/s to 4.55 Mb/s, the packet delivery ratio falls suddenly to 70% and increased up to 72% between 4.55 Mb/s and 4.8 Mb/s. From 4.2 Mb/s, nuOLSRv2 drops a large part of the packet. The packet delivery ratio falls under 70%. With Q-routing, the average PDR is higher (over 70%), but the standard deviation is quite high. Q-routing epoch offers the better average packet delivery ratio than nuOLSRv2 from 4.8 Mb/s. The two versions of Q-routing outperform nuOLSRv2 in PDR only under high load condition (above 4.55 Mb/s). The Fig. 6 shows the average delivery time in function of the background traffic for Q-routing, Q-routing epoch and nuOLSRv2. According to our results, the three protocols offer a comparable average delivery time up to 3.4 Mb/s. With nuOLSRv2, the average delivery time increases from 3.4 Mb/s up to peak at 260 ms at 3.56 Mb/s. It decreases after 3.56 Mb/s but the number of packets contributing to the metric decreases also. There is a singularity for nuOLSRv2 and Q-routing with "epochs" around 3.8 Mb/s. The singularity between 4 Mb/s and 4.8 Mb/s present in PDR is also present in average delivery time. With Q-routing, the average delivery time increased from 3.56 Mb/s to 3.9 Mb/s. It peaks at 60 ms on average. Q-routing offers the best average delivery time except on singular points. The Fig. 7 shows the average jitter in function of the background traffic for Q-routing, Q-routing epoch and nuOLSRv2. The three protocols offer a comparable average jitter up to 3.4 Mb/s. The Q-routing with "epochs" has a better jitter than the original.

Our Q-routing epoch doesn't improve performances in terms packet delivery ratio and in average delivery time. It improves slightly the jitter on a range of background traffic throughput compared to the original. Q-routing delivers the best performance in terms of PDR and average delivery time under high load condition (above 4.5 Mb/s). The high standard deviation can be explained by the instability of the measured latency in wireless communication. This leads Q-routing making some wrong routing choice. This scenario by design puts nuOLSRv2 in difficulty as the best solution is to use the alternative path for the CBR stream.

5.2 Adapted Wireless Irregular Grid

We evaluate Q-routing, Q-routing epoch and nuOLSRv2 on the wireless grid on the two tests cases. The average delivery time, the packet delivery ratio and the jitter are the average of all the CBR streams.

Scenario 3: Located Congestion. The four CBR streams contribute to the average delivery time, the packet delivery ratio and the jitter. The Fig. 8 shows the packet delivery ratio following the throughput per CBR stream for Q-routing, Q-routing epoch and nuOLSRv2. Q-routing outperforms nuOLSRv2. The PDR with Q-routing is up to 44% (at 410 kb/s per CBR) better than with nuOLSRv2. There is no significant difference between Q-routing and Q-routing epoch. The Fig. 9 shows the average delivery time in function of the throughput per CBR stream for Q-routing, Q-routing epoch and nuOLSRv2. Q-routing provides low latency under low load condition (up to 820 kb/s). The latency increased up to overtake the latency with nuOLSRv2. There is no significant difference between Q-routing and Q-routing epoch. The Fig. 10 shows the jitter following the throughput per CBR stream for Q-routing, Q-routing epoch and nuOLSRv2. nuOLSRv2 has the worst average jitter. Q-routing outperforms nuOLSRv2. There is no significant difference between Q-routing and Q-routing epoch.

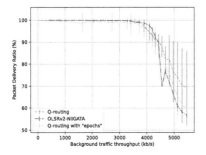

Fig. 5. Packet delivery ratio on the toy example (scenario 2).

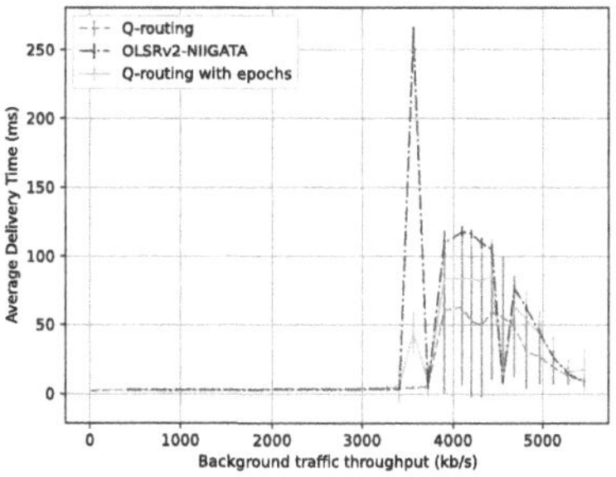

Fig. 6. Average delivery time on the toy example (scenario 2).

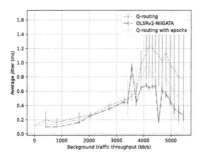

Fig. 7. Average jitter on the toy example (scenario 2).

The two versions of Q-routing outperforms under low load condition because Q-routing can more easily balance the CBR streams. The CBR streams (4, 34) and (35, 5) can use the "upper" path even if the path is longer. nuOLSRv2 uses the upper path only for the CBR stream (5, 35) in the best case. As the link between the nodes 16 and 22 is saturated, nuOLSRv2 loses packets, but also increases the average delivery time. Interestingly, when the throughput per CBR increased, Q-routing loses its advantage in terms of average delivery time face to nuOLSRv2.

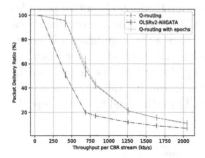

Fig. 8. Packet delivery ratio on the scenario 3

Fig. 9. Average delivery time on the scenario 3

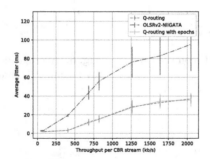

Fig. 10. Average jitter on the scenario 3.

Scenario 4: Diffused Traffic. The 15 CBR streams contribute to the average delivery time, the packet delivery ratio and the jitter. The Fig. 11 shows the packet delivery ratio following the throughput per CBR stream for Q-routing, Q-routing epoch and nuOLSRv2. The three routing protocol have the same shape. The packet delivery ratio decreases when the throughput per CBR increases. Q-routing epoch offers the best packet delivery. However, the difference with Q-routing and nuOLSRv2 is limited. There is 8% between Q-routing epoch and nuOLSRv2 and 3% between the two Q-routing in the best case (at 820 kb/s). The Fig. 12 shows the average delivery time in function of the throughput per CBR stream for Q-routing, Q-routing epoch and nuOLSRv2. As the packet delivery ratio, the curves of the average delivery time have the same shape. On average, nuOLSRv2 is the slowest of the three protocols. Q-routing is up to 1 s faster. Q-routing epoch improve slightly this metric. The Fig. 13 shows the jitter following the throughput per CBR stream for Q-routing, Q-routing epoch and nuOLSRv2. nuOLSRv2 has the worst average jitter. Q-routing epoch offers the best average except between 1.6 Mb/s and 2.7 Mb/s where there is an instability.

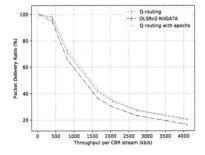

Fig. 11. Packet delivery ratio on the scenario 4.

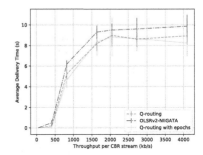

Fig. 12. Average delivery time on the scenario 4.

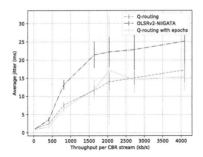

Fig. 13. Average jitter on the scenario 4.

This scenario is the less static in terms of traffic so the performance of Q-routing was quite unexpected due to its greedy behaviour. Q-routing epoch provides a slight improvement but less than expected. The difference of performance between Q-routing and nuOLSRv2 can be explained by the unneeded verbosity of nuOLSRv2. In fact, nuOLSRv2 broadcasts more packets than Q-routing. Those packets are useful in mobility scenarios but this one.

5.3   Discussion

The tests over a simple wireless topology were very encouraging. Q-routing epoch gives the results expected. It returns on the shortest path when the congestion is finished. It also chooses the alternative path to bypass the congestion. Q-routing outperforms nuOLSRv2 and Q-routing in PDR and in average delivery time up to 4.8 Mb/s. For the jitter, the improvement is not so obvious. On the wireless grid, the difference between Q-routing and Q-routing epoch is very slight, even on the scenario designed to favour Q-routing epoch (scenario 4).

Q-routing epoch has a higher computational cost and memory requirement than Q-routing. During the exploration phase, it has to maintain two Q-tables. The size of the Q-table is proportional to the number of 1-hop neighbour and the number of destinations. However, Q-routing epoch can remove staled routes from the Q-table at the end of the exploration phase. The size of the Q-table has an impact on update. On the wireless grid, each node broadcast up to 4 packets per update, so the routing overhead is high. This routing overhead can be reduced but at cost of a computation overhead. Those observations are agreed to [7] on difficulties for Q-routing to scale to large networks.

Another point concerns nuOLSRv2. The different scenarios are not designed to advantage nuOLSRv2. They don't include mobility. Their size in number of nodes is quite limited. For example, the wireless grid is composed of only 32 nodes. nuOLSRv2 implements advanced draft of OLSRv2. But, nuOLSRv2 is not totally compliant with the rfc7181. However, we think reasonably that the performance of nuOLSRv2 reflects the performance of a rfc7181-compliant implementation.

6   Conclusion

In this paper, we present an evaluation of our modification of Q-routing on the wireless standard IEEE 802.11. We experienced it on the professional packet driven simulator Qualnet on several scenarios. Q-routing epoch reacts as expected on the first scenario. The second scenario shows that our modification doesn't improve the performance of Q-routing. However, Q-routing epoch give a slight improvement on the wireless irregular grid compared to the original Q-routing. The two versions of Q-routing outperforms in PDR nuOLSRv2 in all our tests. Except the scenario 2 where the results are similar, they also clearly outperforms in average jitter nuOLSRv2. Nevertheless, the results in average delivery time depend on the scenario. We show that Q-routing doesn't need to be modified to give good results on our wireless grid even with diffused and changing traffic. However, our implementation of Q-routing doesn't have the auxiliary function of OLSRv2 and can't scale like it. So, our results can hardly generalize on specific scenarios or bigger topologies.

References

1. Bitaillou, A., Parrein, B., Andrieux, G.: Q-routing: from the algorithm to the routing protocol. In: Boumerdassi, S., Renault, É., Mühlethaler, P. (eds.) MLN 2019. LNCS, vol. 12081, pp. 58–69. Springer, Cham (2020). https://doi.org/10.1007/978-3-030-45778-5_5

2. Boyan, J.A., Littman, M.L.: Packet routing in dynamically changing networks: a reinforcement learning approach. In: Advances in Neural Information Processing Systems, pp. 671–678 (1994)
3. Clausen, T.H., Dearlove, C., Jacquet, P., Herberg, U.: The Optimized Link State Routing Protocol Version 2. RFC 7181, April 2014. https://doi.org/10.17487/RFC7181. https://rfc-editor.org/rfc/rfc7181.txt
4. Clausen, T.H., Jacquet, P.: Optimized Link State Routing Protocol (OLSR). RFC 3626, October 2003. https://doi.org/10.17487/RFC3626. https://rfc-editor.org/rfc/rfc3626.txt
5. Das, S.R., Perkins, C.E., Belding-Royer, E.M.: Ad hoc On-Demand Distance Vector (AODV) Routing. RFC 3561, July 2003. https://doi.org/10.17487/RFC3561. https://rfc-editor.org/rfc/rfc3561.txt
6. De Couto, D.S.J., Aguayo, D., Bicket, J., Morris, R.: A high-throughput path metric for multi-hop wireless routing. In: Proceedings of the 9th Annual International Conference on Mobile Computing and Networking, MobiCom 2003, San Diego, CA, USA, pp. 134–146. Association for Computing Machinery, September 2003. https://doi.org/10.1145/938985.939000
7. Hendriks, T., Camelo, M., Latré, S.: Q2-routing: a Qos-aware Q-routing algorithm for Wireless Ad Hoc Networks. In: 2018 14th International Conference on Wireless and Mobile Computing, Networking and Communications (WiMob), pp. 108–115, October 2018. https://doi.org/10.1109/WiMOB.2018.8589161. ISSN 2160-4886
8. Kavalerov, M., Likhacheva, Y., Shilova, Y.: A reinforcement learning approach to network routing based on adaptive learning rates and route memory. In: SoutheastCon 2017, pp. 1–6 (2017). https://doi.org/10.1109/SECON.2017.7925316
9. Kavalerov, M., Shilova, Y., Likhacheva, Y.: Adaptive Q-routing with random echo and route memory. In: 2017 20th Conference of Open Innovations Association (FRUCT), pp. 138–145, April 2017. https://doi.org/10.23919/FRUCT.2017.8071304. ISSN 2305-7254
10. Paul, A., Banerjee, A., Maity, S.P.: Residual energy maximization in cognitive radio networks with Q-routing. IEEE Syst. J. 1–10 (2019). https://doi.org/10.1109/JSYST.2019.2926120
11. Serhani, A., Naja, N., Jamali, A.: AQ-routing: mobility, stability-aware adaptive routing protocol for data routing in MANET–IoT systems. Cluster Comput. **23**(1), 13–27 (2019). https://doi.org/10.1007/s10586-019-02937-x
12. Watkins, C.J.C.H., Dayan, P.: Q-learning. Mach. Learn. **8**(3), 279–292 (1992). https://doi.org/10.1007/BF00992698
13. Zhang, W., Ye, Y.: An approximate thermal-aware Q-routing for optical NoCs. In: 2019 IEEE/ACM Workshop on Photonics-Optics Technology Oriented Networking, Information and Computing Systems (PHOTONICS), pp. 22–27, November 2019. https://doi.org/10.1109/PHOTONICS49561.2019.00009

Vehicle Software Update over ICN Architectures

Ali Elgammal[1,2(✉)], Mena Safwat[1,2], Wael Badawy[5], Eslam G. AbdAllah[3],
Marianne A. Azer[2,4], and Changcheng Huang[6]

[1] Valeo, Giza, Egypt
me.safwat@nu.edu.eg
[2] School of Information Technology and Computer Science,
Nile University, Giza, Egypt
{a.elgammal,mazer}@nu.edu.eg
[3] Master of Information Systems Security Management,
Concordia University of Edmonton, Edmonton, AB, Canada
eslam.abdallah@concordia.ab.ca
[4] National Telecommunication Institute, Cairo, Egypt
[5] Badr University, Cairo, Egypt
wael.badawy@buc.edu.eg
[6] Department of Systems and Computer Engineering,
Carleton University, Ottawa, ON, Canada
huang@sce.carleton.ca

Abstract. The Internet Protocol (IP) architecture could not fully satisfy Vehicular Ad-hoc Networks (VANETs) needed efficiency due to their dynamic topology and high mobility. This paper presents a technique to update the software of Electronic Control Units (ECUs) in vehicles using Information Centric Network (ICN) architecture. The proposed technique replaces Flashing Over The Air (FOTA) using IP with FOTA using ICN. The importance of FOTA is illustrated as well as the impact of applying the ICN architecture on VANETs. Through our experiments, we compare between the known FOTA over IP and the newly introduced FOTA technique over ICN.

Keywords: Flashing Over The Air (FOTA) · Information Centric Networking (ICN) · ndnSIM · Vehicle software update · Vehicular Ad-hoc Networks (VANETs).

1 Introduction

In the recent years, data transfer rates have rapidly increased. The number of connected nodes exponentially increases to accommodate the demand of users and services such as mobile phones, vehicles and Internet of Things (IoT). The rapid growth in the number of nodes introduces prime challenges such as resource consumption, mobility, security and scalability to the Internet Protocol (IP) addressing network architecture (host to host). One of the key examples is the

© ICST Institute for Computer Sciences, Social Informatics and Telecommunications Engineering 2021
Published by Springer Nature Switzerland AG 2021. All Rights Reserved
L. Foschini and M. El Kamili (Eds.): ADHOCNETS 2020, LNICST 345, pp. 44–54, 2021.
https://doi.org/10.1007/978-3-030-67369-7_4

Vehicular Ad-hoc Networks (VANETs), where the bottleneck or contingency of data results in loss of connectivity and consequently leads to possible vehicle crashes and people fatal injuries. The increase in network latency or centralized network overhead leads to 1.35 million injuries per year [9].

Information Centric Networking (ICN) reduces the latency of VANETs where information is labeled into objects with descriptors. In ICN, the data source node announces the data availability modeled as an object. The requester node establishs a communication channel to the nearest node to transfer an interest request. The interest request propagates through the intermediate nodes until it reaches the source node. Subsequently, the source node sends the required data reversely to the same routing path without needing to know who the requester is. The data is transferred to the neighboring nodes trough the network, until the data reaches the requester node or the nearest node. In ICN, each node in the routing path can cache the data in the content store to satisfy the same upcoming interests in order to decrease the response latency.

Table 1. IP and ICN architecture comparison

	ICN architecture	IP architecture
Caching	Occurs in all the intermediate nodes in routing path	Occurs in servers only
Naming	Hierarchical/flat	Source/destination address embedded in the packet name
Security	Focusing on object security	Focusing on channel security
Data availability in high mobility nodes	Highly associated/achieved with the cached data versions	Achieved with response latency

One of the main features of ICN is the decoupling between a transmitter and a receiver. The ICN uses a message content instead of destination address. Hence, the source/requester node announces and registers a request using the object name and does not use the node address to reduce the network overhead. ICN takes advantage of the distributed control instead of central control to reduce the bottleneck [11]. Table 1 summarizes the main differences between IP and ICN network architectures [4].

An important applications, called Flashing Over The Air (FOTA) has been required recently in automotive industry. In the following sections, we will describe in detail the network challenges, proposed ICN architecture, and FOTA application [1].

The advances in automotive industry use electronic circuits called Electronic Control Units (ECUs) for better control and automatic operations in the vehicle, they connect vehicles through different networks. The connectivity enables data exchange about local information such as road conditions, or weather. Data exchange between vehicles serves in vehicle ECUs update [8]. Consequently, the VANETs use a large numbers of ECUs with complex hardware and software to run algorithms for Advanced Driver Assistant Systems (ADAS) and autonomous driving. For example, 100 ECUs with 250 embedded/graphic CPUs [14] are used to execute more than 100 million lines of code inside the vehicle for handling vehicle normal operation [15].

ECU's errors, in either software or hardware, result in accidents, injuries and losses. Due to the higher reliability of hardware, the software is a more probable source of defects. Software updates are either regular or on demand. They are necessary to offset the liability of potential errors through vehicle recalls. Currently Original Equipment Manufacturers (OEMs) plan to perform these updates periodically for adding new features, fixing defects and handling security vulnerabilities. ECU software updates occur at the OEM service center. FOTA technology [7] is designed to avoid user inconvenience, unnecessary consumed time, and to manage frequently ECU software update on the fly [2].

FOTA uses software data transfer over wireless communication network and requires the following features: (1) minimal software update time, (2) data integrity, and (3) security goals. The proposed technique of using FOTA over ICN eliminates the need for source node addressing and the specific message routing, which improves the VANETs performance.

In this paper, we run our experiments to evaluate the performance of our proposed technique versus FOTA over IP in VANETs using Named Data Networking Simulator (ndnSIM). The results show that using our proposed technique enhances VANETs performance in all analyzed scenarios. Accordingly, we propose to use the aforementioned ICN advantages in FOTA.

The remainder of this paper is organized as follows. Section II illustrates FOTA and ICN background. Section III demonstrates a platform for FOTA over ICN. Section IV presents FOTA simulation framework. Finally, conclusions and future work are present in Section V.

2   FOTA and ICN Background

This section introduces the FOTA over IP network and the ICN platform in section A and B, respectively. Using the IP network, vehicles receive the updated software through an On Board Diagnostics (OBD) port and then the gateway ECU routes the software data to the required ECU.

The IP network uses a Telematics Control Units (TCU) to interface the vehicle to the network. The vehicles are developed to centralize the remote diagnostics communication via internet [6]. Remote vehicle diagnostics facilitate the vehicle's ECUs software update. When software artifact or vulnerabilities are detected, or new features are added; the ECU supplier updates/releases an updated software version. The following steps describe the positive scenario for FOTA process.

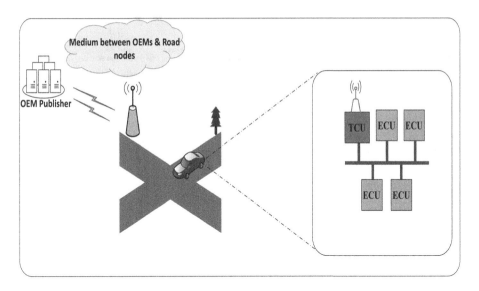

Fig. 1. Flashing over the air, IP network

2.1 Flash over the Air over IP Scenario

As shown in Fig. 1, FOTA over IP is performed by the following steps.

1 - An OEM uploads the new software version to its cloud server.
2 - The cloud server notifies the vehicle with the availability of a new software version.
3 - The main/gateway ECU authenticates the server and accordingly receives the new software data information (metadata).
4 - The main ECU verifies/compares the received metadata with the already flashed version and defines the targeted ECU to be flashed. Then the main ECU decides either to continue the software update or not.
5 - The main ECU receives the new software data, while the vehicle's whole functionalities are running.
6 - The main ECU checks the software integrity and signature, then requests the flash writing from the targeted ECU.

2.2 Information Centric Networking (ICN)

In this section, we present an ICN architecture, specifically Named Data Networking (NDN). An NDN node contains three main data structures. Forwarding Information Base (FIB) memorizes the information about the sent interests. Pending Interest Table (PIT) holds the awaiting information to be satisfied. Content Store (CS) contains the cached data version locally.

The requests and satisfactions in ICN architecture are illustrated in Fig. 2. Node 1 (subscriber 1) sends an interest request "/lib_1/book_ai/2018.txt" to the

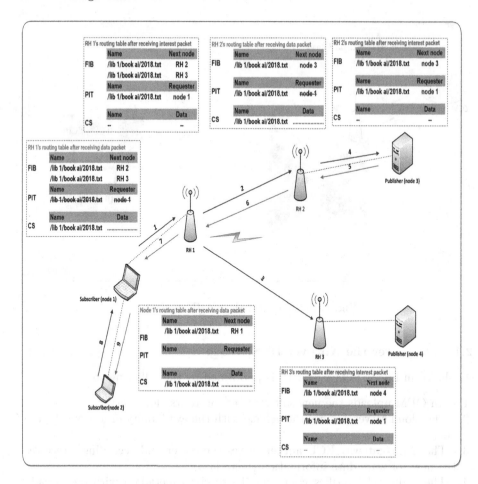

Fig. 2. Data flow in ICN architecture

Resolution Handler 1 (RH_1), RH_1 exports the interest name and searches for the content on its content store. Assuming that RH_1 does not have the requested interest data, RH_1 forwards the interest to RH_2 and RH_3 and stores the interest information in its PIT and FIB.

RH_2 and RH_3 do the same as RH_1, then node 3 (publisher 1) satisfies the "/lib_1/book_ai/2018.txt" interest by forwarding the data back to node 1 on the same routing path. The intermediate nodes between node 3 and node 1 (RH_1, RH_2 and RH_3) store the interest data at the CS then remove the interest request from the PIT.

Node 2 (subscriber 2) sends an interest request "/lib_1/book_ai/2018.txt" to node 1, node 1 responses directly with the interest data from its content store [13].

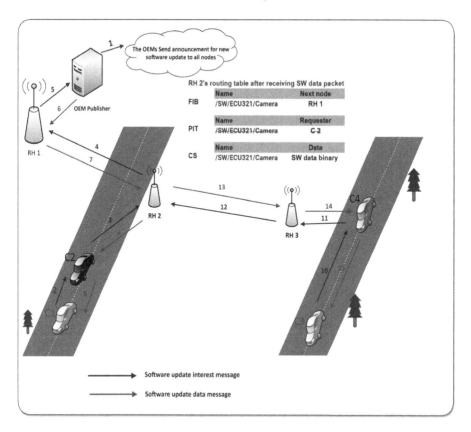

Fig. 3. Software data exchange sequence

3   Proposed Platform for FOTA over ICN

In this section, we propose the vehicle software update through ICN architecture procedure. First, the vehicle manufacturer node announces new software update for specific ECUs in one of their vehicle models. The targeted vehicles in the software update request the data from the nearest node/vehicle and the request propagates towards the data source. New software data is routed back to the requester through the same request path. All the intermediate vehicles/nodes can cache the data to satisfy the upcoming requests. Each OEM has its own technique to identify the software update file naming and versioning schema.

ICN in-network caching refers to caching the response data inside the intermediate vehicles/nodes to decrease the number of requests that are directed to the data provider. Accordingly, the manufacturer node response time is improved. Hence, the software update feature could be delivered in a more efficient manner for the rest of the vehicles.

FOTA over ICN procedure is described in the following steps, and is depicted in Fig. 3. The figure describes the steps while the vehicles are under coverage of ICN network.

1 - The OEM publisher sends an announcement to indicate that there is an updated software version for specific ECU. Vehicle C_1 and C_3 have the targeted ECU.

2 - C_1 sends an interest request to another vehicle C_2.

3 - C_2 adds the C_1's interest to PIT and forwards the request to RH_2.

4 - RH_2 and RH_1 perform the same step as step 3 until interest request reaches the OEM publisher.

5 - The OEM publisher transmits the software chunks to RH_1 then RH_1 transfers the software until reaching C_1. All the intermediate nodes between the OEM publisher and C_1 cache the data in CS.

6 - Once C_1 receives the full software, it checks the validity of the software and then starts the update procedure.

7 - Meanwhile, C_3 requests the updated software from the nearest node C_4.

8 - C_4 and RH_3 repeat step 3 till interest request reaches RH_2, as the RH_2 already has the software update in the CS.

9 - RH_2 forwards the data directly to RH_3.

10 - RH_3 and C_4 save the data in the CS and forward it back to C_3.

11 - C_3 repeats step 6.

Each time a vehicle needs to update the software, there is no need for C3 request to reach the main server (OEM publisher). This reduces the load on the server side and decreases the latency. The latency is decreased as data response takes shorter path and data comes from many nodes to satisfy same interest from different nodes.

4   FOTA Simulation Framework

In this section, our objective is to highlight the flashing time measurements for both IP and ICN networks through simulation experiments using Named Data Network simulator (ndnSIM) [5].

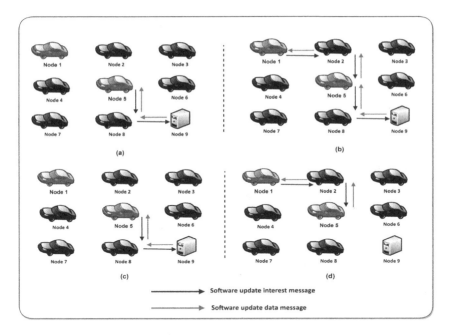

Fig. 4. FOTA Software data exchange for the first scenario 3*3 grid, node 1, 5 act as consumers and node 9 act as a producer. Parts a & b in the figure show FOTA over IP simulation data flow, and parts c & d show FOTA over ICN simulation data flow.

Table 2. Simulated vehicle Software flashing scenarios

Scenario ID	Network topology	Consumer nodes ID	Producer node ID
Scenario_1	Grid of 3*3 nodes	C1:Node_1 C2:Node_5	Node_9
Scenario_2	Grid of 10*10 nodes	C1:Node_1 C2:Node_45	Node_100
Scenario_3	Grid of 15*15 nodes	C1:Node_1 C2:Node_81 C3:Node_129	Node_225

4.1   Simulation Set-Up

ndnSIM is an open source package that uses the Named Data Networking (NDN) protocol stack for the NS-3 simulator [12]. The ndnSIM simulator is widely used to figure out NDN attributes such as FIB, PIT and CS and ICN network [3] [5]. This simulator is based on C++, our simulation parameters are as follow.

- Network Topology: Point to point.
- Routing Strategy: Best route strategy.
- Data Rate: 1 Mbps.
- Packet Size: 1024 Kbytes.

The analyzed case is to transfer one software for specific ECU, transmitted as one segment, and vehicle connectivity is ensured during the software transfer.

Three scenarios are implemented for flashing software with the packet size as descried in Table 2. The producer node "server" has the updated software, and

Consumer vehicles request the updated software from nearest node (in case of ICN) or from the server directly (in case of IP).

4.2 Simulation Results

We used the NetAnim tool to visualize the NS-3 simulator output results by investigating the generated .xml files. In Fig. 4 we present FOTA software data transfer between nodes for the scenarios mentioned earlier.

Figure 4-a & Fig. 4-b show FOTA over IP simulation data flow for the first scenario as follows.

1. - Node 5 "consumer 2" sends a software update request to node 8.
2. - Node 8 forwards the request to node 9 "producer".
3. - Node 9 transmits the software update to node 8.
4. - Node 8 forwards the software update to node 5.
5. - Meanwhile, node 1 requests the updated software from node 2.
6. - Nodes 2, 5 and 8 repeat step 3 until the request reaches node 9 "producer".
7. - Node 9 transmits the software update to node 8.
8. - Nodes 2, 5 and 8 repeat step 4 till software update reaches node 1.

Figure 4-c & Fig. 4-d show FOTA over ICN simulation data flow for the first scenario as follows.

1 - Node 5 "consumer 2" sends a software update request to node 8.
2 - Node 8 adds the node 5's interest to PIT and forwards the request to node 9 "producer".
3 - Node 9 transmits the software update to node 8.
4 - Node 8 caches the data in CS and forwards the software update to node 5.
5 - Meanwhile, node 1 requests the updated software from node 2.
6 - Node 2 adds the node 1's interest to PIT and forwards the request to node 5. Node 5 already has the software update in the CS.
7 - Node 5 forwards the software update directly to node 2.
8 - Node 2 forwards the software update to node 1.

In Fig. 5, we present the experimental results for the three cases, where the data transfer in ICN is faster than data transfer in IP. In IP protocol, the data source is centralized in one node "producer", and hence the producer is the only one that can provide the data. In ICN protocol, the data source is decentralized and the consumers can get the data from the nearest node that has the data in the CS. In scenario 1, the transfer time for the consumer 1 in case of IP is less than by 0.003 and this is due to network protocol and caching time as it is the same node, server, routing path and distance. Using our proposed technique, the data transfer time is reduced by 30% in most of the scenarios.

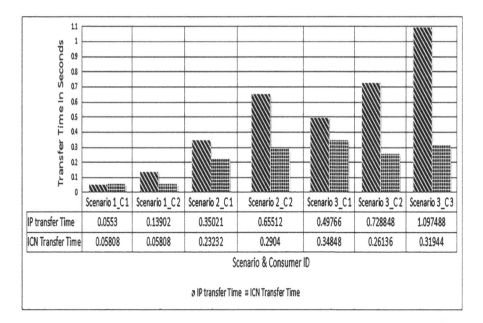

Fig. 5. Experimental results for the three FOTA Scenarios over both IP and ICN networks [1- 3*3 Grid of vehicles "two consumers (C_1 & C_2)" 2- 10*10 Grid of vehicles "two consumers (C_1 & C_2)" 3- 15*15 Grid of vehicles "three consumers (C_1 & C_2 & C_3)"]

5   Conclusions and Future Work

IP networks have several issues such as resource consumption, security, and scalability especially when it comes to vehicles high mobility. With the current type of concerns, researchers take the opportunity to develop new alternative solutions. Information Centric Network (ICN) is one of the proposed alternatives to overcome the IP architecture concerns. This paper presents our novel methodology for providing Flashing Over The Air (FOTA) for vehicle software updates over ICN architectures. This paper proposes and simulates three different FOTA scenarios by changing the number of vehicles, the number of consumers and the network architecture. This simulation is handled using NDN simulator. Results have proven that FOTA over ICN improves many aspects such as software flashing time, network response and servers bottleneck.

In the future, we plan to analyze more scenarios for FOTA over ICN while taking into consideration the application hex data segmentation [10], topology changes and vehicle mobility. This is in addition to analyzing the impact of the possible attacks for both FOTA over IP and FOTA over ICN.

Acknowledgments. The authors would like to acknowledge Valeo Interbranch Automotive Software, Egypt, and Nile university research center.

References

1. Gurmani, M.S., Möller, D.P.F.: Mechanism protecting vehicle-to-vehicle communication. In: Akhilesh, K.B., Möller, D.P.F. (eds.) Smart Technologies, pp. 335–343. Springer, Singapore (2020). https://doi.org/10.1007/978-981-13-7139-4_26
2. Halder, S., Ghosal, A., Conti, M.: Secure ota software updates in connected vehicles: A survey. arXiv preprint arXiv:1904.00685 (2019)
3. Raman, A., Chou, K., Mastorakis, S.: Experimenting with a simulation framework for peer-to-peer file sharing in named data networking. arXiv preprint arXiv:1911.07289 (2019)
4. Yao, H., Li, M., Du, J., Zhang, P., Jiang, C., Han, Z.: Artificial intelligence for information-centric networks. IEEE Commun. Mag. **57**(6), 47–53 (2019)
5. Kato, T., Minh, N.Q., Yamamoto, R., Ohzahata, S.: How to implement NDN manet over ndnSIM simulator. In: 2018 IEEE 4th International Conference on Computer and Communications (ICCC), pp. 451–456. IEEE (2018)
6. Mayilsamy, K., Ramachandran, N., Raj, V.S.: An integrated approach for data security in vehicle diagnostics over internet protocol and software update over the air. Comput. Electr. Eng. **71**, 578–593 (2018)
7. Mirfakhraie, T., Vitor, G., Grogan, K.: Applicable protocol for updating firmware of automotive hvac electronic control units (ecus) over the air. In: 2018 IEEE International Conference on Internet of Things (iThings) and IEEE Green Computing and Communications (GreenCom) and IEEE Cyber, Physical and Social Computing (CPSCom) and IEEE Smart Data (SmartData), pp. 21–26. IEEE (2018)
8. Onuma, Y., Terashima, Y., Nakamura, S., Kiyohara, R.: A method of ECU software updating. In: 2018 International Conference on Information Networking (ICOIN), pp. 298–303. IEEE (2018)
9. Organization, W.H., et al.: Global status report on road safety 2018. World Health Organization (2018)
10. Teraoka, H., Nakahara, F., Kurosawa, K.: Incremental update method for vehicle microcontrollers. In: 2017 IEEE 6th Global Conference on Consumer Electronics (GCCE), pp. 1–2. IEEE (2017)
11. AbdAllah, E.G., Hassanein, H.S., Zulkernine, M.: A survey of security attacks in information-centric networking. IEEE Commun. Surv. Tutorials **17**(3), 1441–1454 (2015)
12. Mastorakis, S., Afanasyev, A., Moiseenko, I., Zhang, L.: ndnSIM 2.0: a new version of the NDN simulator for ns-3. NDN, Technical report NDN-0028 (2015)
13. Fang, C., Yu, F.R., Huang, T., Liu, J., Liu, Y.: A survey of energy-efficient caching in information-centric networking. IEEE Commun. Mag. **52**(11), 122–129 (2014)
14. Georgakos, G., Schlichtmann, U., Schneider, R., Chakraborty, S.: Reliability challenges for electric vehicles: from devices to architecture and systems software. In: Proceedings of the 50th Annual Design Automation Conference, p. 98. ACM (2013)
15. Charette, R.N.: This car runs on code-IEEE spectrum. IEEE Spectrum: Technology, Engineering, and Science News (2009). http://spectrum.ieee.org/green-tech/advanced-cars/this-car-runs-on-code

Joint Mobility-Aware UAV Placement and Routing in Multi-Hop UAV Relaying Systems

Anousheh Gholami[1], Nariman Torkzaban[1], John S. Baras[1(✉)], and Chrysa Papagianni[2]

[1] Department of Electrical and Computer Engineering and the Institute for Systems Research,
University of Maryland, College Park, MD 20742, USA
{anousheh,narimant,baras}@umd.edu
[2] Nokia Bell Labs, Antwerp, Belgium
chrysa.papagianni@nokia-bell-labs.com

Abstract. Unmanned Aerial Vehicles (UAVs) have been extensively utilized to provide wireless connectivity in rural and under-developed areas, enhance network capacity and provide support for peaks or unexpected surges in user demand, mainly due to their fast deployment, cost-efficiency and superior communication performance resulting from Line of Sight (LoS)-dominated wireless channels. In order to exploit the benefits of UAVs as base stations or relays in a mobile network, a major challenge is to determine the optimal UAV placement and relocation strategy with respect to the mobility and traffic patterns of the ground network nodes. Moreover, considering that the UAVs form a multi-hop aerial network, capacity and connectivity constraints have significant impacts on the end-to-end network performance. To this end, we formulate the joint UAV placement and routing problem as a Mixed Integer Linear Program (MILP) and propose an approximation that leads to a LP rounding algorithm and achieves a balance between time-complexity and optimality.

Keywords: Unmanned Aerial Vehicle (UAV) · UAV-aided mobile communications · UAV placement and relocation · Multi-hop relaying · Route optimization

1 Introduction

Over the past decade, UAVs have been adopted in a broad range of application domains, due to their autonomy, high mobility and low cost. Historically, UAVs have been primarily used in the military, usually deployed in hostile territory to reduce risk for aircrew. Recent advances in UAV technologies have made them more affordable and accessible to civilian and commercial applications such as cargo transport, emergency search and rescue, precision agriculture, commercial package deliveries, etc. Moreover, UAVs are seen as a promising solution for next generation wireless networks because of their inherent advantages, including flexible and fast deployment and reconfiguration, as well as a higher chance of having Line-of-Sight (LoS) links leading to less impaired communication channels compared to terrestrial wireless communication systems.

© ICST Institute for Computer Sciences, Social Informatics and Telecommunications Engineering 2021
Published by Springer Nature Switzerland AG 2021. All Rights Reserved
L. Foschini and M. El Kamili (Eds.): ADHOCNETS 2020, LNICST 345, pp. 55–69, 2021.
https://doi.org/10.1007/978-3-030-67369-7_5

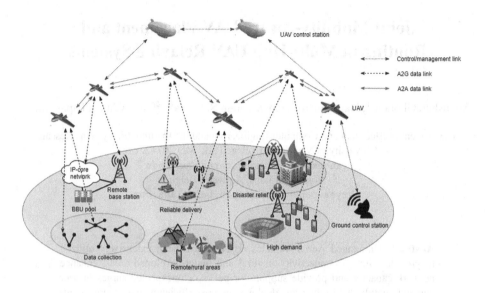

Fig. 1. The architecture and application scenarios of a multi-UAV relay system

According to [28], UAV-aided wireless communications can fall into three representative categories of use cases; (i) UAV-aided ubiquitous coverage, (ii) UAV-aided information dissemination and data collection and (iii) UAV-aided relaying. Focusing on the latter, communication relaying is an effective technique for network coverage extension and throughput maximization. However, a number of key challenges should be addressed in order to use UAVs as mobile relaying nodes, providing broadband communication to users (or user groups) without direct and/or reliable communication links (e.g., in disaster-hit or rural areas [6]). First, efficient algorithms should be devised to place UAVs in a 3D space. The mobility of the UAVs introduces new challenges to the network design problem compared to the traditional static relaying and fixed-infrastructure schemes (e.g. WiFi access-points). Moreover, in order to cover large geographical areas and because of the limited transmission range of UAVs, a swarm of UAVs is needed to route users' traffic demands through wireless multi-hop path(s). Due to the intermittent wireless links and frequent topology changes in such mobile ad hoc networks (MANETs), the traffic routing decision should be considered together with the UAVs placement and relocation. More importantly, such decisions should be adaptive to the topology and traffic pattern changes in a timely manner.

In this study, we consider an aerial platform consisting of multiple UAVs that supports the traffic demand of a ground network. Multi-hop relaying in the next generation of wireless networks will not only facilitate the coverage of more UEs and the support of long-distance communications, but also will be able to handle overloaded networks. Figure 1 illustrates the architecture and application scenarios of such systems. In contrast to the majority of existing studies such as [31] and [27] that solely focus on a single UAV relay and the air-to-ground (A2G) access links with one-hop communication or at most two-hop communications considering also the UAV-to-BS links in UAV-aided cellular networks (e.g. [14]), we exploit a multi-hop aerial relaying platform. Moreover, the rate-constrained UAV-to-UAV (or Air-to-Air, A2A) communications and the connectivity between UAVs are considered in the proposed framework. Although facility placement and traffic routing are usually addressed sequentially as two separate problems, the meaningful interrelation between the two, as discussed in [22] makes it more reasonable to approach them in a single model. Thus, another contribution of this manuscript is jointly optimizing the UAV placement and the routing decisions, when the ground network is quasi-static. We also extend our approach to the case of a mobile ground network and consider the impact of the UAVs' speed, while most of the existing relaying schemes utilize static relay nodes due to the practical constraints on relay mobility and the need for high-throughput links [27]. In order to reduce the system energy consumption and since the propulsion energy consumption of UAVs is typically significantly greater than the energy consumption for communications [16], we avoid unnecessary UAVs' relocation in subsequent snapshots in our solution. The problem is formulated as a mixed-integer linear program (MILP). To reduce the time-complexity and enable real time re-positioning of the mobile relays and routing decision, we propose an approximation algorithm using linear programming (LP) relaxation and a rounding procedure. The proposed approach assumes logically centralized network control i.e., software defined networking (SDN). The controller's global network view in an SDN architecture, renders centralized UAVs placement and adaptive routing strategies feasible [12]. The controller may be placed at a remote ground center, inside the ad hoc network devices as in [20] or at UAVs as shown in Fig. 1.

The paper is organized as follows. Section 2 describes the problem and the system model. In Sect. 3, we introduce a MILP formulation for the optimal UAV placement in the case of a quasi-static ground network and then extend our approach, considering mobility of the nodes, as well as provide our LP-based approximation method. Performance evaluation is presented in Sect. 4, while we provide the overview of the related work in Sect. 5. Finally, in Sect. 6, we highlight our conclusions and discuss our future work.

2   System Model and Problem Description

2.1   Radio Propagation Model

We adopt the model proposed in [1] for the A2G propagation model, where two signal propagation groups are considered; Line-of-Sight (LoS) and Non-Line-of-Sight (NLoS). The latter corresponds to receivers with no Line-of-Sight but still having coverage via strong reflections and diffraction. Additional impairments to the radio channel are caused by scattering and shadowing from the man-made structures in the environment. The occurrence probability of LoS is given by:

$$p_{LoS} = \frac{1}{1 + a\,exp(-b(\frac{180}{\pi}tan^{-1}(\frac{h}{r_{n,l}}) - a))} \tag{1}$$

where a and b are constants depending on the environment, h is the UAV altitude and $r_{n,l}$ is the horizontal euclidean distance between the UAV l and the user equipment (UE)

n. The probability of NLoS is $p_{NLoS} = 1 - p_{LoS}$ and the total A2G path loss (in dB) as a function of $r_{n,l}$ and h is:

$$L(h, r_{n,l}) = p_{LoS}L_{LoS} + p_{NLoS}L_{NLoS},\tag{2}$$

$$L_{LoS} = 20log(\frac{4\pi f_c d_{n,l}}{c}) + \eta_{LoS},$$

$$L_{NLoS} = 20log(\frac{4\pi f_c d_{n,l}}{c}) + \eta_{NLoS}$$

where f_c is the carrier frequency, $d_{n,l} = \sqrt{h^2 + r_{n,l}^2}$ is the distance between UAV l and UE n, η_{LoS} and η_{NLoS} are respectively the average additional losses due to the environment.

We assume that the A2A links are dominated by LoS components resulting in the following free space path loss model:

$$L(r_{u,v}) = 20log(\frac{4\pi f_c r_{u,v}}{c})\tag{3}$$

where $r_{u,v}$ is the distance between UAV u and UAV v. Assuming that an interference-coordination mechanism among adjacent UAVs and users is available, the interference is negligible and the received signal at a node is only affected by Additive White Gaussian Noise (AWGN). Consequently, the coverage radii for the A2G and A2A channels, denoted by R_1 and R_2, satisfy:

$$P_{UE} = L(h, R_1) + \gamma_{min} + \sigma_n^2\tag{4}$$

$$P_{UAV} = 20log(\frac{4\pi f_c R_2}{c}) + \gamma_{min} + \sigma_n^2\tag{5}$$

The QoS requirement is expressed in terms of the minimum received SNR at the receiver (γ_{min}), noise power (σ_n) and maximum transmission power of UAVs (P_{UAV}) and users (P_{UE}), where $P_{UE} \leq P_{UAV}$.

2.2 Problem Description

We discretize time and consider a directed graph $G^t = (V^t, E^t)$ representing the topology of the ground network at snapshot t. The vertex set V^t represents the network nodes and the edge set E^t represents the wireless links, i.e. $(u, v) \in E^t$ if and only if node v can receive data packets directly from node u. We assume that all node-to-node communication is unicast, i.e. each packet transmitted by a node $u \in V^t$ is intended for a unique $v \in V^t$ where $(u, v) \in E^t$. Moreover, each wireless link has a maximum capacity c_{uv}. For the sake of simplicity, the superscript t is dropped in the following.

There are traffic demands between UEs given by a traffic demand matrix D, where the element D_{uv} denotes the amount of demand from the source UE u to the destination UE v. The demand profile can be estimated using existing MANET traffic pattern inference (if a central controller is not available) or the schemes proposed for cellular networks (e.g., [25,29]) which are also applicable here in the presence of the UAV or ground control stations. Due to the limited transmission power of the UEs and in order to reduce the control traffic overhead required for traffic routing, the ground network is partitioned into M clusters, denoted by C_i, $i = 1,...,M$. Each cluster has a cluster head (CH) which functions as a gateway, relaying the cluster total traffic to the aerial platform. Let CH_i, $i = 1,...,M$ denote the ith cluster head. Given D, the inter-cluster traffic demand for a pair of clusters and from CH_i to CH_j is calculated by:

$$TD_{ij} = \sum_{u \in C_i, v \in C_j} D_{uv}, \quad \forall i, j \in \{CH_1,...,CH_M\}$$

We denote by $i \to j$, a traffic flow originated from CH_i and destined to CH_j. The problem considered in this paper entails the optimal placement of at most N_{max} available UAVs as relay nodes to support the traffic demand of the ground origin destination (OD) flows. For each OD flow $i \to j$, a collection of aerial multi-hop paths can be used to route the traffic demand of the flow.

Let $\mathcal{U} = \{u_i, i = 1,...,|\mathcal{U}|\}$ denote the set of potential locations for UAV placement, where v_i stands for the ith location. Here, we assume that all UAVs are placed at the same altitude h; however, it is easy to extend the formulation to a 3D UAV placement where the set $\mathcal{U}$ includes locations at different heights. The following graphs are defined for the problem formulation:

Demand Graph: We model the connectivity and traffic requirements of the ground clusters by a directed graph $G_D = (\mathcal{V}_D, \mathcal{E}_D)$ where, $\mathcal{V}_D = \{CH_1,...,CH_M\}$ is the set of all CHs, and $(i, j) \in \mathcal{E}_D$ if and only if the OD flow $i \to j$ exists for $i, j \in \mathcal{V}_D$.

Network Graph: We introduce a directed graph $G_P = (\mathcal{V}_P, \mathcal{E}_P)$ where $\mathcal{V}_P = \mathcal{V}_D \cup \mathcal{U}$ and $(u, v) \in \mathcal{E}_P$ if and only if $d_{u,v} \leq R_2$ for A2A links, and $d_{u,v} \leq R_1$ for A2G links.

3 Problem Formulation

In this section, the MILP formulations for the optimal UAV placement and traffic routing in both static and mobile ground networks are presented and the proposed LP-based approximation solution is discussed.

3.1 MILP Formulation

Given the network and demand graphs G_P, G_D, we formulate the problem at hand considering the following decision variables:

- A set of binary variables x, where x_u is set to 1 if a UAV is deployed at position $u \in \mathcal{U}$ and 0 otherwise.
- A set of continuous variables f, where f_{uv}^{ij} is the amount of traffic from OD flow $i \to j$ assigned to the link $(u, v) \in \mathcal{E}_P$.
- A set of continuous variables y, where y_{ij} denotes the traffic amount of the OD flow $i \to j$ that is not supported (not delivered).

Table 1. System model parameters and variables

Variables	Description
x_u	Binary decision variable of UAV placement at position u
f_{ij}^{uv}	The amount of (i, j) traffic d assigned to (u, v)
y_{ij}	Total unsupported traffic of the OD pair (i, j)
Parameters	Description
$G_P = (V_P, E_P)$	The network graph of UAVs and ground cluster heads
$G_D = (V_D, E_D)$	The demand graph
M	Number of ground cluster heads
U	The set of UAV potential locations
N_{max}	Available number of UAVs
h	UAVs height
D	Traffic demand matrix of the ground network
TD_{ij}	Traffic demand between the CHs i and j
c_{uv}	Capacity of the link (u, v)

A summary of the system model parameters and variables is given in Table 1. The proposed MILP formulation for the joint UAV placement and traffic routing (**UPR_MILP**) is as follows:

$$\text{minimize} \quad \phi \frac{\sum_{u \in U} x_u}{N_{max}} + (1 - \phi) \frac{\sum_{(i,j) \in E_D} y_{ij}}{\sum_{(i,j) \in E_D} TD_{ij}} \tag{6}$$

Feasibility Constraints:

$$f_{uv}^{ij} \leq x_u c_{uv} \quad \forall (i, j) \in E_D, u \in U, v \in V_p \tag{7}$$

$$f_{uv}^{ij} \leq x_v c_{uv} \quad \forall (i, j) \in E_D, v \in U, u \in V_p \tag{8}$$

$$\sum_{u \in U} x_u \leq N_{max} \tag{9}$$

Flow Constraints:

$$\sum_{v \in V_p} (f_{uv}^{ij} - f_{vu}^{ij}) = \begin{cases} 0 & \forall u \in V_P \backslash \{i, j\}, (i, j) \in V_D \\ TD_{ij} - y_{ij} & u = i, \forall (i, j) \in E_D \\ -(TD_{ij} - y_{ij}) & u = j, \forall (i, j) \in E_D \end{cases} \tag{10}$$

Capacity Constraints:

$$\sum_{(i,j) \in E_D} f_{uv}^{ij} \leq c_{uv} \quad \forall (u, v) \in E_P \tag{11}$$

Domain Constrains:

$$0 \leq f_{uv}^{ij} \quad \forall i,j \in \mathcal{V}_D, u,v \in \mathcal{V}_p \tag{12}$$

$$0 \leq y_{ij} \quad \forall (i,j) \in \mathcal{E}_D \tag{13}$$

$$x_u \in \{0,1\} \quad \forall u \in \mathcal{U} \tag{14}$$

The objective function (6) aims at jointly minimizing the cost of UAV deployment (reflected as the number of deployed UAVs) and the total amount of requested traffic that can not be supported by the network (the total unsupported traffic). We normalize both metrics to be between 0 and 1 in order to avoid the known problem of different range values in Pareto Analysis (i.e. one metric having large value and the other one having small value). Since we have in our formulation two performance objectives (minimizing the number of deployed UAVs and minimizing the unsupported traffic), a full solution of the problem requires the complete tradeoff analysis between these two metrics and finding the Pareto Points or Pareto Frontier of this tradeoff problem. To arrive at Eq. (6), we employed what is known as the "scalarization method" for tradeoff analysis. This method is less computationally intensive. To fully understand the tradeoff between these two metrics using the scalarization method, we need to vary ϕ between 0 and 1. In this way we can compute the convexified Pareto Frontier. Indeed in our experiments, we tested different values for ϕ and selected a relatively small value to promote a solution that primarily enhances the performance of the network by minimizing the unsupported traffic.

Constraints (7) and (8) guarantee that the amount of traffic assigned to an A2G link is nonzero only if an UAV is placed at the aerial end of the link. Constraint (9) limits the maximum number of deployed UAVs, while constraints (10) enforce flow conservation, i.e. the sum of all inbound and outbound traffic for the UAV relays should be zero. Moreover this constraint ensures that for each OD flow $i \rightarrow j$, the inbound (outbound) traffic to j (from i) is $TD_{ij} - y_{ij}$ (the amount of supported traffic). Constraints (11) ensure that the total traffic assigned to a link does not exceed its capacity. Finally, (12), (13) and (14) express the domain constraints.

3.2 MILP Formulation with UAV Mobility Constraints

In the case of mobile UEs or dynamic traffic patterns, **UPR_MILP** can be reapplied periodically in order to update the UAV positions [19]. This update rate can be in the order of seconds [8]. To consider the effect of UAVs maximum speed in a dynamic environment, we add mobility constraints to the optimization problem discussed in the previous section. The maximum speed of UAVs is represented by v_{max} and the time duration of a snapshot is denoted by ΔT. For each $u_i \in \mathcal{U}$, let $\mathcal{B}_i \subset \mathcal{U}$ denote the set of potential locations that the UAV deployed in u_i can reach in one snapshot, i.e. $u_j \in \mathcal{B}_i$ if $d_{i,j} \leq v_{max}\Delta T$.

Given $\mathcal{B}_i$ and the UAV placement decision variables at snapshot $t-1$ ($\boldsymbol{x}^{t-1}$), the UAV mobility constraints at snapshot t can be expressed as:

$$\sum_{u_j \in \mathcal{B}_i} x_j^t \geq \mathbb{1}\{x_i^{t-1} = 1\} \tag{15}$$

Moreover, in order to reduce the propulsion energy consumption of UAVs by avoiding unnecessary and less-effective UAV relocations in consecutive snapshots, we add another term to the objective function (6). The new objective function is:

$$(\phi\frac{\sum_{u\in \mathcal{U}}x_u}{N_{max}}+(1-\phi)\frac{\sum_{(i,j)\in \mathcal{E}_D}y_{ij}}{\sum_{(i,j)\in \mathcal{E}_D}TD_{ij}})+\alpha(max_u|x_u^t - x_u^{t-1}|) \qquad (16)$$

where α is a constant factor determining the balance between the two terms of the objective function. Instead of the maximum function in the new objective and in order to get rid of the absolute value, we define a scalar variable z and add it to the objective function as follows:

$$(\phi\frac{\sum_{u\in \mathcal{U}}x_u}{N_{max}}+(1-\phi)\frac{\sum_{(i,j)\in \mathcal{E}_D}y_{ij}}{\sum_{(i,j)\in \mathcal{E}_D}TD_{ij}})+\alpha z \qquad (17)$$

and we add the following set of constraints to the optimization problem:

$$x_u^t - x_u^{t-1} \leq z \quad \forall u \in \mathcal{U} \qquad (18)$$

$$x_u^{t-1} - x_u^t \leq z \quad \forall u \in \mathcal{U} \qquad (19)$$

The resulting MILP is referred to as **MUPR_MILP** and is an NP-hard problem. However, the decision variables have to be determined in real-time, in response to the network changes. In the subsequent section we employ an LP-relaxation to deal with the time-complexity of the **MUPR_MILP**. A greedy rounding approach is used to obtain the binary solution of the original problem.

3.3   LP Relaxation and Rounding Algorithm

We derive the Linear Programming (LP) model of **MUPR_MILP** by relaxing the binary variables x_u^t or replacing the constraint sets (14) by:

$$x_u^t \in [0,1], \forall u \in \mathcal{U} \qquad (20)$$

The resulting LP is represented by **UPR_LP**. We also define the set $X \subseteq \mathcal{U}$ based on which the following LP denoted by **UPR_LP_reduced**(X) is defined:

$$\textbf{minimize} \quad (\phi\frac{\sum_{u\in \mathcal{U}}x_u^t}{N_{max}}+(1-\phi)\frac{\sum_{(i,j)\in \mathcal{E}_D}y_{ij}}{\sum_{(i,j)\in \mathcal{E}_D}TD_{ij}})+\alpha z \qquad (21)$$

$$\text{s.t} \quad (7)-(12),(18),(19) \qquad (22)$$

$$x_u^t = 1, \quad \forall u \in X \qquad (23)$$

$$x_u^t \in [0,1] \quad \forall u \notin X \qquad (24)$$

We introduce a rounding-based decision-making process (DM-LP) to retrieve the binary decision variables of **MUPR_MILP** at each snapshot by solving a sequence of **UPR_LP_reduced**(X) problems iteratively. Similar approach has been used for solving MILPs in resource allocation problems such as [23]. The proposed solution is shown in Algorithm 1. The set X represents the locations chosen for UAV placement and is updated within each iteration (line (4)). The final X reflects the UAV placement decision. As explained in lines (7)-(9), UAVs are placed deterministically with the priority given to the neighboring locations of the deployed UAVs at the previous snapshot (reflected in the definition of the set S which is constructed by the union of the sets $\mathcal{B}_v$ for $v \in \mathcal{U} : x_v^{t-1} = 1$) in order to not violate the mobility constraints. For example, if two UAVs are placed at locations u_1, u_2 at snapshot $t-1$, the set $\mathcal{B}_1 \cup \mathcal{B}_2$ is first considered for UAV placement at snapshot t so that at least one UAV is placed at one of the locations of $\mathcal{B}_1$ (similarly for $\mathcal{B}_2$). Once all mobility constraints are satisfied, all the remaining potential UAV locations are considered for the placement of new UAVs. In both cases, a UAV is deployed at the position with maximum x value within each iteration (line (9) and (11)). The algorithm terminates when the addition of a new UAV does not reduce the objective function or makes the problem infeasible, i.e. $x_u^t = 0, \forall u \in X$ or equivalently, $x_{u^*}^t = 0$. Finally, the routing decisions are automatically obtained from the f solution of the last iteration. Moreover, the input x is 0 in the first snapshot meaning that any location in $\mathcal{U}$ can initially be considered for UAV placement.

Algorithm 1. DM-LP

Input: $G_p^t, G_D^t, TD^t, x^{t-1}$
Output: x^t, f

1: Initialize $X \leftarrow \emptyset$, *Terminate* $\leftarrow$ *False*
2: **repeat**
3:     **if** not first iteration **then**
4:         $X \leftarrow X \cup \{u^*\}$
5:     **end if**
6:     $\{x_u^t, f_{uv}^{ij}\} \leftarrow$ Solve **UPR_LP_reduced**(X)
7:     $S \leftarrow \cup_{\{v:x_v^{t-1}=1, v \notin X\}} \{argmax_{k \in \mathcal{B}_v} x_k^t\}$
8:     **if** $S \neq \emptyset$ **then**   ▷ Mobility constraints are not satisfied
9:         $u^* = argmax_{u \in S} x_u^t$
10:     **else**   ▷ Mobility constraints are satisfied
11:         $u^* = argmax_{u \notin X} x_u^t$
12:     **end if**
13:     **if** $x_{u^*}^t > 0$ **then**
14:         $x_{u^*}^t = 1$
15:     **else**
16:         *Terminate* $\leftarrow$ *True*
17:     **end if**
18: **until** *Terminate* $==$ *False*
19: **return** x^t, f

It is important to note that compared to **MUPR_MILP** which is intractable for large networks, the proposed approximation algorithm calls the LP solver at most $|N_{max}| + 1$ times. In the next section, we provide numerical results to evaluate the performance of the proposed approach.

4 Performance Evaluation

In this section, we benchmark out proposed decision-making process, DM-LP, against the exact solution, denoted as DM-MILP and the connectivity-based approach proposed in [19], namely DM-Conn. We also compare the performance of the mobile and static UAV deployment approaches. We use the CPLEX commercial solver for solving our MILP model using the branch-and-bound method, while the method used to solve the LP is primal-dual SIMPLEX. All experiments are carried out on an Intel Xeon processor at 2.3 GHz with 8 GB memory. We consider 10 km × 10 km square region and CHs are distributed according to a Matern cluster process [7] with the number of clusters changing between $2 - 11$. The cluster density mean and cluster radius are 10 and 1000 m. We use the Reference Point Group Mobility (RPGM) model introduced in [9]. In this model, GUs in a cluster tend to coordinate their movement and the movement of each CH determines the behavior of the entire group. One example of such mobility is the movement of rescue teams during disaster relief. In our experiments, CHs move according to RWPM and their speed is distributed uniformly according to $U(5, 40)m/s$. We consider a grid with the total number of 100 points at height h as the potential UAV positions. The ground network flows are generated according to a Bernoulli distribution with the parameter $\lambda = 0.04$ while the traffic demand for each pair is chosen with equal probability among the values 0.2, 0.4, and 0.6 Mbps. Unless stated otherwise, simulation parameters are provided in Table 2. Based on the simulation parameters, the A2G communication range $R_1 = 2214$ m and the corresponding A2A communication range

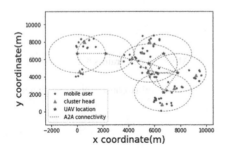

| **Fig. 2.** DM-MILP UAV placement | **Fig. 3.** DM-LP UAV placement |

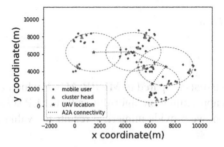

Fig. 4. DM-Conn UAV placement [19]

is $R_2 = 3774$ m calculated from Eqs. (4) and (5). In the following, the numerical results are provided for two experiments.

Static Ground Network. In this experiment, we consider a fixed network with 9 clusters and a 10×10 UAV location grid. Figure 2, 3 and 4 illustrate the UAV placement solution of DM-MILP, DM-LP, DM-Conn strategies. It can be observed that all the clusters are covered by UAVs in all three cases. The number of deployed UAVs in DM-Conn is less than the other two approaches, since D-Conn only ensures the A2G, A2A connectivity and A2G link capacity constraints, not the end-to-end traffic delivery. As a result, the supported traffic of DM-Conn is 67%, while both DM-MILP and DM-LP fully support the traffic demands in this example. This experiment highlights the need for joint UAV placement and traffic routing in multi-hop UAV relaying systems.

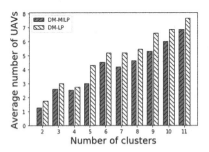

Fig. 5. Number of UAVs: DM-LP vs. DM-MILP

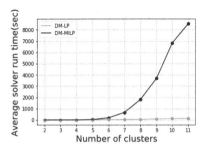

Fig. 6. Solver runtime: DM-LP vs DM-MILP

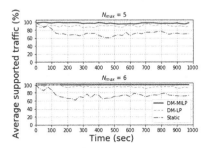

Fig. 7. Average percentage of supported traffic

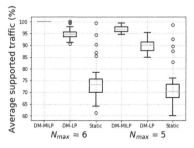

Fig. 8. Average percentage of supported traffic profile

Mobile Ground Network. In this experiment, the proposed DM-LP is benchmarked against DM-MILP and a static UAV deployment in a dynamic ground network. Figure 5 depicts the number of relays deployed based on DM-MILP and DM-LP, as an indicator of the deployment cost. The results are averaged over 20 snapshots. There are no hard limits imposed on the maximum number of UAVs, i.e. their number is only constrained by the number of potential UAV positions on the grid ($|\mathcal{U}|$). As a result, traffic demands are fully supported, while the difference in the average number of deployed UAVs is at most 2 more for the approximation algorithm. With regards to time complexity, as depicted in Fig. 6, DM-MILP follows an exponential growth, whereas the DM-LP method has an approximately linear time growth with respect to the number of clusters. Under the current evaluation environment, the real time operation of a network comprised of up to 6 clusters can be supported. However, DM-LP's linear time-complexity would guarantee real time support for larger network instances with a more powerful system.

Figure 7 shows the average total supported traffic per snapshot for a ground network of 10 clusters, following DM-LP, DM-MILP and a static UAV deployment where the UAVs locations are obtained from the solution of DM-MILP for the first snapshot. Figure 8 depicts the profile of the average supported traffic for the same scenarios over snapshots. The results are averaged over 5 random networks. Overall, the deviation of the DM-LP from the optimal solution is on average 7% and 5% when $N_{max} = 5$ and $N_{max} = 6$ respectively. Note that 6 UAVs are enough to fully support the traffic demand of the generated network instances as DM-MILP achieves 100% traffic support in this experiment. This demonstrates the ability of the proposed LP-based scheme to generate good solutions, for a limited number of available UAVs. Moreover, a static UAV deployment with even an optimal initial deployment resulted in a maximum of 40% unsupported traffic, highlighting the need for a dynamic UAV deployment solution.

The four figures together shows how the mobility capability of UAVs can be exploited to achieve higher traffic delivery in a mobile ground network and demonstrates that the proposed DM-LP approach trades only a small degree of optimality for fast retrievable solutions.

5 Related Work

Deployment of UAVs has extensively been a topic of research with different objectives, such as the maximization of the downlink (DL) throughput [15,24] and DL received signal strength (RSS) [5]. In contrast, we explore a UAV-assisted communication system considering both uplink (UL) and DL traffic streams. Authors in [1,2,17] investigate the usage of UAVs to maximize the covered area with respect to the UAV altitude, antenna gain and minimum received power of users. In [21], the coverage probability of a reference ground user is evaluated for a 3D UAV movement process characterized by the RWPM and uniform mobility models. In [3], authors propose a UAV-assisted cellular network and maximize the revenue, that is proportional to the number of covered users. However, in order to fully satisfy the QoS requirement of the users in a multi-hop wireless network, the end-to-end traffic delivery should be considered which is more challenging than a coverage problem. Regarding energy efficiency, Mozaffari et al. [18] applied optimal transport theory to minimize total DL transmission power. Optimizing the flight radius and speed to improve energy efficiency is also addressed in [26].

The required number of aerial UAVs is minimized in [10,19]. Authors in [19] propose a UAV placement algorithm taking into account the connectivity between UAVs

Table 2. Simulation parameters

Parameters	Description
$(a, b, \eta_{LoS}, \eta_{NLoS})$	$(9.61, 0.16, 1.0, 20.0)$ for urban environment
UAVs altitude h	2000 m
Carrier frequency f_c	2 GHz
Thermal noise power σ^2	−90 dBm
SNR threshold γ_{min}	−4 dBm
E_{GU}, E_{UAV}	20 dBm, 110 dBm
v_{max}	55 m/s
Snapshot duration ΔT	25 s

and the clusters demands; however, the constraints on the UAVs mobility and the A2A links capacity are ignored. Authors in [4] and [13] considered multi-hop wireless backhauling in UAV-aided networks. In [4], U. Challita and W. Saad seek to form a multi-hop backhaul network in the sky connecting small ground base station through formation of a bidirectional tree structure. Different from [4], we consider both A2A and A2G links and jointly optimize the UAV placement and routing. In [13], the authors optimized the UAV placement, power and bandwidth allocation in an UAV-enabled multihop backhaul with fixed number of UAVs. In our case, we minimize the number of deployed UAVs in addition to imposing a constraint on the maximum number of UAVs. In contrast to [30] which investigates the trajectory design and power allocation strategies for a single fixed ground source-destination, we consider a general mobile ground network consisting of multiple traffic flows which makes the UAV relays trajectory design and traffic routing more challenging and out of the scope of the set-up in [30]. Authors in [11] consider the placement and resource allocation problem of multi UAV relays for a ground network with multiple traffic flows; however they ignore the mobility of the ground nodes and how it affects the UAV locations and other decision variables.

6   Conclusion

In this article, we propose a framework for joint UAV placement and route optimization in a multi-hop UAV relaying communications system, taking into account the mobility of the ground nodes, the capacity of A2A and A2G links, UAVs mobility constraints and UAVs propulsion energy consumption. We model the problem as a MILP, and then propose an efficient LP-based approximation algorithm to effectively reduce the time-complexity of our model, achieving a near-optimal solution. The numerical simulations provide insights on the effect the users' mobility and the dynamic relocation of UAVs on the decision making process and the service degradation. Among our future directions are to consider the control/management layer resource allocation problem and investigate the computation offloading and service placement problem together with the resource allocation in a mobile edge computing setup.

68 A. Gholami et al.

Acknowledgment. The research of A. Gholami, N. Torkzaban and J.S. Baras, was partially supported by ONR grant N00014-17-12622 and by a grant from the Lockheed Martin Corporation.

References

1. Al-Hourani, A., Kandeepan, S., Lardner, S.: Optimal lap altitude for maximum coverage. IEEE Wirel. Commun. Lett. **3**(6), 569–572 (2014)
2. Alzenad, M., El-Keyi, A., Yanikomeroglu, H.: 3-D placement of an unmanned aerial vehicle base station for maximum coverage of users with different QoS requirements. IEEE Wirel. Commun. Lett. **7**(1), 38–41 (2017)
3. Bor-Yaliniz, R.I., El-Keyi, A., Yanikomeroglu, H.: Efficient 3-D placement of an aerial base station in next generation cellular networks. In: 2016 IEEE International Conference on Communications (ICC), pp. 1–5. IEEE (2016)
4. Challita, U., Saad, W.: Network formation in the sky: unmanned aerial vehicles for multi-hop wireless backhauling. In: GLOBECOM 2017–2017 IEEE Global Communications Conference, pp. 1–6. IEEE (2017)
5. Galkin, B., Kibilda, J., DaSilva, L.A.: Deployment of UAV-mounted access points according to spatial user locations in two-tier cellular networks. In: 2016 Wireless Days (WD), pp. 1–6. IEEE (2016)
6. Gholami, A., Fiaz, U.A., Baras, J.S.: Drone-assisted communications for remote areas and disaster relief. arXiv preprint arXiv:1909.02150 (2019)
7. Haenggi, M.: Stochastic Geometry for Wireless Networks. Cambridge University Press, Cambridge (2012)
8. Han, Z., Swindlehurst, A.L., Liu, K.R.: Optimization of manet connectivity via smart deployment/movement of unmanned air vehicles. IEEE Trans. Veh. Technol. **58**(7), 3533–3546 (2009)
9. Hong, X., Gerla, M., Pei, G., Chiang, C.C.: A group mobility model for ad hoc wireless networks. In: Proceedings of the 2nd ACM International Workshop on Modeling, Analysis and Simulation of Wireless and Mobile Systems, pp. 53–60 (1999)
10. Kalantari, E., Yanikomeroglu, H., Yongacoglu, A.: On the number and 3D placement of drone base stations in wireless cellular networks. In: 2016 IEEE 84th Vehicular Technology Conference (VTC-Fall), pp. 1–6. IEEE (2016)
11. Kang, Z., You, C., Zhang, R.: Placement learning for multi-UAV relaying: a gibbs sampling approach. In: ICC 2020–2020 IEEE International Conference on Communications (ICC), pp. 1–6 (2020)
12. Li, B., Fei, Z., Zhang, Y.: UAV communications for 5G and beyond: recent advances and future trends. IEEE Internet Things J. **6**(2), 2241–2263 (2018)
13. Li, P., Xu, J.: UAV-enabled cellular networks with multi-hop backhauls: placement optimization and wireless resource allocation. In: 2018 IEEE International Conference on Communication Systems (ICCS), pp. 110–114. IEEE (2018)
14. Lyu, J., Zeng, Y., Zhang, R.: UAV-aided offloading for cellular hotspot. IEEE Trans. Wirel. Commun. **17**(6), 3988–4001 (2018)
15. Merwaday, A., Guvenc, I.: UAV assisted heterogeneous networks for public safety communications. In: 2015 IEEE Wireless Communications and Networking Conference Workshops (WCNCW), pp. 329–334. IEEE (2015)
16. Mozaffari, M., Saad, W., Bennis, M., Nam, Y., Debbah, M.: A tutorial on UAVs for wireless networks: applications, challenges, and open problems. IEEE Commun. Surv. Tutor. **21**(3), 2334–2360 (2019)

17. Mozaffari, M., Saad, W., Bennis, M., Debbah, M.: Efficient deployment of multiple unmanned aerial vehicles for optimal wireless coverage. IEEE Commun. Lett. **20**(8), 1647–1650 (2016)
18. Mozaffari, M., Saad, W., Bennis, M., Debbah, M.: Optimal transport theory for power-efficient deployment of unmanned aerial vehicles. In: 2016 IEEE International Conference on Communications (ICC), pp. 1–6. IEEE (2016)
19. Perumal, S., Baras, J.S., Graff, C.J., Yee, D.G.: Aerial platform placement algorithms to satisfy connectivity, capacity and survivability constraints in wireless ad-hoc networks. In: MILCOM 2008–2008 IEEE Military Communications Conference, pp. 1–7. IEEE (2008)
20. Poularakis, K., Qin, Q., Marcus, K.M., Chan, K.S., Leung, K.K., Tassiulas, L.: Hybrid SDN control in mobile ad hoc networks. In: 2019 IEEE International Conference on Smart Computing (SMARTCOMP), pp. 110–114. IEEE (2019)
21. Sharma, P.K., Kim, D.I.: Random 3D mobile UAV networks: mobility modeling and coverage probability. IEEE Trans. Wirel. Commun. **18**(5), 2527–2538 (2019)
22. Torkzaban, N., Gholami, A., Baras, J.S., Papagianni, C.: Joint satellite gateway placement and routing for integrated satellite-terrestrial networks. In: ICC 2020–2020 IEEE International Conference on Communications (ICC), pp. 1–6 (2020)
23. Torkzaban, N., Papagianni, C., Baras, J.S.: Trust-aware service chain embedding. In: 2019 Sixth International Conference on Software Defined Systems (SDS), pp. 242–247. IEEE (2019)
24. Wu, Q., Zeng, Y., Zhang, R.: Joint trajectory and communication design for multi-UAV enabled wireless networks. IEEE Trans. Wirel. Commun. **17**(3), 2109–2121 (2018)
25. Yu, C., et al.: Modeling user activity patterns for next-place prediction. IEEE Syst. J. **11**(2), 1060–1071 (2015)
26. Zeng, Y., Zhang, R.: Energy-efficient UAV communication with trajectory optimization. IEEE Trans. Wirel. Commun. **16**(6), 3747–3760 (2017)
27. Zeng, Y., Zhang, R., Lim, T.J.: Throughput maximization for UAV-enabled mobile relaying systems. IEEE Trans. Commun. **64**(12), 4983–4996 (2016)
28. Zeng, Y., Zhang, R., Lim, T.J.: Wireless communications with unmanned aerial vehicles: opportunities and challenges. IEEE Commun. Mag. **54**(5), 36–42 (2016)
29. Zhang, C., Zhang, H., Qiao, J., Yuan, D., Zhang, M.: Deep transfer learning for intelligent cellular traffic prediction based on cross-domain big data. IEEE J. Sel. Areas Commun. **37**(6), 1389–1401 (2019)
30. Zhang, G., Yan, H., Zeng, Y., Cui, M., Liu, Y.: Trajectory optimization and power allocation for multi-hop UAV relaying communications. IEEE Access **6**, 48566–48576 (2018)
31. Zhang, S., Zhang, H., He, Q., Bian, K., Song, L.: Joint trajectory and power optimization for UAV relay networks. IEEE Commun. Lett. **22**(1), 161–164 (2017)

Analysis and Performance of Topology Inference in Mobile Ad Hoc Networks

J. David Brown[✉], Mazda Salmanian, and Tricia J. Willink

Defence Research and Development Canada, Ottawa, Canada
{david.brown,mazda.salmanian,tricia.willink}@drdc-rddc.gc.ca

Abstract. This paper examines the performance of a strategy for mapping the topology of a mobile ad hoc network (MANET), providing insight for network defenders to understand how much information an adversary could discern about a target network. Using this topology inference strategy, a network eavesdropper collects frame emission start- and end-times and uses these to detect the presence of link layer acknowledgements between devices and ultimately constructs a network topology. We show how the performance of this simple strategy varies as a function of the amount of data collected by the eavesdropper over time, the size of the target network, the speed of the nodes, and the nodes' data generation rate. We derive analytical results that allow for the rapid computation of expected true positive rate and false positive rate for topology inference in a MANET; these are compared against simulation results. The analytical results are used to derive a sensible window of observation over which to perform inference, with guidance on when to discard stale data. The results are also used to recommend strategies for network defenders to frustrate the performance of an adversary's network inference.

Keywords: Network topology inference · Mobile ad hoc networks (MANET) · Traffic analysis · Cyber analytics

1 Introduction

The reconnaissance phase, in which an adversary gathers information about its intended target, is typically one of the first steps in any cyber-attack. In performing reconnaissance against a wireless ad hoc network, an important consideration is deriving the logical network topology: identifying which nodes have direct communication links with one another. A logical topology is either assumed or acquired as a pre-condition in many cyber and electronic warfare (EW) attacks. For instance, a simple man-in-the-middle attack [1] requires knowledge of where in the network to insert or capture packets; targeted jamming attacks such as in [2] require a topology map to achieve the greatest effect. Even for attacks in which knowing the target topology is not a pre-condition, having the topology map can lead to a greater impact; for example, the well-known wormhole [3] or black hole attacks [4] are most effective when they target known weak points in the network. Whether assumed or acquired, a known logical topology is the basis for an effective attack.

L. Foschini and M. El Kamili (Eds.): ADHOCNETS 2020, LNICST 345, pp. 70–86, 2021.
https://doi.org/10.1007/978-3-030-67369-7_6

In this paper, we present a general approach to topology inference in a mobile ad hoc network (MANET) and we analyze its performance. We derive analytical estimates for link detection accuracy and error rate, and we validate these through simulation. We also explore the relationship between node velocity and node traffic generation rate, leading to recommendations for defensive techniques to frustrate an adversary's topology inference.

Many works examining topology discovery assume that it is possible to probe the network in some fashion. For instance, [5] and [6] present techniques to infer a network topology using ICMP probes, where certain nodes in the network discard or ignore ICMP messages and others respond unreliably. While [5] and [6] are intended for mapping enterprise networks, these methods could also be effective in a wireless MANET in the case where an adversary had a packet injection capability but was not able to see the entire network from a single location. In [7], the difficulty of relying on ICMP is acknowledged, and another technique is introduced wherein non-ICMP probe messages are sent and the timing of the probes is measured to infer a topology; once again, however, the method assumes that it is possible to inject probes to which the network will respond. The M-iTop algorithm [8] adopts a different strategy that infers a network topology by vastly overestimating the number of components in the network and then paring them down through careful merging by relying on observed messages from known nodes within the network.

In unencrypted wireless networks using known communication protocols, it is generally understood that a global eavesdropper could determine the nearest-neighbour network topology without any probes simply by observing the link layer (or MAC) source and destination addresses for all packets in the network, inferring that source and destination nodes share a common link. Previous work in [9] identifies traffic flows in a MANET where the network is encrypted above the link layer and the MAC is obfuscated according to an anonymizing routing protocol such as in [10]. In this case, two-way communication between nodes over a short time period can still be used to perform one-hop topology inference based on short-term obfuscated identifiers (not fixed MAC addresses per se). End-to-end flow inference in a MANET is also explored in [11], which examines the correlation of packet timing and size across all nodes in the network to infer the presence of flows between certain parties; although not specifically focused on topology inference, it is a reasonable step to infer the network topology as well using this technique. While the technique in [11] shows promise, its performance is quite sensitive to tuning parameters and does not appear to be robust in the face of anonymizing routing protocols. In the case where encryption is extended to the link layer such that the MAC itself is encrypted, simple source-destination matching analyses are no longer possible.

This paper expands on a previous study [12], which assumes that an adversary detects direct links (i.e., direct point-to-point connections) between nodes in the network by observing the timing of link-layer messaging between the nodes. Specifically, an adversary observes acknowledgements (ACKs) sent in response to regular packet data and infers the existence of links between senders and receivers. By design, a link-layer ACK is typically an immediate short response following a link-layer data message between neighbouring nodes. In principal, these ACKs could be detected through packet timing analysis alone, even when encrypted, and without requiring access to headers or payloads (indeed, the authors of [13] state without proof that a static network topology can be inferred in this manner). However, as we observed in [12], even for static networks using a simple ACK-based topology inference method, it is not evident *a priori* how much data must be observed to ensure the inferred network topology is accurate; nor is it evident what impact network size, network node range, and traffic flow frequency can have on that accuracy.

Our focus in this paper moves beyond static inference and examines a MANET with a continually changing topology. Our aim is to characterize the limitations and accuracy of such an ACK-based inference scheme, in which observed links become stale due to mobility-induced topology changes. These topology changes present a challenge to the accuracy of the inference scheme when one attempts to determine which links are still "fresh".

In this paper we make the following contributions:

1) We derive an analytical estimate of the accuracy of ACK-based topology inference in a MANET;
2) We provide supporting simulations that demonstrate the accuracy of the analytical estimate and give an intuitive sense of the roles of node velocity, node range, traffic flow frequency, and network size in performing topology inference;
3) We propose a method to select a sensible observation window size over which to perform inference (i.e., to decide when ACK messages are no longer "fresh" enough to be used to infer links); and
4) We offer guidance on how nodes in a network can frustrate the accuracy of the ACK-based traffic analysis by shaping the timing of their emissions as a function of the nodes' velocities.

The rest of the paper is organized as follows. Section 2 introduces the network and mobility model, along with basic assumptions and notation. In Sect. 3, we derive formulas that describe the correct detection rate and false detection rate for an ACK-based topology inference scheme. Simulations in Sect. 4 validate the derived formulas and show how performance varies with network size, node range, traffic load, and node velocity; this section also includes methods to select a window size for inference, and suggestions for network defenders. Section 5 summarizes our contributions with a brief conclusion.

2 Model, Assumptions and Notation

Following the notation in [14] (pp. 811–812), we represent a MANET of n nodes as a graph $G = (V, E)$, which describes a set of $V = \{1, 2, ..., n\}$ vertices representing the mobile nodes connected by edges $E \in V \times V$. We adopt the well-known random geometric graph (RGG) model (documented extensively by Penrose [15]) where we assume that nodes are positioned uniformly at random in a square area of dimensions X by X meters; any two nodes i and j are considered "neighbours" with a link between them (and hence an edge in the graph G) if the distance between the nodes, d_{ij}, is less than the network transmission range in meters, R. A route exists between two nodes if there exists a set of edges in E that connect the nodes through a set of vertices in V.

Nodes in the network generate traffic randomly according to a Poisson process at an average rate of λ packets per second; for each packet generated, a node selects a (routable) destination at random and transmits the packet over a potentially multi-hop route, where the average number of hops in the network is denoted by h.

Nodes move about from their initial positions following a random direction mobility model ([14], Chapter 7), where for mathematical tractability in Sect. 3 we assume all nodes travel at the same speed, v, and bounce off the boundary of the square area without pausing. While the set of nodes V never changes, the edges (i.e., the links, E) in G change over time as nodes move around in the square. Adopting a discrete-time model, we use the notation G_k to refer to the graph of the nodes in the network at time step k. Furthermore, the $n \times n$ adjacency matrix A_k is derived from G_k and describes the presence or absence of links between nodes; A_k consists of entries $a_{ij}[k] \in \{0,1\}$ for each pair of vertices (i, j) such that an edge exists between i and j if $a_{ij}[k] = 1$ and does not exist otherwise. We assume that links are symmetric such that $a_{ij}[k] = a_{ji}[k]$ for all (i, j).

In performing topology inference, we are interested in finding estimates $\hat{a}_{ij}[k]$ for each value of $a_{ij}[k]$ in A_k. If $a_{ij}[k] = \hat{a}_{ij}[k]$, then our inference about an edge between i and j is correct; otherwise it is incorrect. Using standard confusion matrix formulas [16], we can write the true positive rate (TPR) for the network-wide topology inference at time instant k as

$$TPR_k = \frac{1}{L_k} \sum_{i \in V} \sum_{j \in V \mid j < i} a_{ij}[k] \cdot \hat{a}_{ij}[k], \tag{1}$$

where L_k is the total number of edges in G_k; the TPR captures the percentage of links that have been correctly identified by a set of topology inference estimates $\hat{a}_{ij}[k]$ over all i and j. Likewise, the false positive rate (FPR) describes the percentage of non-links that have been falsely is identified as links and is computed using

$$FPR_k = \frac{1}{L_{max} - L_k} \sum_{i \in V} \sum_{j \in V \mid j < i} \left(1 - a_{ij}[k]\right) \cdot \hat{a}_{ij}[k], \tag{2}$$

where $L_{max} = n \cdot (n - 1)/2$ is the maximum possible number of links in a network of n nodes, and $L_{max} - L_k$ is the number of non-links in the network at instant k. Note that throughout the paper, we often drop the subscript k denoting the time step on TPR and FPR, though context should make it clear.

In modeling ACK-based topology inference, we assume a global eavesdropper that can observe the timing of all emissions from all nodes in the network and is able to distinguish these emissions from one another. We assume each unicast communication between any two adjacent nodes produces an identifiable ACK response, allowing the eavesdropper to infer the presence of the link. Note that the intent of our analysis here is not to determine how well we can identify ACKs, but to characterize the performance and limitations of a link-based inference scheme in a mobile network with a changing topology. A key realization from this last point is that while our work in this paper focuses on an ACK-based topology inference scheme, the results would apply equally well to any link-based topology inference scheme in which the transmission of a unicast packet allowed the eavesdropper to reliably infer the presence of a link between the source and destination of the packet.

3 Analytical Characterization of Topology Inference

Consider a MANET with n nodes represented by a random geometric graph with n vertices, where each node moves in an independently selected random direction with velocity v and generates traffic according to a Poisson process. In this section, we derive analytical expressions for the expected true positive and false positive rate of a link-based topology inference scheme operating in such a network. We introduce the notation T_k and F_k to represent the expected number of links correctly identified and falsely identified, respectively, at time step k. Thus, the expected true positive and false positive rates are expressed as $\text{TPR}_k = T_k/L$ and $\text{FPR}_k = F_k/(L_{max} - L)$, where L is the average number of links in the network and $L_{max} = n(n-1)/2$ and corresponds to the maximum possible number of links in the network.

Without loss of generality, consider the case where the duration of the time step from time k to $k+1$ is such that on average a single node in the network generates exactly one packet; this amounts to effectively choosing a time step size of $\Delta k = 1/\lambda n$. On average, a single unicast packet traverses h hops from source to destination; successfully observing ACK messages for each hop produces evidence for h links in the network arising from this unicast message. From time step k to $k+1$, we expect the average number of correctly identified links, T_k, to increase by some amount in response to this new evidence. In the absence of mobility, at time step k we would expect that some fraction of the h newly observed links are already known; in fact, the average number of observed links that are already known is simply h scaled by the expected true positive rate in the previous instant, $\text{TPR}_k = T_k/L$. Thus, for a static network we can write

$$T_{k+1} = T_k + h\left(1 - \frac{T_k}{L}\right). \tag{3}$$

Now, in a network with mobility, from time instant k to $k+1$, the nodes will have moved some distance, resulting in some number of link breakages (denoted here by L_{break}) and some number of new links (denoted here by L_{new}). Similar to the discussion above, we would expect that some fraction of the link breakages would have been previously (correctly) identified as true links, and this fraction would be given by the true positive rate in the previous time step, TPR_k; the fact that they are no longer links thus reduces the number of correctly observed links, T_{k+1}, by $E\{L_{break}\} \cdot (T_k/L)$, where $E\{L_{break}\}$ is the average number of link breakages expected over one time step.

Furthermore, some of the new links generated through mobility would have been previously (incorrectly) identified as links due to false detection, with this fraction of links given by the false-positive rate $F_k/(L_{max} - L)$. The result is that these newly formed links will now count among correct links, increasing T_{k+1} by $E\{L_{new}\} \cdot F_k/(L_{max} - L)$. Finally, as noted in [17], in a spatially constrained MANET with our constant-velocity mobility model we expect link generation and link breakage rates to be equal (on average), leading to $L_\Delta = E\{L_{break}\} = E\{L_{new}\}$, where L_Δ represents the average number of links broken (and created) in time step k to $k+1$. Incorporating the effects of mobility into Eq. (3) for T_{k+1} yields

$$T_{k+1} = T_k + h\left(1 - \frac{T_k}{L}\right) + L_\Delta\left(\frac{F_k}{L_{max} - L} - \frac{T_k}{L}\right). \tag{4}$$

Developing an expression for F_{k+1} follows in a similar fashion. Assuming links are detected accurately through ACK observations, the source of errors in our topology inference will arise primarily from out-of-date (stale) links that have broken due to node mobility. During time step k to $k + 1$ there will be $E\{L_{break}\}$ links broken and $E\{L_{new}\}$ links generated on average (where $E\{L_{break}\} = E\{L_{new}\} = L_\Delta$, as before). Some fraction of the links that break will have been previously correctly inferred, with this fraction given by TPR_k; these will now be in error, thus increasing the number of false positives, F_{k+1}, by $E\{L_{break}\}\cdot(T_k/L)$. Likewise, some fraction of the new links would have been previously incorrectly inferred, as given by FPR_k; these will now be correct, thus decreasing F_{k+1} by $E\{L_{new}\}\cdot F_k/(L_{max} - L)$. This results in an expression for F_{k+1} given by

$$F_{k+1} = F_k - L_\Delta\left(\frac{F_k}{L_{max} - L} - \frac{T_k}{L}\right). \tag{5}$$

An expression for L_Δ can be found by adapting the work in [18], in which it is shown that the link break and generation rates in a MANET with constant-velocity nodes are given by $(8/\pi)\rho Rv$, where ρ is node density. This expression provides the average link break and generation rate per unit time as seen from the point of view of single node. To be consistent with our time step size and notation, we scale this expression by a factor of $(1/n\lambda)$ seconds/message. Additionally, we are interested in the link break/generation rate of the network, not just that seen by a single node—this requires that we scale the expression by a factor of $(n/2)$, where the factor of 2 arises since for all nodes in the network any link break/generation is viewed by the two nodes forming the link and we only want to count these once. With these modifications, we obtain the expression

$$L_\Delta = \frac{4}{\pi^2} \cdot \frac{N_{av}}{R} \cdot \frac{v}{\lambda}, \tag{6}$$

where we have also made the substitution $\rho = N_{av}/(\pi R^2)$, with N_{av} denoting the average number of neighbours seen by nodes in the network.

The expressions in (4) and (5) for T_{k+1} and F_{k+1} comprise a system of coupled first-order difference equations. Armed with Eqs. (4), (5) and (6), we now have analytical expressions to generate true positive and false positive rates for ACK-based topology inference in a MANET, given its size (n), node velocity (v), range (R), and traffic generation rate (λ). These expressions can be evaluated rapidly up to any desired time step, k, using simple programming, with initial conditions of $T_0 = F_0 = 0$. In evaluating (4), (5) and (6), values of N_{av} can be computed using the expression in [19], and the average number of links, L, is found using $L = \lambda N_{av}/2$. Values for the average number of hops, h, can be computed from simple network simulations, or using estimates such as those in [20].

Note that Eqs. (4), (5) and (6) are not specifically reliant on a particular choice of MANET routing protocol such as AODV (ad hoc distance vector) routing or OLSR (optimum link state routing). However, the average number of hops in the network can be influenced by the choice of such protocols; for instance if all routes were (unwisely) chosen to maximize the number of hops per route, this would clearly yield a different value for h than choosing to minimize the number of hops. In this paper, as discussed in more detail in Sect. 4, our simulations use shortest-path routes; thus in evaluating TPR and FPR, above, we use an estimate for h based on shortest-path routing [20]. Of interest is that in static networks, we observed in [12] that a subset of links naturally form a part of multiple routes, making them more likely to be re-used as time goes on by a factor measured at roughly $(1 + (h - 1)T_k/L)^2$. Were a different routing protocol selected that did not explicitly minimize hops, a different estimate for h would be required, but this is beyond the scope of this paper.

We show in Sect. 4 that our expressions for expected TPR and FPR generate results that align very closely with network simulation.

4 Simulations and Analytical Results

We completed a series of simulations in MATLAB, where we considered the effect of varying network size, node range, node speed and traffic generation rate on the performance of an ACK-based topology inference scheme. In selecting parameters for our simulations, we considered small networks representative of military tactical network deployments. It is of interest for users of such networks to understand how much information an adversary might infer about their network topology. Simulation parameters are summarized in Table 1 and discussed below.

Table 1. Simulation parameters for MANET scenarios.

Simulation parameter	Values
Area of operation	Square area, 3000 m × 3000 m
Number of nodes (n)	8, 16, 24
Radio transmission range (R)	750 m, 1125 m, 1500 m
Node speed (v)	1 m/s, 3 m/s, 10 m/s
Average transmission rate per node (λ)	0.5 packets/s, 1 packet/s, 2 packets/s

A typical tactical network can be structured around the basic sub-unit of an infantry Section, which consists of approximately 8-10 nodes. Sections can operate independently or in groups of up to three, where three Sections are organized as a Platoon (approximately 24 nodes). Our simulations consider networks of sizes 8, 16, and 24 nodes, representing a single Section, two Sections operating together, and a Platoon.

Following guidance in [21], we consider a scenario where nodes travel in a square area of operation of size 3000 m × 3000 m. We assume that nodes have transmission ranges between 750 m to 1500 m, in line with performance expectations for existing high-bandwidth multi-hop radios. For simplicity of the model, all nodes move at the same speed, travelling at speeds of either 1 m/s (walking speed), 3 m/s (jogging speed), or 10 m/s (moderate vehicle speed). Each node randomly generates packets at a rate determined by a Poisson process with a mean, λ, of 0.5, 1, or 2 packets/s.

In conducting a single simulation run, we select values for each of n, R, v, and λ from Table 1. Nodes are placed uniformly at random in the area of operations and move at speed v, changing directions when they encounter the edges of the area. Nodes generate traffic, which is transmitted via a shortest-path multi-hop route to intended (randomly selected) destinations.

During the course of a single simulation run, an ideal eavesdropper collects the timing of packets for all network transmissions and estimates the existence of ACKs by comparing the timestamp of each newly observed frame to the timestamp of the previously observed frame. If the difference between the two frames is less than a given threshold, the newly observed frame is deemed to be an ACK to the previous frame, indicating a link between the sources of the ACK and the previous frame. ACKs are assumed to be generated sufficiently rapidly (and are sufficiently short) that the time difference between a frame and its corresponding ACK is small enough to ensure correct detection of all ACKs.

Inferred links in a single run are compared against the known instantaneous ground truth of the network topology at every time step k, allowing for the computation of single-run TPR and FPR as functions of k. Average TPR and FPR are computed by repeating each single-run simulation 100 times (with new randomized node placement each time) and averaging all the single-run TPR and FPR values at each time step.

In Sect. 4.1, our plots examine the expected TPR and FPR as a function of k, without an attempt to drop old (stale) information; this is done to get a clear understanding of how correct and incorrect inference evolves over time. In Sect. 4.2 we explore how to select an appropriate time window to focus only on recently observed ACKs to limit the proliferation of inference errors due to stale information.

4.1 Effect of Range, Network Size, Node Speed, and Traffic Rate on Inference

To explore the effect of range, size, speed, and traffic generation rate on topology inference, we vary each of R, n, v and λ individually and plot the resulting average TPR and FPR against time step k (where to compare against estimates in (4) and (5), k is the time for the network to generate one new message, on average).

Figure 1 shows the effect of different transmission ranges, R, under mobility. We see that for lower values of R, the TPR increases more rapidly, while the FPR increases less rapidly than for higher R values. These results are intuitively satisfying, since a network with smaller R will have more hops on average between any source-destination pair; thus, a single source transmission is likely to hop more times through the network, revealing more links, leading to a higher TPR. Another factor that leads a smaller R to yield a higher TPR is that a smaller R results in a network with fewer links to discover, meaning that each transmitted message in the network provides proportionally more information. Likewise, with respect to false positives, a smaller R will result in a larger number of "non-links" in the network[1]; thus a single erroneously detected link will constitute a smaller fraction of the total non-links in the network, leading to a smaller FPR.

Figure 1 also shows agreement between the simulation results—shown as solid and dashed curves—and our analytical predictions derived from Eqs. (4) and (5), shown as dotted curves.

---

[1] A non-link in this context is a pair of nodes for which there is no direct 1-hop connection. There are, on average, $L_{max} - L$ non-links in the network.

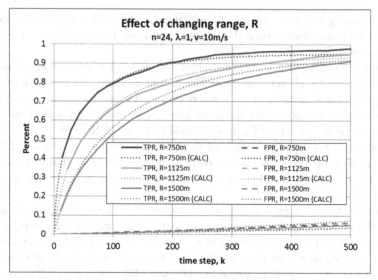

Fig. 1. Effect of transmission range, R, on the average true positive rate (TPR) and false positive rate (FPR) for MANET with $n = 24$, $v = 10$ m/s, $\lambda = 1$ packet/s.

The effect of network size on topology inference is shown in Fig. 2, which plots TPR and FPR for values of $n = 8$, 16, and 24. We observe that in a network with fewer nodes, there is a more rapid increase in both TPR and FPR compared to a larger network. The intuition behind TPR increasing faster for a smaller network is similar to what was described above for a network with lower range: the smaller network has comparatively fewer links to discover, meaning that the percentage of correctly inferred links is larger for each observed ACK. For FPR, however, the case is different here since a smaller network also has fewer potential non-links—this means that every error in inference (though infrequent) has a greater impact on the FPR compared to a larger network. Once again, we see that our simulations agree quite well with the analytical estimates in predicting the effect of network size on inference.

Figures 3 and 4 examine the effects of node velocity and data transmission rate on topology inference. A higher node velocity results in a more rapid increase in FPR; this is expected since faster nodes result in a more rapidly changing topology, meaning that links are broken more frequently—this in turn means that previously observed links become errors after a shorter period of time. An opposite phenomenon is observed for data transmission rate: a faster transmission rate means that for the same number of observed transmissions, k (with on average one new message occurring per time step k) we observe relatively fewer errors. This occurs since more transmissions occur in a shorter period of time, meaning there is less time for them to become stale. Note that this effect on FPR would be less apparent were we to scale the x-axis as a function of time as opposed to the discrete time step k (where we multiply k by $1/n\lambda$ to obtain time in seconds, as discussed in Sect. 3); instead we would observe a separation in TPR curves such that TPR rises more rapidly for larger values of λ.

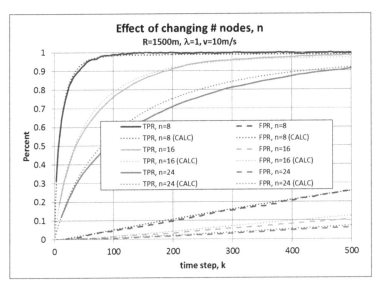

Fig. 2. Effect of network size, n, on the average true positive rate (TPR) and false positive rate (FPR) for MANET with $R = 1500$ m, $v = 10$ m/s, $\lambda = 1$ packet/s.

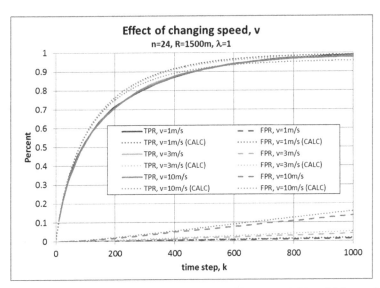

Fig. 3. Effect of node speed, v, on the average true positive rate (TPR) and false positive rate (FPR) for MANET with $n = 24$, $R = 1500$ m, $\lambda = 1$ packet/s.

Figures 3 and 4 suggest that node velocity and data transmission rate are important and related network metrics when it comes to characterizing the performance of topology inference. In fact, from Eq. (6), we observe that the rate of link breakage (and creation) in the network is a function of the ratio v/λ. We define a new term, $\gamma = v/\lambda$ with units

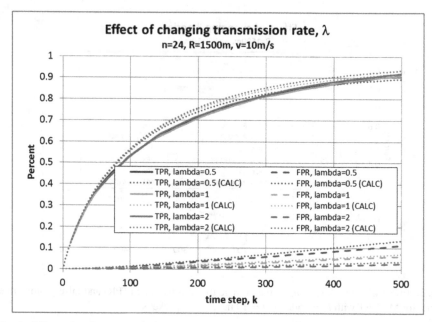

Fig. 4. Effect of packet transmission rate, λ, on the average true positive rate (TPR) and false positive rate (FPR) for MANET with $n = 24$, $R = 1500$ m, $v = 10$ m/s.

of meters/packet—ultimately this refers to the expected distance in meters that a node would travel before generating one packet. Based on (4), (5) and (6), we would expect that TPR and FPR (as functions of k) should depend only on the ratio γ, and not on the individual values of v and λ. Figure 5 plots simulation results for TPR and FPR, showing that as long as v and λ change in sync and maintain a constant ratio, γ, our performance is unchanged.

4.2 Selecting Window of Observation for Topology Inference

In Sect. 4.1, the expected true positive rate and false positive rate were plotted assuming all inference data is retained for the duration of the simulation. In practice, since the network is mobile we would expect that older data would become less relevant; indeed, in our model the primary source of false positives arises from links that were (correctly) inferred in the past and which no longer exist.

One potential means of reducing errors is to simply use a sliding window, such that topology inference is only performed using data that is newer than some threshold (i.e., fits within the time window)[2]. We would expect that by limiting our observations to a sliding window of m time steps the expected TPR and FPR would reach steady state

---

[2] In this work, we consider fixed time windows where all data in the window is treated equally until its age exceeds the window size. An alternative for future work would be to include a decay factor where data has less impact on an inference decision as it ages, as opposed to a strict step function like with our window.

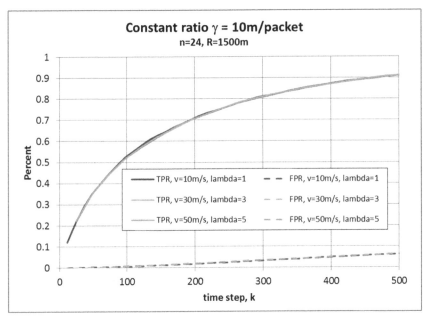

Fig. 5. TPR and FPR in a MANET with constant $\gamma = 10$ m/packet, with $n = 24$ and $R = 1500$ m.

given by the values of TPR[m] and FPR[m] from our plots in Sect. 4.1. In fact, this is precisely what we observe in Fig. 6, where we apply several window sizes to the data in our simulation.

A larger window size results in a higher expected TPR, but also results in a higher expected FPR. The question is how to select an appropriate window size when performing topology inference. Ultimately, the answer depends upon the particular goals of the adversary performing the inference and what is deemed an acceptable[3] trade-off between TPR and FPR. One well-known method to choose a balance between TPR and FPR in diagnostic or binary decision problems is to maximize Youden's J statistic (sometimes called the informedness)[4], where $J_k = \text{TPR}_k - \text{FPR}_k$ [22]. Figure 7 shows a plot of J, TPR and FPR for a network with $n = 24$, $R = 1500$ m, $v = 10$ m/s and $\lambda = 1$ packet/s. Finding the value at which J_k is maximized is a simple matter of finding the value for k at which $J_{k+1} - J_k = 0$; this is shown by the highlighted area in Fig. 7.

In Fig. 8 we plot the J statistic for a range of values of $\gamma = v/\lambda$. We use Eqs. (4) and (5) to compute the TPR and FPR curves that inform the J statistic in this case. The recommended window size as a function of γ is shown in Fig. 9. We observe that the

---

[3] We note that the relationship between TPR and FPR for binary classification problems often involves plotting TPR versus FPR as a receiver operating characteristic (ROC) curve; however, for our purposes it is more informative to observe these values plotted against a common axis.

[4] Youden's J statistic is typically expressed as $J = $ sensitivity $+$ specificity $- 1$. The sensitivity of a measurement in statistics is equal to the TPR, and the specificity is (1-FPR). These substitutions lead to $J = \text{TPR} - \text{FPR}$. The intuition behind the J statistic is that it is the point on the ROC curve furthest from chance.

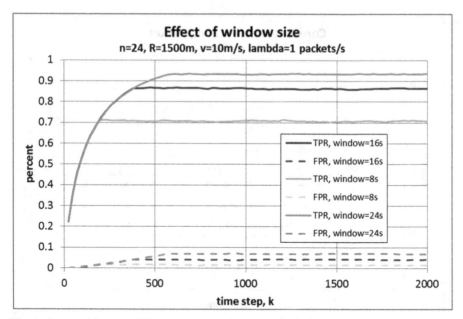

Fig. 6. True positive rate (TPR) and false positive rate (FPR) for topology inference based on data constrained to a sliding window.

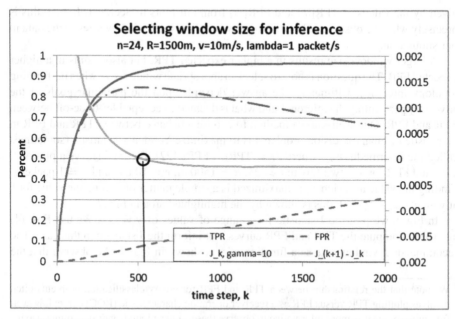

Fig. 7. Selecting a window size for topology inference by maximizing TPR - FPR.

window size decreases as γ increases. This result largely agrees with the intuition gained in Sect. 4.1. If the nodes are moving faster (larger v), then data will become stale more quickly and we should have a smaller window size k; similarly if the network produces data more slowly (smaller λ), we will accumulate less data before it gets stale and thus would have a smaller window size, k (where once again, k is the number of discrete time steps in the window and can be converted to time in seconds by scaling by $1/n\lambda$).

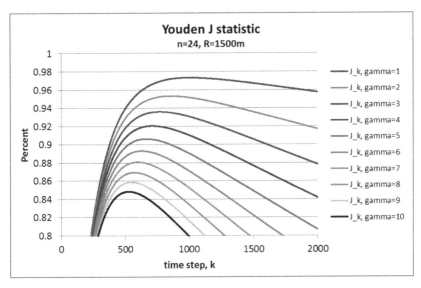

Fig. 8. The J statistic is shown for a range of values, $\gamma = v/\lambda$.

Figure 8 provides an interesting conclusion for users wishing to limit an adversary's success in performing network topology inference. We observe that the ultimate success rate of inference (as described by the J statistic) is lower for higher values of γ. Thus, where feasible, increasing node speed or decreasing data transmission rate (or both) will succeed in increasing the value γ, leading to poorer inference. While a network operator may have little control over node speeds, data rate is more fungible. A network operator with a desired set-point for γ could in theory adjust data rates, beacons, and flow control to keep the ratio γ within a desired range depending upon node speed and network dynamics.

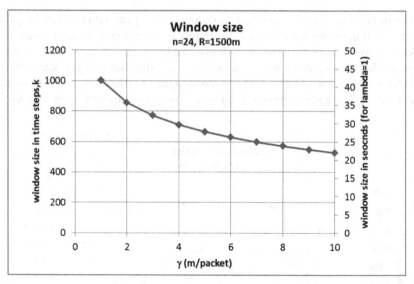

Fig. 9. Recommended window size for topology inference showing that window size decreases as a function of γ.

5 Conclusion

This paper characterized the performance of an ACK-based topology inference scheme for mobile ad hoc networks. We derived accurate analytical estimates that allow for rapid computation of the network-wide topology inference true positive rate and false positive rate, assuming constant velocity nodes in a MANET modeled as a random geometric graph. We validated our analytical estimates through extensive simulations; the simulations showed how topology inference is influenced by network size, node transmission range, node speed, and data transmission rate.

Based on our analysis, we identified valuable conclusions for network operators wishing to reduce an adversary's ability to perform topology inference: increasing the network size (i.e., the number of nodes in the network) where possible will require an adversary to collect more data over a longer period of time to identify all network links; increasing the ratio of node speed to data transmission rate will reduce the adversary's accuracy in topology inference—this can be accomplished by increasing node speed, decreasing transmission rate, or both.

Our analysis in this paper made a number of simplifying assumptions regarding the adversary's eavesdropping capability and the network dynamics. In future work, we plan to examine the effect of limited adversary range (as opposed to an ideal adversary that can listen to the entire network); heterogeneous network nodes that operate at different velocities and generate data at different rates; and how the timing data of higher-layer network protocol information (beyond link-layer ACKs) can be incorporated.

References

1. Vanhoef, M., Piessens, F.: Advanced WiFi attacks using commodity hardware. In: Proceedings of 2014 Annual Computer Security Applications Conference, New Orleans LA, USA (2014)
2. Eisen, J., Watson, S., Willink, T.: Location constrained jamming: surgical link removal using local graph partitioning. In: Proceedings of 2018 International Conference on Military Communications and Information Systems (ICMCIS), Warsaw, Poland (2018)
3. Hu, Y.C., Perrig, A., Johnson, D.B.: Packet leashes: a defense against wormhole attacks in wireless networks. In: Proceedings of 22nd Annual Joint Conference of the IEEE Computer and Communications Societies, San Francisco, USA (2003)
4. Puray, M., Palod, P.: Black-hole attack in MANET: a study. Int. J. Adv. Res. Comput. Eng. Technol. **5**(3) (2016)
5. Jin, X., Ken Yiu, W.P., Gary Chan, S.H., Wang, Y.: Network topology inference based on end-to-end measurements. IEEE J. Sel. Areas Commun. **24**(12), 2182–2195 (2006)
6. Gunes, M.H., Sarac, K.: Resolving anonymous routers in internet topology measurement studies. In: Proceedings of IEEE INFOCOM 2008, Phoenix AZ, USA (2008)
7. Malekzadeh, A., MacGregor, M.H.: Network topology inference from end-to-end unicast measurments. In: Proceedings of 27th International Conference on Advanced Information Networking and Applications Workshops, Barcelona, Spain (2013)
8. Silvestri, S., Holbert, B., Novotny, P., La Porta, T., Wolf, A., Swami, A.: Inferring network topologies in MANETs applied to service redeployment. In: Proceedings of 24th International Conference on Computer Communication and Networks (ICCCN), Las Vegas NV, USA (2015)
9. Liu, Y., Zhang, R., Shi, J., Zhang, Y.: Traffic inference in anonymous MANETs. In: Proceedings of 7th Annual IEEE Communications Society Conference on Sensor, Mesh and Ad Hoc Communications and Networks (SECON), Boston MA, USA (2010)
10. Zhang, Y., Liu, W., Lou, W.: Anonymous communications in mobile ad hoc networks. In: Proceedings of IEEE INFOCOM 2005, Miami FL, USA (2005)
11. Chang, H., Shan, H.: End-to-end flow inference of encrypted MANET. In: Proceedgins of IEEE 3rd International Conference on Information Science and Technology, Yangzhou, China (2013)
12. Brown, J.D., Salmanian, M., Willink, T.J.: Topology inference of multi-hop wireless networks. DRDC Scientific Report, DRDC-RDDC-2018-R300 (2019)
13. He, T., Wong, H.Y., Lee, K.: Traffic analysis in anonymous MANETs. In: Proceedings of IEEE Military Communications Conference (MILCOM), San Diego CA, USA (2008)
14. Roy, R.R.: Handbook of Mobile Ad Hoc Networks For Mobility Models. Springer, Boston (2011)
15. Penrose, M.D.: Random Geometric Graphs. Oxford University Press, Oxford (2003)
16. Fawcett, T.: An introduction to ROC analysis. Pattern Recogn. Lett. **27**(8), 861–874 (2006)
17. Samar, P., Wicker, S.B.: On the behavior of communication links of a node in a multi-hop mobile environment. In: Proceedings of MobiHoc Conference, Tokyo, Japan (2004)
18. Cho, S., Hayes, J.P.: Impact of mobility on connection stability in ad hoc networks. In: Proceedings of IEEE Wireless Communications and Networking Conference (WCNC), New Orleans LA, USA (2005)
19. Bakhshi, B., Khorsandi, S.: Node connectivity analysis in multi-hop wireless networks. In: Proceedings of IEEE Wireless Communications and Networking Conference (WCNC), Sydney Australia (2010)
20. Younes, O., Thomas, N.: Analysis of the expected number of hops in mobile ad hoc networks with random waypoint mobility. Electron. Notes in Theoret. Comput. Sci. **275**, 143–158 (2011)

21. Chapman, B.J.: Bounding the force employment concept. Technical Memorandum, Defence R&D Canada Centre for Operation Research and Analysis (2009)
22. Powers, D.M.W.: Evaluation: from precision, recall and F-measure to ROC, informedness, markedness and correlation. J. Mach. Learn. Technol. 2(1), 37–63 (2011)

A Stochastic Traffic Model for Congestion Detection in Multi-lane Highways

El Joubari Oumaima[1]([✉]), Ben Othman Jalel[1,2], and Vèque Véronique[1]

[1] Université Paris Saclay, CNRS, CentraleSupélec,
Laboratoire des signaux et systèmes, 91190 Gif-sur-Yvette, France
oumaima.eljoubari@centralesupelec.fr
[2] Université Sorbonne Paris Nord, Villetaneuse, France

Abstract. Vehicular Ad Hoc Networks (VANETs) represent a significant leap forward in the deployment of intelligent transport systems. These networks enable vehicles to instantly exchange traffic information with the aim of smoothing traffic flows and intensifying drivers comfort. In this context, this study addresses the issue of traffic congestion description and detection in multi-lane highways. By making use of collected information, a Markov chain based mobility model is proposed to predict the future road traffic states. Based on the obtained stationary distribution probabilities, performance criteria in steady-state are inferred and computed for different road configurations. The numerical results validate the model demonstrated in the paper.

Keywords: VANETs · Mobility model · Vehicular traffic · Markov chain

1 Introduction

The advancement of wireless network infrastructure has led to the emergence of a new type of networks dedicated to supporting intelligent traffic management, called VANETs. These networks would allow real-time communication and information exchange between moving vehicles equipped with wireless communication devices. Therefore, VANETs can offer a solution to many transportation issues affecting the efficiency of transport operations such as traffic congestion, safety, and fuel consumption. Considering that congestion is such a potential threat to public safety, economy and air quality, there is a strong need for faster detection of future congestion and saturation points. This depends heavily on the availability of accurate and realistic traffic forecasts. The classical methods for traffic prediction such as Google Maps and Waze depend primarily on centralized approaches to calculate traffic jams using historical and real-time traffic data. The major drawbacks of these methods is that they perform poorly in areas with little or no activity and they require a large data storage capacity. With the benefits granted by VANETs, a shift to a fully distributed traffic estimation becomes feasible. Based on locally collected traffic information via V2V or V2I

© ICST Institute for Computer Sciences, Social Informatics and Telecommunications Engineering 2021
Published by Springer Nature Switzerland AG 2021. All Rights Reserved
L. Foschini and M. El Kamili (Eds.): ADHOCNETS 2020, LNICST 345, pp. 87–99, 2021.
https://doi.org/10.1007/978-3-030-67369-7_7

communications, vehicles can automatically calculate estimates of future traffic distributions and reacts accordingly.

As such, the main focus of this study is to develop a decentralized traffic estimation approach in a multi-lane highway environment. Principles of Markov chain theory are used to build a model able to describe the temporal evolution of the traffic state as a random process. Markov chain theory has been widely used in various fields of research [1–3], to study systems characterized by uncertainty. As events in the system occur in continuous time, the model is constructed as a continuous-time Markov chain (CTMC) with a finite number of states. The stationary distribution will be obtained by applying a numerical approach [3]. Following that, performance indicators such as average density, congestion rate and average sojourn time will be described and computed. The network performance is evaluated in terms of the derived performance metrics by varying different parameters including arrival rate, average speed, and the number of lanes.

The remainder of this paper is structured as follows. Section 2 provides a brief literature review. Section 3 comprises the proposed model for highway traffic forecasting along with the definition of steady-state probabilities. In Sect. 4, the performance measures are defined and the numerical results of the model are demonstrated for two different scenarios. Our concluding and suggestions for future researches are given in Sect. 5.

2 Related Work

In this section, the body of related work that is available on vehicular mobility modelling is reviewed.

Generally, there are two classes of vehicular mobility models [4]: trace based mobility models (TBMM) and synthetic mobility models. The trace based models derive mobility patterns of moving vehicles from real world traces [5–7]. These models provide more credible spatial and temporal measurements and are more suitable for large scale and complex scenarios. However, they highly depend on the availability of large datasets of recorded vehicle trajectories. Several projects have been conducted to collect mobility traces such as OpenStreetMap [8] and CRAWDAD [9]. Still, these small-sized GPS datasets require the involvement of many participants to be more useful in the future.

Synthetic models describe the mobility of vehicles based on mathematical approaches, and are classified into five categories:

Stochastic models are simplistic models that describe the movements of nodes as a random process, where speed and paths are usually randomly chosen. A number of studies have presented stochastic mobility models such as City section [4], Freeway and Manhattan [10]. Nagel and Schreckenberg [11] addressed the issue of vehicular mobility in single lane-freeways. This method was extended in [12] to take into account drivers' reactions to velocity and headway distance. These models are widely applied because of their limited data demands and their easy implementation since they model traffic dynamics with a minimal level of details. However, they require further improvements to mimic real-world driving behaviors such as lane change, queues forming and stop-and-go phenomenon.

Traffic stream models describe traffic flow as a hydrodynamic phenomenon and they involve the three major macroscopic characteristics of traffic stream: speed, density and flow. The most extensively used model within this category is Lighthill-Whitham-Richards (LWR) [13,14]. Based on kinematic waves, the authors consider that the traffic flow is a continuous function of density and predict the evolution of traffic flow along arterial roads and near shock waves. The LWR framework was used as a bedrock in [15] and [16] to study the dynamics of queues at intersections. Traffic stream models manage to capture the overall traffic behavior with low details. However, bringing a solution to these models is time consuming and cumbersome when incoming flow varies continuously in time.

Car following models take into account measures such as the headway distance and the speed of nearby vehicles to display the behavior of each individual vehicle. Authors in [17] introduced a velocity threshold to maintain the safety distance from the leading car in single-lane roads. The previous work was extended in [18] to tackle the issue of lane changing. Another model was introduced in [19] to emulate the lane-change behavior in multiple-lane roads by using Bayesian reasoning. Generally, these models are more precise and provide an accurate description of traffic which increases the computational complexity, especially for large scale simulations. Besides, the overall dynamics of the system cannot be captured.

Behavioural models were inspired from the fields of biological physics and artificial intelligence. They are built based on behavioral rules conducted by social influences, rational decisions or actions following a stimulus-reaction process. Legendre *et al.* [20] introduced the first behavioral model to describe human mobility. Later, the model was improved to fit in the case of vehicular traffic. The work proposed in [21] involves describing the behaviour of the driver such as the response to the abrupt braking of the preceding vehicle. An improved behavioural model was proposed in [22] to emulate various mobility characteristics that can't be inferred from recorded driving traces. The model allows to generate simulation measures consistent with real traces. Although the aforementioned models appear to successfully provide a mobility description close to the actual real world, they cannot be applied for large-scale scenarios as they require complex calculations.

Queue models are constructed to study queue lengths and delays of vehicles waiting in queues by applying basic probabilistic distributions. Gawron [23] was the first to introduce a queuing model dedicated to vehicular traffic. In [24], a queuing model was developed for signal control optimization at isolated intersections. Cremer and Landenfeld [25] developed a model for signalized intersections while capturing the effects of spill-back phenomena. Authors in [26] presented a model that takes into account the streets topology to describe mobility at intersections and along the streets. The main reason why queue models are used is their ability to model complex systems. Moreover, they can be easily deployed as they are based on restrictive assumptions. Their major drawback is that the waiting queue in each street are described independently. Thus, they overlook the importance of coordinating the vehicles crossing the intersection and lane changing.

Our approach differs from other works as we aim to address the congestion issue in multiple-lane free-flow highways in the context of VANETs by implementing a stochastic model that describes and predicts traffic density and travel time based on traffic information collected by vehicles at the start point of the highway. The lane change behavior is also described based on the density of the lanes. The proposed model is to be implemented in vehicles and has shown its effectiveness to cover all aspects of mobility in highway environments, as it is demonstrated in Sect. 4 through analytical results of different scenarios.

3   Proposed Model

In this section, the continuous time Markov chain model for future traffic state prediction is first presented, then the steady state probabilities are derived.

In order to formulate the proposed CTMC, the notations which will be used throughout the rest of the paper are introduced in Table 1.

Table 1. Notations

$\mathcal{N}$	Set of road lanes
N	Total number of lanes
Len	Length of a highway section
Sp	Average speed on a highway section
i	Index value for lane i
C	Lane capacity
α_i	Weight of lane i
D_i	Density of lane i
R	Lane change probability matrix
R_{ij}	Lane change probability from lane i to j
λ	Arrival rate of vehicles
λ_i	Arrival rate of vehicles at lane i
μ	Service/Departure rate of vehicles
μ_i	Service/Departure rate of vehicles at lane i
t	Temporal variable
$X(t)$	Multivariate random vector representing the traffic condition of the system at time t
$X_i(t)$	Random variable representing the traffic condition of lane i at time t

(contniued)

Table 1. *(contniued)*

Ω	State space
x,y,z	Values of X(t)
P	Transition probability matrix
p_{xy}	Transition probability from state x to state y
π	Steady-state probability distribution
L_i	Average number of vehicles at lane i
W_i	Average time spent in lane i
VC_i	Average volume-to-traffic ratio of lane i

The developed model considers a highway of N lanes, where it's assumed that all lanes are of equal capacity C. The set of lanes will be denoted $\mathcal{N}$. Each lane i is assigned a weight α_i relative to its position on the road, such as $\alpha_i > \alpha_j$ if lane j is at the left side of lane i, and $\sum\limits_{i \in \mathcal{N}} \alpha_i = 1$. The weight of a lane i is defined by the following formula:

$$\alpha_i = \frac{N - i + 1}{N!} \tag{1}$$

Figure 1 illustrates an example of a single direction highway, while Fig. 2 represents the highway diagram as a queue system.

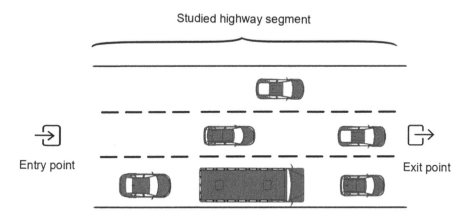

Fig. 1. An example of a highway road segment.

Similarly to works in [1,2,26], we assume arrivals of vehicles at the start point occur at a rate λ according to a Poisson process and service times have an exponential distribution with a rate parameter $\mu = \frac{Sp}{Len}$, where Len is the length of the highway segment and Sp the average speed of vehicles. Arrival rates at

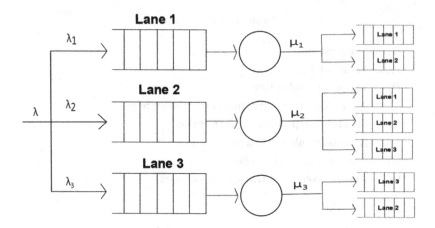

Fig. 2. A highway road segment as a queue system.

each lane are defined by their position on the road, such that the right lane has a higher arrival rate than the left lane. This was expressed as the following formula:

$$\lambda_i = \lambda \times \alpha_i \tag{2}$$

Similarly to the arrival rates, the service rates are defined in a way that the right lane has a lower service rate than the one on the left of the road. This condition can be expressed as:

$$\mu_i = \mu \times \frac{1}{\alpha_i} \tag{3}$$

The traffic state of the studied segment is represented by a vector of multiple random variables corresponding to the number of vehicles on each lane as follows:

$$X(t) = \{X_1(t), X_2(t), ..., X_N(t)\} \tag{4}$$

As each lane can only handle a limited number of vehicles, the following constraint must be satisfied:

$$\forall i \in \mathcal{N}, 0 \le X_i(t) \le C \tag{5}$$

The collection of possible values of $X(t)$ forms the state space Ω of the Markov chain.

A change in the system's state can be caused by one of the following events:

- A vehicle arriving at the start point of the highway;
- A vehicle arriving at the end point of the highway;
- A vehicle changing lanes.

P is used to denote the transition matrix of the Markov chain, where its elements p_{xy} is the transition probability of state x to state y. In order to define

P, R the lane change probability matrix is first expressed. Given D_i the density of lane i which represents the actual number of vehicles travelling on lane i, R_{ij} the probability a vehicle changes from lane i to an adjacent lane j is defined as below:

$$R_{ij} = \begin{cases} 1 - \dfrac{D_j}{\sum\limits_{k \in \mathcal{N}} D_k \cdot \mathbb{1}_{(i-k=1 || i-k=-1)}} & \text{if } i \text{ and } j \text{ are adjacent lanes} \\ 0 & \text{otherwise} \end{cases} \tag{6}$$

Given the arrival, service and lane change rates, the transition probability from each state x to state y $((x,y) \in \Omega^2$ and $x \neq y)$ can be established:

$$p_{xy} = \begin{cases} \lambda_i & \text{if a vehicle arrives at the start point of lane } i \\ \mu_i & \text{if a vehicle arrives at the end point of lane } i \\ R_{ij} & \text{if a vehicle changes from lane } i \text{ to lane } j \\ -\sum\limits_{z \in \Omega \setminus \{x\}} p_{xz} & \text{if } x = y \\ 0 & \text{otherwise} \end{cases} \tag{7}$$

The stationary distribution vector π is defined by the steady-state statement such as $\pi P = \pi$. By applying the rate-conservation principle, π can be obtained. Given the transition probability matrix P defined previously and the equilibrium vector π, the balance equation is expressed as follows:

$$\pi_x \cdot \sum_{y \in \Omega \setminus \{x\}} \left(\sum_{i \in \mathcal{N}} \lambda_i \cdot \mathbb{1}_{(p_{xy}=\lambda_i)} + \sum_{i \in \mathcal{N}} \mu_i \cdot \mathbb{1}_{(p_{xy}=\mu_i)} + \sum_{i \in \mathcal{N}} \sum_{j \in \mathcal{N} \setminus \{i\}} R_{ij} \cdot \mathbb{1}_{(p_{xy}=R_{ij})} \right) =$$

$$\sum_{y \in \Omega \setminus \{x\}} \pi_y \left(\sum_{i \in \mathcal{N}} \lambda_i \cdot \mathbb{1}_{(p_{yx}=\lambda_i)} + \sum_{i \in \mathcal{N}} \mu_i \cdot \mathbb{1}_{(p_{yx}=\mu_i)} + \sum_{i \in \mathcal{N}} \sum_{j \in \mathcal{N} \setminus \{i\}} R_{ij} \cdot \mathbb{1}_{(p_{yx}=R_{ij})} \right)$$

To compute the stationary vector of the transition rate matrix P, the Grassmann-Taksar-Heyman (GTH) algorithm [27] is applied.

4   Performance Indicators and Numerical Results

To demonstrate the validity of the proposed approach, numerical solutions are presented in this section.

4.1   Performance Indicators

From the obtained vector π, L_i the long-run average number of vehicles on lane i is first computed using the following formula:

$$L_i = \sum_{x \in \Omega} \pi_x \cdot x_i \tag{8}$$

The average volume-to-capacity ratio VC_i of lane i can be inferred from L_i as below:

$$VC_i = L_i/C \tag{9}$$

Based on Little's law formula, W_i the average sojourn time a vehicle spends on lane i is calculated as follow:

$$W_i = \frac{1}{\lambda_i} \cdot \sum_{x \in \Omega} \pi_x \cdot x_i \tag{10}$$

4.2 Numerical Results

The values used to find the numerical solution are based on samples extracted from highD dataset [28] that offers measurement data collected at German highways. Table 2 summarizes the values of the settings used.

Table 2. Values used for numerical resolution

Parameter	Scenario 1	Scenario 2
Highway length	400 m	200 m
Number of lanes	3	Varies from 1 to 4
Per-lane capacity	18	8
Average speed	33 m/s	25-30-35 m/s
Time unit	1 min	1 min
Arrival rate	Varies from 0 to 10	5 vehicles/time unit

First, different values of arrival rates are tested to analyse the impact of this parameter on the performance of a highway section of 400 m long. The studied highway is composed of three lanes and only one travel direction is considered similarly to the configuration previously presented in Fig. 1.

Figure 3 illustrates the average number of vehicles on each highway section lane. Generally, left lanes are usually used for passing or when traffic on right lanes is congested. It can be observed from the results that density decreases from the right lane to left one, which is a clear proof that the information obtained reflects the realistic behavior of traffic.

The chart in Fig. 4 represents the congestion rates corresponding to each lane. The curves show the same results as the previous one. It can be seen that the congestion rate on the first lane increases rashly compared to the other two lanes. The congestion rate of the upper lane grows more slowly. The average sojourn time per lane is depicted in Fig. 5 and shows that the average driven time grows as the traffic density rises. It can also be noticed that the travel speed considerably slows down on the most congested lane.

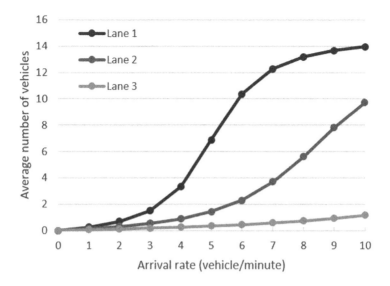

Fig. 3. Average number of vehicles vs. Arrival rate.

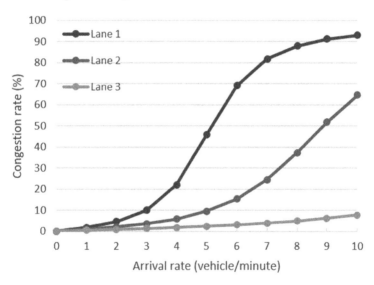

Fig. 4. Congestion rate vs. Arrival rate.

In a different test, we consider a highway section 200 m that handles at most 8 vehicles at the same time. We derive the performance measures for different numbers of lanes and average speeds to capture how these settings affect the performance. The estimated average number of vehicles versus the number of lanes is shown in Fig. 6, for three different values of the average speed. It's noted that having more lanes increases the capacity of the road allowing to handle

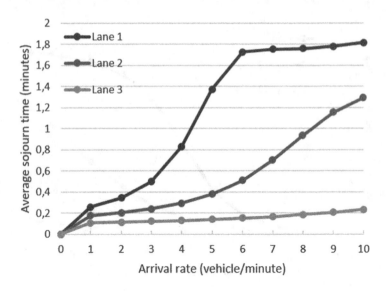

Fig. 5. Average sojourn time vs. Arrival rate.

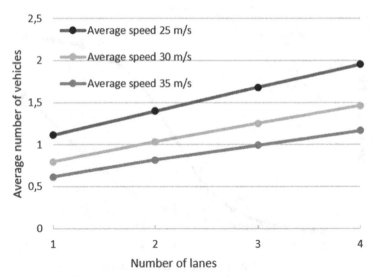

Fig. 6. Average number of vehicles vs. Number of lanes.

more vehicles. In addition, a significant reduction of density can be noticed when average speed increases specially for roads with multiple lanes.

As observed in Fig. 7, the overall congestion rate of the freeway is substantially higher for a single-lane highway than a multi-lane. From the results, it can also be deduced that speed is a major contributor to the congestion. A slight increase of the speed can allow to drop the congestion rate by 4% for single-lane highways. The average sojourn time depicted in Fig. 8 demonstrates that

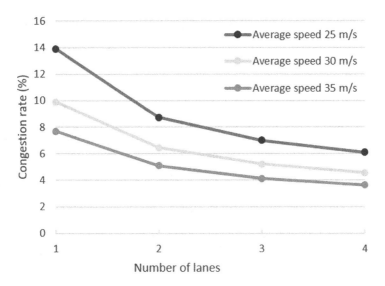

Fig. 7. Congestion rate vs. Number of lanes.

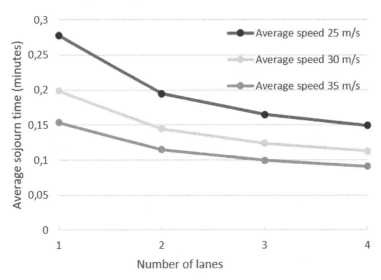

Fig. 8. Average sojourn time vs. Number of lanes.

multi-lane roads allow shorter journey times compared to single-lane roads. It can also be observed that the model accurately reproduces the travel delays brought on by low velocities.

From the presented results we can assume that the first lane is more seriously affected by congestion as more drivers tend to stay in the right most lane except in heavy traffic. The obtained estimates can be used to design lane change assistance to ease congested lanes and increase utilization of fast lanes. Moreover, intelligent speed assistance systems can be designed to adapt the velocity of vehicles depending on the estimated circumstances.

5   Conclusions

Congestion has become a serious issue that the majority of countries are facing. It does not solely affect the efficiency of transportation systems, but also the environmental and economic welfare. Thus, methods for congestion detection are vital to the improvement of transportation infrastructure. The availability of accurate estimates of future congestion points will make it easier to manage traffic flows. This study focuses on developing a mobility model for multi-lane highways using Markov chains. The proposed model allows to forecast the distribution of traffic over highway lanes and then derives synthetic measures that represent important performance indicators for congestion assessment. The evaluation results highlight the potential contribution of the proposed model to mitigating traffic congestion. This study was limited to highway traffic. For future work, it is planned to address the applicability of the model on urban environments.

References

1. Kafi, M.A., Ben-Othman, J., Mokdad, L., Badache, N.: Performance analysis and evaluation of REFIACC using queuing networks. Simul. Model. Pract. Theory **71**, 15–26 (2017)
2. Mokdad, L., Ben-Othman, J., Nguyen, A.T.: DJAVAN: detecting jamming attacks in vehicle ad hoc networks. Perform. Eval. **87**, 47–59 (2015)
3. Mokdad, L., Ben-Othman, J., Yahya, B., Niagne, S.: Performance evaluation tools for QoS MAC protocol for wireless sensor networks. Ad Hoc Netw. **12**, 86–99 (2014)
4. Davies, V.A.: Evaluating mobility models within an ad hoc network. Master's thesis, advisor: Tracy Camp. Department of Mathematical and Computer Sciences, Colorado School of Mines (2000)
5. Vetriselvi, V., Parthasarathi, R.: Trace based mobility model for ad hoc networks. In: Third IEEE International Conference on Wireless and Mobile Computing, Networking and Communications (WiMob 2007), p. 81. IEEE, October 2007
6. Förster, A., Bin Muslim, A., Udugama, A.: TRAILS-A trace-based probabilistic mobility model. In: Proceedings of the 21st ACM International Conference on Modeling, Analysis and Simulation of Wireless and Mobile Systems, pp. 295–302, October 2018
7. Beiró, M.G., Panisson, A., Tizzoni, M., Cattuto, C.: Predicting human mobility through the assimilation of social media traces into mobility models. EPJ Data Sci. **5**(1), 1–15 (2016). https://doi.org/10.1140/epjds/s13688-016-0092-2
8. Haklay, M., Weber, P.: OpenStreetMap: "user-generated street maps.". IEEE Pervasive Comput. **7**(4), 12–18 (2008)
9. Kotz, D., Henderson, T.: CRAWDAD: a community resource for archiving wireless data at Dartmouth. IEEE Pervasive Comput. **4**(4), 12–14 (2005)
10. Bai, F., Sadagopan, N., Helmy, A.: The IMPORTANT framework for analyzing the Impact of Mobility on Performance Of RouTing protocols for Adhoc NeTworks. Ad Hoc Netw. **1**(4), 383–403 (2003)

11. Nagel, K., Schreckenberg, M.: A cellular automaton model for freeway traffic. J. Phys. I **2**(12), 2221–2229 (1992)
12. Zhang, G., Xu, W.: Cellular automaton traffic model considering driver's reaction to velocity and headway distance with variable possibility of randomization. In: IOP Conference Series: Materials Science and Engineering, vol. 392, no. 6, p. 062024. IOP Publishing, July 2018
13. Lighthill, M.J., Whitham, G.B.: On kinematic waves II. A theory of traffic flow on long crowded roads. Proc. Roy. Soc. Lond. Ser. A Math. Phys. Sci. **229**(1178), 317–345 (1955)
14. Richards, P.I.: Shock waves on the highway. Oper. Res. **4**(1), 42–51 (1956)
15. Liu, H.X., Wu, X., Ma, W., Hu, H.: Real-time queue length estimation for congested signalized intersections. Transp. Res. Part C Emerg. Technol. **17**(4), 412–427 (2009)
16. Yang, H., Rakha, H., Ala, M.V.: Eco-cooperative adaptive cruise control at signalized intersections considering queue effects. IEEE Trans. Intell. Transp. Syst. **18**(6), 1575–1585 (2016)
17. Briesemeister, L.: Group membership and communication in highly mobile ad hoc networks (2001)
18. Krauß, S.: Microscopic modeling of traffic flow: investigation of collision free vehicle dynamics. Doctoral dissertation (1998)
19. Pop, M.D., Proştean, O., Proştean, G.: Multiple lane road car-following model using Bayesian reasoning for lane change behavior estimation: a smart approach for smart mobility. In: Proceedings of the 3rd International Conference on Future Networks and Distributed Systems, pp. 1–8, July 2019
20. Legendre, F., Borrel, V., de Amorim, M.D., Fdida, S.: Modeling mobility with behavioral rules: the case of incident and emergency situations. In: Cho, K., Jacquet, P. (eds.) AINTEC 2006. LNCS, vol. 4311, pp. 186–205. Springer, Heidelberg (2006). https://doi.org/10.1007/11930181_14
21. Gipps, P.G.: Behavioral car-following model for computer simulation. Transport. Res. **15**(2), 105–111 (1981)
22. Kharrazi, S., Almén, M., Frisk, E., Nielsen, L.: Extending behavioral models to generate mission-based driving cycles for data-driven vehicle development. IEEE Trans. Veh. Technol. **68**(2), 1222–1230 (2018)
23. Gawron, C.: An iterative algorithm to determine the dynamic user equilibrium in a traffic simulation model. Int. J. Mod. Phys. C **9**(03), 393–407 (1998)
24. Mirchandani, P.B., Zou, N.: Queuing models for analysis of traffic adaptive signal control. IEEE Trans. Intell. Transp. Syst. **8**(1), 50–59 (2007)
25. Cremer, M., Landenfeld, M.: A mesoscopic model for saturated urban road networks. In: Traffic and Granular Flow, vol. 97, pp. 169–180 (1998)
26. Mohimani, G.H., Ashtiani, F., Javanmard, A., Hamdi, M.: Mobility modeling, spatial traffic distribution, and probability of connectivity for sparse and dense vehicular ad hoc networks. IEEE Trans. Veh. Technol. **58**(4), 1998–2007 (2008)
27. Grassmann, W.K., Taksar, M.I., Heyman, D.P.: Regenerative analysis and steady state distributions for Markov chains. Oper. Res. **33**(5), 1107–1116 (1985)
28. Krajewski, R., Bock, J., Kloeker, L., Eckstein, L.: The highD dataset: a drone dataset of naturalistic vehicle trajectories on German highways for validation of highly automated driving systems. In: 2018 21st International Conference on Intelligent Transportation Systems (ITSC), Maui, HI, pp. 2118–2125 (2018). https://doi.org/10.1109/ITSC.2018.8569552

Flexibility of Decentralized Energy Restoration in WSNs

Osama I. Aloqaily[✉]

University of Ottawa, Ottawa, Canada
Osama.Aloqaily@uottawa.ca

Abstract. Wireless Rechargeable Sensor Networks (WRSNs) have become more and more popular thanks to the advances in wireless power transfer and battery material. The strategy followed by the charger to decide which sensor to be recharged next, is considered *effective* if only few sensing holes exist at any time, and their duration is short-lived. Ideally, the strategy will allow the system to be *immortal*; that is, all sensors are operational at all times. A recharging strategy is said to be *flexible* if it is effective for a wide range of parameters (i.e., for different applications).

In this paper, we analyze a simple decentralized recharging strategy which is based on local learning, operates without any a-priori knowledge of the network, has small memory requirements, and uses only local communication. We study the effectiveness and the flexibility of such a technique under a variety of ranges of the network parameters, showing its applicability to various contexts. We focus on three classes of applications that differ in network size (number of sensors), level of sensitivity of collected data, transmission rate, battery capacity, and type of mobile charger used to replenish energy. Our experiments show that in all these different settings, this simple local learning strategy is highly effective, achieving total immortality or near immortality in all cases.

Keywords: Adaptive · Decentralized · Recharging · Mobile charger · WRSN · Local learning

1 Introduction

1.1 Energy Restoration

Wireless sensor networks (WSNs) are used in a wide range of applications; they consist of small devices, called sensor nodes, deployed in a targeted area to monitor, collect, and report information on the surrounding environment. In the majority of applications, the sensors are powered by batteries of limited (usually small) capacity. When the battery becomes depleted, the sensor stops being operational, creating a sensing hole (and possibly a coverage hole) in the

© ICST Institute for Computer Sciences, Social Informatics and Telecommunications Engineering 2021
Published by Springer Nature Switzerland AG 2021. All Rights Reserved
L. Foschini and M. El Kamili (Eds.): ADHOCNETS 2020, LNICST 345, pp. 100–115, 2021.
https://doi.org/10.1007/978-3-030-67369-7_8

network. Unless remedial action is taken, eventually the entire network stops operating.

The earliest approaches to extend the WSN lifetime focused on reducing the energy consumption of the sensors (e.g., [6]); These approaches however only delay the inevitable demise of the network.

To prolong the life of the network almost indefinitely it is indeed necessary to restore the depleted energy in the network. Various approaches to energy restorations considered in the literature are *endogenous*, consisting of enhancing the sensors by adding capabilities that would enable them to recharge their battery. An example of such an approach is the proposal to provide the sensors with *energy harvesting* equipment to collect energy from surrounding resources [1,9,25]. This approach suffers from resource fluctuation and small harvested energy amounts that are not enough to fulfill sensors operations.

Another proposal has been to equip the sensors with *mobility* and location capabilities, so they can move to a recharging station when the battery level becomes too low, recharge, and then return (e.g., [24,32]).

All these proposals require sensor nodes of substantially increased complexity (and thus cost); this fact severely limits their feasibility and applicability.

An important popular alternative, that does not require more complex sensors, consists of using a mobile entity (robot, vehicle, etc.) that acts as a *mobile energy charger* (MC), moving in the environment and restoring the energy supply to nodes in need. This *exogenous* approach, intensively studied from a theoretical point of view, is becoming increasingly more practical and relevant due to the recent breakthrough in the area of *wireless energy transfer* technology by Kurs *et al.* [16,17]; once this technology becomes fully developed, the MC should be able to recharge a battery efficiently without the need of wires and plugs, with energy generated elsewhere.

1.2 Effectiveness, Immortality, and Flexibility

The idea behind this approach is simple: the mobile charger MC moves through the network recharging depleted nodes, with possible stops to an (exterior) recharging station to renew its own energy capacity (although most studies assume the latter to be infinite). The MC decides which sensor it should recharge next according to some strategy, with the objective of keeping the network functioning forever.

The *effectiveness* of a strategy is evaluated in terms of two measures: How many sensors are operational at any one time (called *operational size* or *coverage*), and for how long a sensing hole lasts (called *disconnection time*). The ideal situation, called *immortality* [29], is when the coverage is complete and disconnection time is nil; that is, when all sensors are operational at all times.

These two measures, coverage and disconnection time (and thus, the effectiveness), depend on a multitude of factors, including the number of sensors, the battery capacity, the size of the sensing area, and the power of the MC (e.g., speed, charging distance, charging time); these factors vary from one application to another, depending on the type of application. This means that the effectiveness of recharging strategies may vary greatly in different application settings. Hence another important measure of a restoration strategy is its *flexibility*, that is its capacity to be effective for a wide range of parameters, i.e., in several different applications.

1.3 Main Contributions

In this paper, we analyze the effectiveness in a variety of applications of the simple fully decentralized MC strategy introduced in [2] that, unlike previous strategies, is based on local learning, operates without any a-priori knowledge of the network, has small memory requirements, and uses only local communication.

We focus on three classes of application settings. The first class includes applications characterized by a small number of sensors deployed in a relatively small area, low data sensitivity, and low transmission rate; it is well suited for a robot charger. The second includes applications characterized by a moderate number of deployed sensors, highly sensitive data, and a high transmission rate; it describes settings suitable for both robots or vehicles. The third class, which is more suitable for a vehicle charger, includes applications characterized by a large number of deployed sensors in large areas, and low transmission rate.

In all cases, we evaluate the effectiveness of the strategy in terms of *operational size*: the number of sensors that are maintained operational at any given time, and *disconnection time*: the time from the moment a sensor becomes no longer operational to the time when the MC serves it.

We show that in all three settings the system reaches immortality (all nodes are always operational), or near immortality (90% of the nodes are always operational and if a node becomes non-operational it does so only once, and never for more than 1% of the network lifetime). In other words, in spite of its simplicity, the strategy is highly effective in all three distinct classes of application settings, showing its flexibility.

The paper is organized as follows. The next subsection contains a concise review of related work; Sect. 2 introduces the model; the proposed strategy is described in the Subsect. 2.2; the experimental results and their discussion are contained in Sect. 3; Sect. 4 concludes this paper.

1.4 Related Work

Several strategies have been proposed, studied and analyzed. In the following, we do not consider *off-line* strategies (i.e., those that assume knowledge of the future events) but only *online* strategies.

A popular approach used in the existing work is based on *centralized* strategies where the sensors report their energy levels (directly or through a base station) either at regular intervals of time, or when their battery level reaches a certain threshold. This is the case, for example, of *on demand* policies (e.g., see [18,26,33]). Furthermore, centralized algorithms are used to solve optimization problems requiring global system information (e.g., [10,18,26,29,30,33]). In particular, in [33] the sensors report their energy levels periodically, and the recharging order is computed by the MC using a centralized algorithm which solves a global optimization problem; in [26], a centralized solution is provided to maximize the ratio of recharging time to vehicles idling time; in [18], each node periodically sends its energy data (e.g., energy level, consumption rate, etc.) to the base station that, based on this data, centrally determines the charging schedule and communicates to the MC through long range radio; a network utility maximization problem is solved in [10]. Other centralized policies have been studied in [12,15,23].

Some *decentralized* strategies have also been devised; in [21], the authors aim to maximize the sensors' lifetime by minimizing the charging tour length and maximizing the charging utility gain; at the same time, the mobile charger receives a reward for every successful recharging process. The authors assume that the mobile charger has finite energy and the maximum number of served requests is limited; in [3], the authors proposed that the network has limited energy and investigated in the optimal ratio of energy assigned to the mobile charger relative to energy assigned to the sensors. Also, they tested full charging versus partial charging. Finally, they tested their hypothesis under several trajectories.

However, the energy restoration process is limited in the sense that there is a bound on the total amount of energy that can be put into the system; in [8] a decentralized energy restoration strategy based on a global circular order of the nodes. Their findings proved the importance of giving a decentralized approach. However, they assumed that the mobile charger follows a trajectory known a-priori. Recently, we have proposed a simple fully decentralized MC strategy that, unlike previous strategies, is based on local learning, operates without any a-priori knowledge of the network, has small memory requirements, and uses only local communication [2].

Finally, some work has considered the use of multiple MCs in various settings; see for example [7,19,22,28].

Let us remark that, to the best of our knowledge, the effectiveness measures considered here as well as the notion of flexibility, have not been explicitly considered in the literature. The only exceptions are [2,8], where however the focus is only on the effectiveness of the proposed strategies and the analysis is limited to restricted cases.

2   Model and Strategy

2.1   The Network

Let $\mathcal{S} = \{s_1 \dots, s_n\}$ be a set of n *sensor nodes*, distributed randomly in a two-dimensional square area. Each node has sensory equipment that allows it to monitor its surroundings; it also has provision for wireless communication. The sensors are homogeneous, and the batteries have the same capacity E_{max};

however, depending on their activities, sensors might consume their batteries, and thus deplete their batteries, at different rates.

In this paper, we use the power consumption model of [29] (also employed in [5,14]). Let $P(s)$ denote the energy consumption rate at sensor node $s \in \mathcal{S}$; $P(s)$ is given by the following equation:

$$P(s) = \rho \cdot \sum_{\substack{p \neq s \\ p \in \mathcal{S}}} f_{j,s} + \sum_{\substack{p \neq s \\ j \in \mathcal{S}}} C_{s,j} \cdot f_{s,j} + C_{s,B} \cdot f_{s,B} \tag{1}$$

where: $\rho \cdot \sum_{\substack{p \neq s \\ p \in \mathcal{S}}} f_{j,s}$ is the reception power consumption, ρ is the energy consumption for receiving one unit, and $f_{j,s}$ is the flow rate between node j and node s; $\sum_{\substack{j \neq s \\ p \in \mathcal{S}}} C_{s,j} \cdot f_{s,j} + C_{s,B} \cdot f_{s,B}$ is the transmission power consumption, where $C_{s,j} = \beta_1 + \beta_2(d_{s,j})^\alpha$, where β_1 and β_2 are distant dependent constants, $d_{s,j}$ is the transmission distance, and α is the path loss index, $C_{s,B}$ is the energy consumption for transmitting one bit of data between node s and base station B. Since sensing the environment requires negligible energy compared with sending and receiving operations, it is considered null. All interactions assume the existence of an ideal MAC Layer, which provides a reliable wireless communication channel by guaranteeing collision-free access to the medium and eliminating interference due to simultaneous transmissions.

Any sensor where the current energy level L of its battery is below a predefined threshold τ_1 is considered in need of recharge and is said to be *at risk*. When its level falls below a predefined threshold $\tau_2 < \tau_1$, the sensor becomes *non-operational*: it stops its sensing activities, thus creating a sensing hole in the network, and it uses its remaining energy only for the limited local communication required to be recharged.

A special mobile entity, called *Mobile Charger* (MC), is deployed in the system to re-charge the sensors in need. The MC is equipped with power transfer technology, and it can charge a sensor when in its proximity. The MC is equipped with a large battery of capacity E_{MC} (initially fully charged), this capacity is used for moving and recharging purposes in the robot-based MC, while it is used for only recharging sensors in the Vehicle-based MC.

The capacity is assumed to be sufficient to charge all the sensors at least once. When the MC battery reaches a given threshold, the MC travels back to the *Service Station* (SS). The SS has fast charging equipment or battery replacement equipment to guarantee fast service time. The SS might be connected to the electricity grid or might have large energy storage that stores energy from various renewable or nonrenewable energy sources. After its battery is recharged or replaced, the MC continues the sensors' charging process.

The decision of which sensor should be recharged next defines the *recharging strategy* employed. The objective of the recharging strategy is to keep the network functioning forever, keeping the number of operational sensors at any one time as large as possible, and the duration of sensing hole as small as possible. Hence the *effectiveness* of a recharging strategy $\mathcal{A}$ is measured in terms of the number of operational sensors and the duration of sensing holes. More precisely, the *operational size*, or *coverage*, at time t under $\mathcal{A}$ (denoted by $Coverage(\mathcal{A}, t)$) is the number of operational nodes at that time; note that the coverage implicitly measures the number $Holes(\mathcal{A}, t) = n - Coverage(\mathcal{A}, t)$ of the sensing holes at time t. The *disconnection time* for node x at time t under $\mathcal{A}$ (denoted by $Disconnect(\mathcal{A}, t, x)$) is the amount of time x had been inactive when last serviced by the mobile charger before or at time t; that is, it measures how long the sensing hole created by x lasts.

Given a recharging strategy $\mathcal{A}$ for the sensor network $\mathcal{S}$, the network achieves *complete immortality* if, within finite time (i.e., after a transient), 100% of the sensors are operational at all time. We also say that $\mathcal{S}$ achieves *near immortality* under $\mathcal{A}$ if, within finite time (i.e., after a transient), 90% of sensors are operational at any time *and* the total disconnection time of a sensor is at most 1% of the network's lifetime.

2.2   The Charging Strategy

We describe the *Local-Learning* fully decentralized recharging strategy used in this paper. In this strategy, the MC starts without any a-priori knowledge of the sensors' location, their initial charges, nor their consumption rates.

Instead of letting the nodes report their energy levels (directly or through a base station) periodically or when the battery level reaches a certain threshold (e.g., *on demand* policies), the MC gathers the battery energy levels of the neighbouring nodes as it moves through the network. This eliminates long distance communications between the MC and the nodes, without need for clustering, cluster management, or cluster-head elections.

The collected data is used by the MC to learn online the dynamics of the network nodes and to build a fully dynamic charging schedule. More precisely, the data is used by the MC to determine, using a simple heuristic, to which node it should move to recharge next. This mechanism provides a continuous gathering of energy information and, in turn, a fully dynamic energy depletion prediction.

In more details, the algorithm behaves as follows. Upon start-up, the MC makes two rounds of exploration of the network, collecting data from the encountered nodes and their neighbours, servicing those that need recharging. Since the MC is initially located close to the BS, the MC communicates with the BS to collect all the available information about the one-hop nodes that communicate directly with the BS, and computes the distance to each of those nodes.

The MC visits the sensors in a greedy fashion, closest unvisited neighbor first, and backtracking once all the sensor's neighbors have been visited. In each visit, the MC records the location of each sensor, its battery level $L_1(s)$ (resp. $L_2(s)$), the current time $t_1(s)$ (resp. $t_2(s)$) for the first (resp,. second) visit, and neighbors' locations; if the MC encounters any sensor with energy $L(s) < \tau_1$, it recharges it. By the end of the two traversals of this startup stage, the MC has constructed a vector of size n with the collected information of the sensors, providing a complete map of the network as well as the means to estimate the future needs of the sensors. The consumption rate $\delta(s)$ of each sensor S is computed as $\delta(s) = (L_2(s) - L_1(s))/(t_2(s) - t_1(s))$. Next, the MC calculates the traveling time to all sensors. Let t be the current time, $d(s, t)$ be the distance from MC to node s at time t, and V be the speed of MC. Then, the time that it would be required for MC to reach s is $\Delta t = d(s, t)/V$. Finally, the calculated consumption rate and travel time are used to estimate the Expected Energy $L_{Exp}(s)$ of the sensor s at time $t + \Delta t$ as follows:

$$L_{Exp}(s) = L_2(s) - \delta(s) \cdot (t - t_2(s) + \Delta t)$$

The next sensor to be charged is chosen to be the one with lowest expected energy: $\min_{s \in S}\{L_{Exp}(s)\}$.

This policy is used for all the subsequent rounds (the *charging rounds*): the MC continues to move greedily, to record the current state of charge values, to record the current time stamp and to update the expected energy values of each sensor it encounters, so that the charging schedule is always based on the most up-to-date information.

Preliminary results have shown that such a strategy is highly effective [2], achieving the same results as those in the specific centralized settings of [13, 29].

3   Results and Discussions

The goal of this study is to determine the *flexibility* of this simple and efficient energy restoration strategy; that is, whether it would be highly effective in settings arising in different types of applications. To this end, we have carried out a large number of experiments under a variety of ranges of the network parameters, and analyzed the results in three classes of applications.

Perhaps surprisingly, we find that the strategy is highly effective, achieving total immortality or near immortality in all cases.

In this section, we describe the experimental setup and the main application settings considered. We then present and analyze the results.

3.1   General Parameters and Experimental Setting

To analyze the effectiveness of the Local-Learning strategy and evaluate its flexibility, we consider different network sizes, varying the number n of sensors between 100 and 600 ($n = 100, 200, 300, 400, 500, 600$), deployed in a square area of variable size (from $200\,\mathrm{m} \times 100\,\mathrm{m}$ to $1000\,\mathrm{m} \times 1000\,\mathrm{m}$). We use three types of sensor battery capacities ($780\,\mathrm{mAh}/1.2\,\mathrm{v}$, $1.2\,\mathrm{Ah}/2.5\,\mathrm{v}$, $1.2\,\mathrm{Ah}/3.7\,\mathrm{v}$), considered in [28, 29, 34], which are equivalent to ($E_{max} = 3.37\,\mathrm{KJ}, 10.8\,\mathrm{KJ}, 15.98\,\mathrm{KJ}$) respectively. The power consumption coefficients (Eq. 1) are $\rho = 50\,\mathrm{nJ}$, $\beta_1 = 50$ nJ/b, $\beta_2 = 0.0013\,\mathrm{pJ}/(\mathrm{b.m}^4)$, and $\alpha = 4$ (see [11, 13, 26, 29]). The initial state of charge of each sensor is a random ratio (20%–70%) of E_{max}; a sensor is considered non-operational if the state of charge is below 5% of E_{max}. At each time unit (1 min of 6 months of simulated time), a sensor sends and receives a random number of packets of size [1–10]Kbit.

The MC consumes 5 J/m for moving, and radiated power with efficiency $\eta = 95\%$ [13]. We consider two charging times ($\gamma = 30, 78$ [29,34]) expressed in minutes. To reflect different types of mobile chargers (vehicle or robot), we consider different speeds (v = 1 m/s, 2 m/s, 5 m/s) and battery capacities (E_{MC} = (216, 770) KJ).

For the experimental evaluation, we use a discrete event simulator developed in MATLAB. For each combination of the values of the parameters, we have run 100 executions. In each execution, the simulated time is 6 months, with time unit 1 min. In each execution, we compute the effectiveness of the Local-Learning strategy by computing the *average* operational size and *average* disconnection time over the simulated time.

3.2   Applications and Settings

In this work we particularly focus on three classes of applications that differ in network size (the number of sensors), level of sensitivity of collected data, transmission rate, battery capacity, and type of MC used to replenish energy.

The first class, *APP1*, contains applications where the number of sensors is small, sensors have small batteries, the sensitivity of the data is low, transmission rate is low, and a robot is more appropriate as a MC. This class includes for example the application that measures soil humidity [27], where 100 sensors or less are deployed, the collected data is not sensitive so the transmission rate is low, the coverage area is rather small (200 × 200 m); because of the size and the nature of the area in this setting a robot is an appropriate choice for MC.

In the second class, *APP2*, which includes the application of the tracking intruders movement [20], the collected data is highly sensitive, the number of sensors is moderate, and the transmission rate is high. For example, in [20], 200 sensors were deployed in a small area of (200 × 100 m); depending on the combination of the various parameters, both robot and vehicle could be suitable choices for the MC.

In the third class, *APP3*, which includes the barrier intruder detection application [31], there is high sensitivity of collected data, the number of sensors is large, the transmission rate is small (e.g., data are sent only if an intruder crosses the borders), and the more suitable MC is a vehicle or a drone. For example, [4] deploys 300–600 sensors in area of 400 × 400, while [31] deploys 200–400 sensors in an area of 800 × 400 m. In our experiments, we consider the worst setting: the largest area (800 × 400 m) and the largest number of sensors (300–600).

Table 1 indicates the specific ranges of parameters associated to these three application classes.

3.3   Experimental Results

In this section we describe the performance of the system in the three considered settings.

Table 1. Application classes

	APP1	APP2	APP3
n	100	200–300	300–600
Area	200 m × 200 m	200 m × 100 m	800 m × 400 m
E_{max}	3.37 kJ	(10.8, 15.98) KJ	(10.8, 15.98) kJ
τ	674 J	2160, 3196 J	2160 J, 3196 J
τ_1	168 J	540 J, 799 J	540 J, 799 J
E_{MC}	216 kJ	216 kJ, 770 KJ	770 KJ
v	1 m/s, 2 m/s	1 m/s, 2 m/s, 5 m/s	5 m/s
E_{Move}	5 J/m	5 J/m	5 J/m
γ	78 min	{30, 78} min	30 min
λ (Kbit)	1–6	1–10	1–8

Robot MC vs. Vehicle MC. In the experiments, we use two types of mobile chargers with different characteristics, a robot-based MC and a vehicle-based MC. In the robot-based MC, the MC battery capacity is small and the charging time is high since the robot has limited space and weight to carry. On the other hand, in the vehicle-based MC, we have plenty of space, and the vehicle can carry more advanced equipment as well as a larger battery; thus, the charging time is short and the MC battery capacity is large.

In particular, for vehicle-based MC, we considered a battery capacity of 770 KJ, a speed of 5 m/s, and a charging time of 30 min. On the other hand, for robot-based MC we assumed a battery capacity of 216 KJ, a speed of 1,2 m/s and a charging time of 78 min.

APP1

The ideal outcome of an energy replacement strategy for an MC is to ensure that the networks becomes immortal; that is, no sensor ever becomes non-operational, even for a small amount of time.

Interestingly, the experimental results show that the Local-Learning strategy achieves precisely this outcome for all networks whose settings are in the application class *APP1*. More precisely, for all such network settings, after the initialization stage (without any knowledge of the network), the Local-Learning strategy keeps the network perpetually operating with no sensor ever depleting its battery (see Fig. 1). In other words, the Local-Learning strategy achieves *complete immortality* for the entire class *APP1*.

APP2

For this class of applications, where the area covered by the sensors is of medium size, both a robot and a vehicle could be suitable. For the setting corresponding to the use of a vehicle-based MC, the Local-Learning strategy achieves *complete immortality*. Indeed, as shown in Fig. 2-(a), in this case, no sensor ever becomes non-operational.

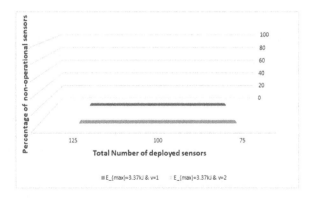

Fig. 1. APP1: Percentage of non-operational sensors.

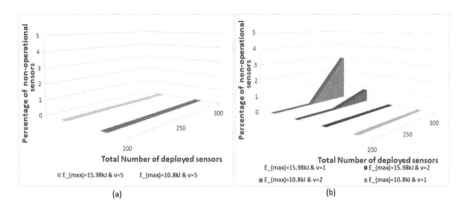

Fig. 2. APP2: Percentage of non-operational sensors (%)

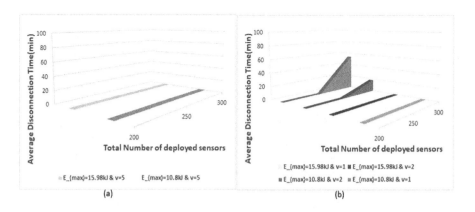

Fig. 3. APP2: Average disconnection time (minutes)

The results for a robot-based MC are also very good. Figure 2-(b) shows the percentage of non-operational sensors using a robot-based MC for various combinations of speed and risk threshold and we can observe that the non-operational sensors never exceed 6% of the total number of sensors and the percentage is often much lower than that. In correspondence to these settings, Fig. 3 shows that the average disconnection time for a sensor that gets depleted is never more than 1 hour.

We also observed how many times a sensor can become non-operational because of a depleted battery noticing that no sensor becomes non-operational more than once. That is, when the MC is a robot, over the entire simulated period of 6 months,

Summarizing, for all network settings in *APP2*, after the initialization stage (without any knowledge of the network), the Local-Learning strategy let the network achieve *complete immortality* if the MC is a vehicle, and *near immortality* when the MC is a robot.

APP3

Also for this class of applications, which are vehicle-based, the results applying the Local-Learning strategy are excellent. We obtain *complete immortality* for all combinations of parameters, with one exception. The exception is when the number of sensors is the highest (600).

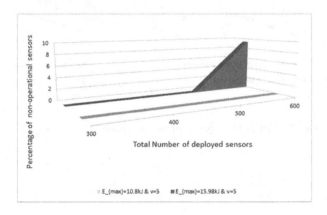

Fig. 4. APP3: Percentage of non-operational sensors for various sensors' battery capacities.

In correspondence of this setting, during the simulated lifetime (6 months), at any time, no more than 10% of the sensors become non-operational (see Fig. 4). Furthermore, a sensor never becomes depleted more than once, and the average disconnection time is never more than 5 h (see Fig. 5). In other words, in this case, the network achieves *near immortality*.

Summarizing, for all network settings in *APP3*, after the initialization stage (without any knowledge of the network), the Local-Learning strategy let the network always achieve *near immortality* and often *complete immortality*.

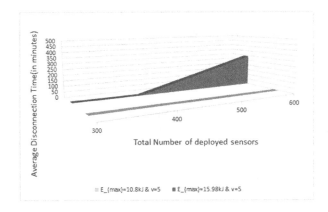

Fig. 5. APP3: average disconnection time using a robot MC.

3.4 Additional Results and Insights

To test further the flexibility of our approach, we have run experiments varying some of the parameters also beyond the three classes of applications. In particular, we tested $E_{max} = 3.37$ KJ, $E_{max} = 10.8$ KJ, $E_{max} = 15.98$ in all three settings, we employed $\gamma = 30$ min and $\gamma = 78$ min, under the worst conditions of all the other parameters, and we extended the size of the area where the sensors are deployed. Simulating the strategy under this wider range of variables leads to the following observations:

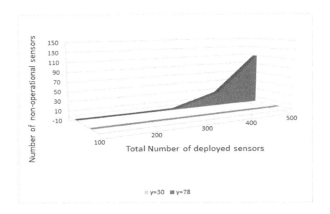

Fig. 6. Number of non-operational sensors with various charging rates: $E_{max} = 3.37$ kJ, $v = 1$, $\lambda = (1\text{–}10)$ Kbit, area of 1000 m × 1000 m

- The smaller the recharging time γ, the better the performance of the strategy. This is not surprising since less recharging time gives the MC more time to visit all the sensors before they get depleted. With recharging time up to $\gamma = 30$ min our approach achieves immortality even under the worst condition of the other parameters (large networks, small sensor battery, low MC speed), as shown in Fig. 6.
- Clearly, larger sensor battery capacities lead to better performance; from our experiments, however, we observe that $E_{max} = 10.8$KJ is the best choice of battery capacity among the ones tested because such batteries are cheaper than the ones with capacity $E_{max} = 15.98$ KJ, and its use achieves almost the same results as the ones obtained with $E_{max} = 15.98$. Decreasing the capacity, we start observing a decrease in performance; in fact, with $E_{max} = 3.37$ KJ we have an increase in the number of non-operational sensors (although their disconnections are still short-lived).
  Under the most unfavorable choice of parameters the increase becomes noticeable, while still not excessive and always below 14%; this happens in correspondence of transmission rate $\lambda = (1$–$10)$ Kbit, charging time $\gamma = 78$ m, and a large area of 1000 m × 1000 m (see Fig. 7).
- All three applications scenarios have been simulated also in larger areas without any decrease in performance. In fact, as Fig. 8 shows, the percentages of non-operational sensors is always below 10%, even in the worst possible condition of battery capacity.

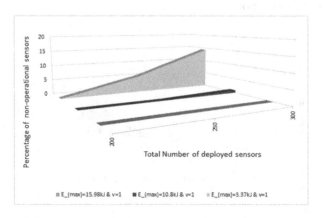

Fig. 7. Percentage of non-operational sensors with various E_{max}: $\lambda = (1$–10 Kbit$)$, $\gamma = 78$ min, area of 1000 m × 1000 m.

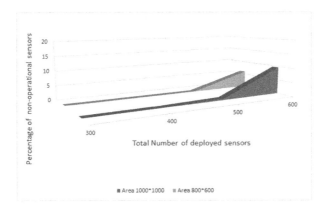

Fig. 8. APP3: Percentage of non-operational sensors in various areas with $\lambda = (1-6$ Kbit$)$, $E_{max} = 3.37$ kJ, $\gamma = 30$ min.

4 Conclusions

In this paper we considered the problem of recharging WSN using a mobile charger. In particular, we studied the applicability of a simple decentralized local learning strategy on a wide range of application parameters: number of sensors, size of the area in which they are deployed, and mobile charger characteristics (speed, battery capacity, charging time, etc.). We found that in all those settings, the strategy achieves complete immortality, or near immortality with the occasional disconnections being very short-lived. This shows the high flexibility of this strategy to changes in the system parameters. The success of the method is due to the ability of the mobile charger to "learn" the global distribution of battery discharges; we are now studying its behavior under variations in the battery discharging patterns, to assess its adaptability to changes. An open direction of investigation is the analytical study in support of the experimental results.

Acknowledgment. I would like to thank Prof. Nicola Santoro and Prof. Paola Flocchini for their helpful guidance and discussions.

References

1. Akhtar, F., Rehmani, M.: Energy replenishment using renewable and traditional energy resources for sustainable wireless sensor networks: a review. Renew. Sustain. Energy Rev. **45**, 769–785 (2015)
2. Aloqaily, O., Flocchini, P., Santoro, N.: Achieving immortality in wireless rechargeable sensor networks using local learning. In: 7th IEEE International Symposium on Networks, Computers and Communications (ISNCC), pp. 1–6 (2020)
3. Angelopoulos, C.M., Nikoletseas, S., Raptis, T.P., Raptopoulos, C., Vasilakis, F.: Improving sensor network performance with wireless energy transfer. Int. J. Ad Hoc Ubiquitous Comput. **20**(3), 159–171 (2015)

4. Chang, C.Y., Hsiao, C.Y., Chang, C.T.: QoS guaranteed surveillance algorithms for directional wireless sensor networks. Ad Hoc Netw. **81**, 71–85 (2018)
5. Chang, J., Tassiulas, L.: Maximum lifetime routing in wireless sensor networks. IEEE/ACM Trans. Netw. **12**(4), 609–619 (2004)
6. Chen, Y., Zhao, Q., Krishnamurthy, V., Djonin, D.: Transmission scheduling for optimizing sensor network lifetime: a stochastic shortest path approach. IEEE Trans. Signal Process. **55**(5), 2294–2309 (2007)
7. Dai, H., Wu, X., Xu, L., Chen, G., Lin, S.: Using minimum mobile chargers to keep large-scale wireless rechargeable sensor networks running forever. In: Proceedings of 22nd International Conference on Computer Communications and Networks (ICCCN), pp. 1–7 (2013)
8. Flocchini, P., Omar, E., Santoro, N.: Effective energy restoration of wireless sensor networks by a mobile robot. Int. J. Netw. Comput. **10**(2), 62–83 (2020)
9. Gaikwad, S., Ghosal, M.: Energy efficient storage-less and converter-less renewable energy harvesting system using MPPT. In: 2017 2nd International Conference for Convergence in Technology (I2CT), pp. 971–973 (2017)
10. Guo, S., Wang, C., Yang, Y.: Mobile data gathering with wireless energy replenishment in rechargeable sensor networks. In: IEEE INFOCOM 2013 - IEEE Conference on Computer Communications, pp. 1932–1940 (2013)
11. Han, G., Jiang, J., Shen, W., Shu, L., Rodrigues, J.: IDSEP: a novel intrusion detection scheme based on energy prediction in cluster-based wireless sensor networks. IET Inf. Secur. **7**(2), 97–105 (2013)
12. He, L., Gu, Y., Pan, J., Zhu, T.: On-demand charging in wireless sensor networks: theories and applications'. In: Proceedings of 10th IEEE International Conference on Mobile Ad-Hoc and Sensor Systems (MASS), pp. 28–36 (2012)
13. Heinzelman, W.R., Chandrakasan, A., Balakrishnan, H.: Energy-efficient communication protocol for wireless microsensor networks. In: Proceedings of the 33rd Annual Hawaii International Conference on System Sciences, vol. 2, pp. 10, January 2000
14. Hou, Y., Shi, Y., Sherali, H.: Rate allocation and network lifetime problems for wireless sensor networks. IEEE/ACM Trans. Netw. **16**(2), 321–334 (2008)
15. Jiang, L., Wu, X., Chen, G., Li, Y.: Effective on-demand mobile charger scheduling for maximizing coverage in wireless rechargeable sensor networks. Mob. Netw. Appl. **19**(4), 543–551 (2014)
16. Kurs, A., Karalis, A., Moffatt, R., Joannopoulos, J.D., Fisher, P., Soljačić, M.: Wireless power transfer via strongly coupled magnetic resonances. Science **317**(5834), 83–86 (2007)
17. Kurs, A., Moffatt, R., Soljačić, M.: Simultaneous mid-range power transfer to multiple devices. Appl. Phys. Lett. **96**(4), 044102 (2010)
18. Li, Z., Peng, Zhang, W., Qiao, D.: J-RoC: a joint routing and charging scheme to prolong sensor network lifetime. In: 19th IEEE International Conference on Network Protocols (ICNP), pp. 373–382 (2011)
19. Liang, W., Xu, W., Ren, X., Jia, X., Lin, X.: Maintaining large-scale rechargeable sensor networks perpetually via multiple mobile charging vehicles. ACM Trans. Sensor Netw. **12**(2), 14:1–14:26 (2016)
20. Lino, C., Navarro, T., Calafate, C.T., Diaz-Ramirez, A., Manzoni, P., Cano, J.: Intruder tracking in WSNs using binary detection sensors and mobile sinks. In: 2012 IEEE Wireless Communications and Networking Conference (WCNC), pp. 2025–2030, April 2012

21. Ma, Y., Liang, W., Xu, W.: Charging utility maximization in wireless rechargeable sensor networks by charging multiple sensors simultaneously. IEEE/ACM Trans. Netw. **26**(4), 1591–1604 (2018)
22. Madhja, A., Nikoletseas, S., Raptis, T.: Distributed wireless power transfer in sensor networks with multiple mobile chargers. Comput. Netw. **80**, 89–108 (2015)
23. Peng, Y., Li, Z., Zhang, W., Qiao, D.: Prolonging sensor network lifetime through wireless charging. In: Proceedings of 31st IEEE Real-Time Systems Symposium, pp. 129–139, November 2010
24. Santoro, N., Velazquez, E.: Energy restoration in mobile sensor networks. In: Mitton, N., Simplot-Ryl, D. (eds.) Wireless Sensor and Robot Networks, pp. 113–142 (2014)
25. Sharma, H., Haque, A., Jaffery, Z.A.: Solar energy harvesting wireless sensor network nodes: a survey. J. Renew. Sustain. Energy **10**(2), 023704 (2018)
26. Shi, Y., Xie, L., Hou, T., Sherali, H.: On renewable sensor networks with wireless energy transfer. In: IEEE INFOCOM 2011 - IEEE Conference on Computer Communications, pp. 1350–1358 (2011)
27. Surez Barón, J.C., Suáirez Barón, M.J.: Application of SHT71 sensor to measure humidity and temperature with a WSN. In: 2014 IEEE 9th Ibero American Congress on Sensors, pp. 1–7, October 2014
28. Wang, C., Li, J., Ye, F., Yang, Y.: NETWRAP: An NDN based real-time wireless recharging framework for wireless sensor networks. IEEE Trans. Mob. Comput. **13**(6), 1283–1297 (2014)
29. Xie, L., Shi, Y., Hou, Y.T., Sherali, H.D.: Making sensor networks immortal: an energy-renewal approach with wireless power transfer. IEEE/ACM Trans. Netw. **20**(6), 1748–1761 (2012)
30. Xie, L., Shi, Y., Hou, Y.T., Lou, W., Sherali, H.D.: On traveling path and related problems for a mobile station in a rechargeable sensor network. In: Proceedings of the Fourteenth ACM International Symposium on Mobile Ad Hoc Networking and Computing, MobiHoc 2013, pp. 109–118. Association for Computing Machinery, New York (2013)
31. Xu, P., Wu, J., Shang, C., Chang, C.: GSMS: a barrier coverage algorithm for joint surveillance quality and network lifetime in WSNs. IEEE Access **7**, 159608–159621 (2019)
32. Zhang, Y., Zhou, Z., Zhao, D., Barhamgi, M., Rahman, T.: Graph-based mechanism for scheduling mobile sensors in time-sensitive WSNs applications. IEEE Access **5**, 1559–1569 (2017)
33. Zhao, M., Li, J., Yang, Y.: Joint mobile energy replenishment and data gathering in wireless rechargeable sensor networks. In: Proceedings of IEEE 23rd International Teletraffic Congress (ITC) (2011)
34. Zhou, P., Wang, C., Yang, Y.: Self-sustainable sensor networks with multi-source energy harvesting and wireless charging. In: IEEE INFOCOM 2019 - IEEE Conference on Compute Communications, pp. 1828–1836, April 2019

Carrot and Stick: Incentivizing Cooperation Between Nodes in Multihop Wireless Ad Hoc Networks

Karol Rydzewski[✉] [iD]

Gdańsk University of Technology, Gdańsk, Poland
k.rydzewski@o2.pl

Abstract. A novel, holistic approach to cooperation incentivization in multihop wireless ad hoc networks is introduced. The concept utilizes a reputation metric to tailor a response to rational nodes' behavior and thus promote cooperation while balancing network traffic among network nodes and protecting well-behaving nodes from excessive network load. The solution aims at deterring selfish optimization techniques which may result in network-wide Path Delivery Ratio (PDR) degradation.

Keywords: Ad-hoc wireless network · Cooperation · Behavior · Selfishness · Reciprocity · Autonomous agents · Reputation

1 Introduction

In a multihop wireless ad hoc network a node communicating with a remote node, located outside of its radio range, needs help from other, transit, nodes to relay its packets to the destination. As there is no infrastructure and centralized network administration, the nodes self-organize their networking. In a public, open network every node can be managed by a different entity which is selfishly interested in maximizing its network performance, while minimizing its cost. Additionally, some optimization algorithms may result in a selfish nodal behavior. In this environment it is easy to imagine a network which is under-performing or collapses because its users do not wish to cooperate with each other. In fact, research shows that selfishness is favoured in current network standards as it often results in a better network performance [1] at a cost of standard-compliant nodes which become selfless "suckers" and experience downgraded network service. Selfish strategy offers better performance in comparison to a compliant strategy. However, if this strategy is widespread in a network, everyone observes severely limited network performance which, in extreme cases, may result in a network collapse as few, or none, nodes are willing to cooperate. End-to-end packet forwarding cooperation is of primary focus in this work.

This work was funded by National Science Centre, Poland under grant No.UMO-2016/21/B/ST6/03146.

L. Foschini and M. El Kamili (Eds.): ADHOCNETS 2020, LNICST 345, pp. 116–129, 2021.
https://doi.org/10.1007/978-3-030-67369-7_9

A prominent solution to selfish nodes problem is an implementation of a reputation system. The goal of such a system is to reliably detect nodal behavior and assign a reputation metric which will inform other nodes about past behavior of a particular node. This metric enables nodes across the network to decide how they should behave in future interactions with this node. In a typical reputation system, at least two subsystems can be identified: firstly, a *reputation deduction subsystem*, which translates nodal behavior to a reputation value, and secondly, a *reputation response subsystem*, which determines nodal response to other nodes' reputation—typically in terms of misbehavior avoidance (better service levels) and misbehavior deterrence (minimizing the number of uncooperative nodes in the network). Section 2 surveys different concepts of using reputation in multihop wireless ad hoc networks.

Recently, two *reputation deduction subsystem* algorithms were published [2,3] capable of producing accurate reputation values for multihop wireless ad hoc networks transit nodes, robust to packet losses and changes of nodal behavior. Furthermore, our preliminary research promise satisfactory reputation rendering capabilities of these algorithms in a mobile ad hoc network environment. The intent is to use the reputation metrics produced by either of the algorithms as an input to the *reputation response subsystem* outlined in this work.

This work presents a novel concept for using reputation metric to promote cooperation between selfish nodes by providing incentives for cooperative nodes and punishing misbehaving ones—thus fulfilling both "carrot" and "stick" parts of the approach. The purpose of this approach is to discourage nodes from misbehavior by making it to appear costly in contrast to the cooperation. In addition, the solution addresses a common problem of a reputation-driven routing which results in overloading well-behaving nodes and offloading misbehaving nodes, hence further boosting incentives for cooperation.

The remainder of this work is structured as follows: Sect. 2 surveys state of the art, Sect. 3 details the model, Sect. 4 outlines the *Stick and Carrot* approach, Sect. 5 discusses preliminary evaluation results, Sect. 6 concludes this paper.

2   Related Works

Reputation systems are one of the prominent concepts addressing the problem of extensive network nodes' autonomy giving rise to nodal selfishness, causing a negative impact on multihop wireless ad hoc networks. A number of areas particularly susceptible to this kind of impact were identified, such as Quality of Service (QoS) [4] and the packet forwarding service [1]. Some works on reputation systems focus solely on assigning an accurate reputation value to each and every network node. Knowing others' inclination to cooperation is a fundamental step in building a successful reputation system. However, it cannot be the only one as having the reputation of a particular value is not a self-contained goal and does not cause any implications to the subject of this rating, nor for holders of this information [5].

One, vital use of the reputation values produced by a *reputation deduction subsystem* is mitigation of misbehaving nodes, thus improving the level of service for nodes within the network. One, notable example of such use is a mechanism called Pathrater [6,7], which selects paths avoiding misbehaving nodes. The misbehaving node in Pathrater's context is a node that provides the packet forwarding service below a certain, predefined threshold. Other authors [8,9], point out that routing around misbehaving nodes in fact rewards them as they are free from costs associated with forwarding others' packets and can still have their packets delivered without obstructions. By analogy, this approach in fact punishes nodes of a good reputation with more transit traffic to forward. Additionally, confining transit nodes' selection to a subset of nodes performing above a predefined threshold may result in no paths available for packets transmission, while there might be some under-performing, more costly options available. A similar algorithm, mitigating the problem of the limited transit nodes' pool was presented in [10], where the best available path was selected—without lower limit of acceptable reputation. Both [9] and [10] recognize a problem of favouring the best performing nodes which result in lack of possibilities for low reputation nodes to improve their rating. [9] addresses this problem with a traffic shedding approach, which routes more traffic via nodes of low reputation and reduces the number of packets sent via cooperative nodes. This approach, however, impacts well-behaving nodes with poor network performance and offers no incentives for nodes to use this approach in a real-life scenario.

Another, equally important, use of reputation is punishment for misbehavior, where nodes of poor reputation receive limited service or, in some cases, their forwarding requests are entirely rejected. It is realised either by forwarding packets with a probability equal to the source node's reputation [11] or a binary decision based on a predefined reputation threshold to entirely drop or forward all packets from a particular node (permanently or temporarily) [12]. The concept of rewarding or punishing nodes for their past behavior, by any node in a network, is called indirect reciprocity and originates from evolutionary biology and game theory [13]. A typical approach is to respond to node's reputation in kind, providing the level of service equal to node's previously observed forwarding behavior, as it is conveyed by the reputation value. This strategy is called tit-for-tat. In [13] a set of evolutionary best performing strategies, modeled as infinitely repeated games, were developed. Apart from indirect reciprocity response, it was found that the best strategies involve a punishment for inadequate response to the reputation. Similar findings were reported in [12].

In some systems [12,14] a game theoretic approach is explicitly defined to model the rise of the misbehavior as well as to incentivize the nodes to cooperate. This approach clearly explains the origins of misbehavior in multihop wireless ad hoc networks and shows that the situation, without additional incentivization mechanisms, is equivalent to Prissoner's Dillema and Tragedy of the Commons [15], where rational nodes are bound to misbehave. A solution to this problem can be found in game theory, which proves that a thoughtful design of the *reputation response subsystem* may effectively foster cooperation between the network nodes.

3 Model

In the presented model we use bold face to denote sets, capital letters for nodes and lowercase letters for various metrics. The model concerns a network of nodes from a finite set **N**, which can change over time as nodes join and leave the network. Our model concentrates on a packet forwarding service in a mulitihop wireless ad hoc network. In such a network, when a source node (S) wants to send a packet to a remote destination node (D), located outside of S's radio range, it must request other, transit nodes to forward it's packets to D. Transit nodes form a path, $\mathbf{P}_{SD}$, accordingly to a selected routing algorithm, in order to fulfil the packet forwarding request. Nodes within the path retain a full decision autonomy, in particular, how to respond to each S's forwarding request: forward it or drop it. Arguably, the node's decision is made based on some rational premises. In a longer perspective, each transit node can forward all requested packets, drop some or all the packets. It is assumed that the nodal forwarding ratio, g_X, called further nodal behavior, is an internally predefined number and the node is making an effort to provide the service as close as possible to g_X. g_X is a real number in $[0,1]$, where 0 represents a node dropping all packet forwarding requests and 1 a node forwarding every request. The g_X is considered a quasi-static number; it is expected that, in a well-designed system, g_X seldom change as the nodes pick a number which secures their equilibrium point, resulting in the best network performance for them (e.g. bandwidth, latency) at an acceptable price (e.g. bandwidth used, battery life). A source node, S, in such a network expects a path delivery ratio (PDR), p_{SD}, equal to the product of transit nodes' behaviors (1):

$$
p_{SD} = \begin{cases} \prod_{X \in \mathbf{P}_{SD}} g_X, & \mathbf{P}_{SD} \neq \varnothing \\ 1, & \mathbf{P}_{SD} = \varnothing \end{cases} \tag{1}
$$

This model intentionally omits possible transmission errors as this is an intricate phenomenon without clearly defined relationships and deserves an in-depth study. In this approach the reputation system simply treats any event influencing (1) as a measurement error. [2] and [3] prove this approach to be successful in accurately rendering actual nodal behavior, g_X, despite adverse conditions such ass, transmission errors and behavior changes. Furthermore, in a well-designed network, various transmission errors affect relatively small percentage of packets and a successful *reputation deduction subsystem* is expected to deduce g_X correctly despite the errors. Hence, the *reputation response subsystem*, defined in a higher abstraction layer, relatively to the *reputation deduction subsystem* and transport protocols, can assume that the error level is negligibly low.

The *reputation deduction subsystem* monitors the network and produces a reputation metric for each node X. We assume following for the reputation value:

1. Is a real number within [0,1] range, where 0 represents a complete absence of cooperation and 1 a completely cooperative node.
2. Is known to any other node in the network.
3. Closely resembles actual node's behavior. Some discrepancies are permissible, however, in principle, they should be minor or temporary. Evaluation of the *Carrot and Stick* approach in an error-prone environment is deferred to the future.

We assume that a node X working in such a network is a rational node, which observes the network, its reputation and makes adjustments to its behavior, routing and other means under its control. An intent of this behavior is to maximize X's network performance while reducing the costs of networking. Both gain and cost functions can render to be multifactor and complicated relationships. Arguably, both metrics can be simplified to a root cause which is a number of X's packets successfully delivered in relation to the total number of packets sent, o_X, for the network gain and a number of packets forwarded on behalf of other nodes, c_X, for the cost. In this perspective, primary optimization problem for the node X becomes (2):

$$1^{\text{st}} \text{ maximize: } o_X = \overline{p_X}$$
$$2^{\text{nd}} \text{ minimize: } c_X \tag{2}$$
$$\text{subject to: } g_X \in [0, 1]$$

where: $\overline{p_X}$ denotes an average observed PDR for all paths originating from X. Performance maximization has a priority over cost minimization in this optimization problem.

Analysis of (2) may lead to a conclusion that a node which is not generating any network traffic has no motivation to behave cooperatively. However, it is important to note that it is unreasonable for such a node to be connected to a network if they do not plan to communicate with anyone as a mere cost of having the receiver enabled along with the cost of periodical exchange of network management traffic cannot be justified and becomes an expendable expense. All other nodes should maintain a reputation level which ensures an optimal o_X at all times, even for infrequent communication needs, as an opportunity for rebuilding reputation might not be readily available.

4   Carrot and Stick Approach

This section outlines high-level means of the *Carrot and Stick* approach and its use of network nodes' reputation. A primary goal of a *reputation response subsystem* is to improve well-behaving nodes' network performance while discouraging nodal misbehavior. *Carrot and Stick* approach addresses both parts by providing the best possible performance for fully cooperative nodes and a gradually deteriorating service for the ones who choose misbehavior.

Figure 1 depicts a complete reputation system operations and *Carrot and Stick* place in the behavior-perception-reputation-reaction feedback loop. The *Carrot and Stick* approach relies on reputation metrics calculated by a *reputation deduction subsystem* from observed PDR and, indirectly, g_X. Based on these metrics all *Carrot and Stick* calculations are made. The method directly influences nodal behavior toward source nodes as well as network routing. It is expected that *Carrot and Stick's* operations will affect rational nodes' decisions and their behavior toward other nodes, prompting the subsequent cycle of the system.

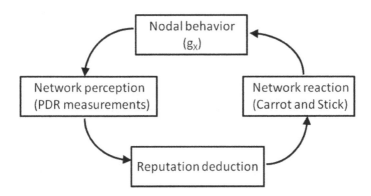

Fig. 1. The graph depicts a behavior-perception-reputation-reaction feedback loop of the entire proposed reputation system. *Carrot and Stick* is a part of this system, using reputation to respond to nodal behavior. The nodes, experiencing *Carrot and Stick* response, react by changing their behavior to optimize their gain and cost (2).

A core component of the *Carrot and Stick* subsystem is an algorithm determining reciprocal reaction of a transit node to the reputation of the source node. The approach is inspired by the indirect reciprocity and tit-for-tat strategies, however *Carrot and Stick* responds to misbehavior with an enhanced severity, thus the response mechanism is called *enhanced indirect reciprocity*. A behavior of a transit node, Y, towards the source node, S is determined accordingly to (3):

$$b_{YS} = \begin{cases} g_S - (g_Y - g_S), & g_S < g_Y \\ g_Y, & g_S \geqslant g_Y \end{cases} \tag{3}$$

For the sake of simplicity, in (3) we assume that the reputation of a node is equal to its behavior, which is not always true. In an actual implementation the reputation value should be used, as g_X can rarely be directly observed by other nodes. Furthermore, a node can directly control its g_X; its reputation, although closely correlated, is not available for direct manipulation by a node.

Since Eq. (3) changes nodal behavior, it influences the PDR expected by the source node. Hence, the formula for PDR calculation (1) transforms to (4):

$$p_{SD} = \begin{cases} \prod_{Y \in \mathbf{P}_{SD}} b_{YS}, & \mathbf{P}_{SD} \neq \varnothing \\ 1, & \mathbf{P}_{SD} = \varnothing \end{cases} \tag{4}$$

The second component of the *Carrot and Stick* approach is a *Reputation-based Balanced Routing* (RBR) which uses both information about the reputation of all the nodes and *enhanced indirect reciprocity* PDR estimations (4). The routing mechanism selects a route which promises the best possible PDR, maximum p_{SD}, for a given source node communicating with a destination node. The specific implementation of the RBR algorithm is not defined to provide flexibility to choose best-performing algorithm suitable for a specific network. The RBR in this view is a route cost metric rather than a full-fledged routing algorithm.

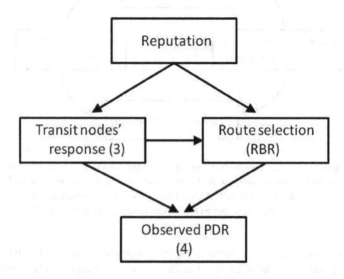

Fig. 2. The diagram depicts *Carrot and Stick's* use of reputation. Transit nodes build their response using source nodes' reputation and (3). The source nodes experience transit nodes response through their observed PDR (4). In parallel, RBR-based routing mechanism, using publicly known reputation values and (3), selects transit nodes that promise the best PDR possible for a given source node, which results in observed PDR (4).

Figure 2 summarizes how *Carrot and Stick* use reputation to influence individual nodes' gain (2) by interfering with their observed PDR (4). (3), determining transit nodes' response to source nodes' reputation, is the fundamental component of the entire response system as it directly impacts source nodes' gains by forwarding or dropping their packets accordingly to *enhanced indirect reciprocity* concept. The second component of the system is the RBR. Such a routing is a rational step, complimentary to the *enhanced indirect reciprocity*, as it allows nodes to maximise their PDR and gain when operating in a network implementing (3).

Enhanced indirect reciprocity and RBR tandem is designed to provide the best possible network performance for cooperative nodes and deteriorating performance for misbehaving ones. Additional, feature of this approach is deflecting misbehaving nodes' traffic from cooperative nodes which further improves cooperative nodes' performance and incentivizes misbehaving nodes to improve their service (2).

It is assumed that the *reputation deduction subsystem* is monitoring how nodes adhere to *Carrot and Stick* principles and punish those who offer different service level than expected (3). It is expected that the reputation system will punish nodes offering both lower and higher level of service as this strategy was proven to be the most effective in [13]. Some tolerance for minor discrepancies is desirable.

The rational nodes by means of the optimization algorithm (2) and their knowledge about the network[1], are expected to react to the *Stick and Carrot* operations and adjust their behavior to yield the best possible network performance. An in-depth evaluation of this dynamic and a study of optimal optimization strategies is deferred to future work.

5   Evaluation

This section presents results of a preliminary evaluation of the *Carrot and Stick* approach in numerical simulations in a custom-developed environment. The goal of this work is to validate if the approach is actually capable to reward cooperative nodes and punish misbehaving ones and if it is possible to incentivize misbehaving nodes to improve their behavior by offering better service level for cooperating nodes only. Two basic simulations were performed: the first one evaluates PDR observed by a source node of varying g_X interacting with one and later with three transit nodes of varying g_Y; the second simulation evaluates PDR observed by randomly selected source nodes, communicating with random destinations, placed within a 100-node network.

Figure 3 presents a simple one source vs. one transit node interaction where a transit node Y is requested to forward source node X's packets. The whole spectrum of possible g_X and g_Y values (with 0.01 step) were examined. It is clear that the fully cooperative X ($g_X = 1$) can always expect the best possible forwarding service irrespective from Y's behavior. X risks receiving no service at all from the well behaving Y if it chooses $g_X \leq 0.5$ (triangular plateau in the lower part of the plot). The lower the X's behavior is the narrower becomes the pool of nodes available for cooperation with them and the lower becomes o_X. In all cases, X achieves highest PDR, when interacting with Y, which $g_Y = g_X$ (diagonal, falling "ridge" in middle of the plot). Additionally, Fig. 3 illustrates c_X in an interaction with X. The higher g_Y is the higher c_X becomes. The optimization problem (2) in this simple case clearly states that X should choose $g_X = 1$ as maximizing o_X has priority over minimizing c_X.

---

[1] Relevant information may include, but is not limited to: transit and source traffic sizes along with the reputation of the nodes in the vicinity.

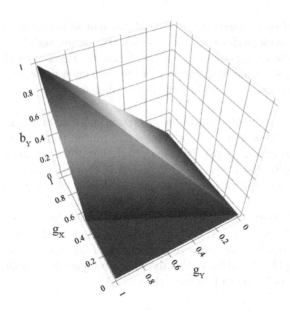

Fig. 3. Behavior (b_{YX}) of a transit node Y towards a source node X, relative to both X (g_X) and Y (g_Y) behaviors.

In networks without the *reputation response subsystem*, missing a misbehavior punishment mechanism, analogous chart renders a flat, tilted surface where $b_{YS} = g_Y$ and b_{YS} value is irrespective to g_X. In such a network o_X depends solely on a probability of cooperating with Y node of a given g_Y value. A rational node in such a network following (2) algorithm will chose not to cooperate at all as this way it will maximize its o_X and minimize c_X.

A simple tit-for-tat $(b_{YS} = g_S g_Y)$ response strategy yields a similar result to *Carrot and Stick*. The major differences are: nonlinear trajectory of b_{YS} and absence of discriminating bonus (3) for higher reputation nodes forwarding packets of relatively lower reputation nodes. In this network, the best X's routing strategy, irrespective of g_X, is to always seek highest available g_Y. In such a scenario high-reputation nodes may become overwhelmed with congestive traffic (see Fig. 6), which reduces their o_X and they may decide to lower their behavior to improve their o_X and lower c_X. This might be even more distinct in other, more elaborate optimization strategies, which take other performance metrics into account.

The node X relaying its packets via multiple transit nodes sees the PDR as a product of transit nodes' behaviors (4). Figure 4 presents X's interaction with three transit nodes, all of which have the same behavior g_Y. Keeping the highest possible behavior is consistently the best strategy, ensuring the best possible o_X in all settings. With decreasing g_X or g_Y the source node experiences a steeper PDR degradation and the best strategy for a misbehaving node is, invariably, to choose transit nodes of similar behavior to g_X, yielding $p_k = g_X{}^3$.

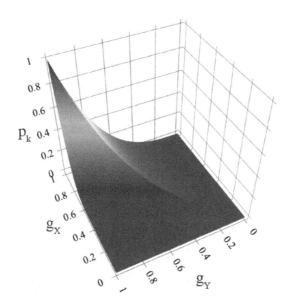

Fig. 4. PDR (p_k) observed by a node X of behavior g_X relaying its packet via three transit nodes, all of which have the same behavior, equal to g_Y

Another numeric experiment involved a network, consisting of 100 nodes, randomly placed on a 500×500 m plain. Each node in this network had a constant 150 m. communication range and randomly[2] assigned g_X value. A simple, rudimentary routing protocol, based on the RBR concept, was implemented, returning a path with the best available expected PDR (4) and of maximal length of 10 transit nodes. The same routing algorithm, picking a path of highest PDR for a given source node, was used in all presented cases. In such a network a 1000 random source-destination pairs were drawn and the routing algorithm returned the best available path between them. To ensure that the results are independent from a specific topology and g_X placement, each experiment's setup was run 10 times, each with different, random nodes' placement and behavior.

Figure 5 presents results of the simulations on the simplified networks. Figures present PDRs observed by the source nodes in relation to the source nodes' g_X. Each dot represents an average PDR observed by a single node. Direct connections, i.e. without transit nodes, were not taken into account. Figure 5a) plots results for networks with *Carrot and Stick* concept implemented (PDR calculated with (3) and (4)). PDR results for the popular tit-for-tat algorithm $(b_{YX} = g_X g_Y)$ are presented in Fig. 5b). The shape of both plots is similar, however the plot for *Carrot and Stick* is visibly steeper and levels at PDR=0 for g_X lower than 0.5. The reason for this, apart from the differences between algorithms themselves, is the distribution of g_X among the nodes in the simu-

---

[2] Normal distribution: mean = 1, standard deviation = 0.4; the draw is repeated if $g_X \notin [0, 1]$.

lation (normal distribution, favouring well-behaving nodes) which results in a relatively small number of significantly misbehaving nodes ($g_X < 0.5$) to interact with each other. In tit-for-tat networks the best strategy for a misbehaving source node is to send its traffic via the best behaving nodes available, whereas in a network implementing *enhanced indirect reciprocity*, the best bet is to use similarly behaving transit nodes. Figure 5c) depicts observed PDR in networks where nodes does not react to the source node reputation and their $b_{YX} = g_Y$.

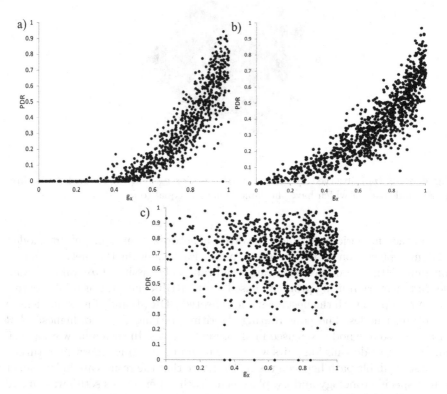

Fig. 5. PDR observed by source nodes in relation to their behavior g_X. Each dot represents an average PDR observed by a single node through the simulation. Chart a) presents results from networks implementing *Carrot and Stick*, b) networks operating accordingly to tit-for-tat approach and c) results from networks without any punishment mechanism.

Figure 6 depicts a total number of sessions where a node acted as a transit node in relation to its g_X. Figure 6a) plots results for *Carrot and Stick* algorithm, Fig. 6b) for tit-for-tat and Fig. 6c) for networks without reciprocity algorithm implemented. The total number of sessions in each simulation was equal to one thousand (each plot present results from 10 identical runs of the simulation) and direct connections are not plotted here. The rudimentary routing algorithm in all experiments was picking the best path available. The most important difference in these results is a balance between how fully cooperative nodes are loaded in comparison to the rest of the nodes. The most heavily used cooperative nodes in networks where *Carrot and Stick* is implemented carry at least two times less traffic then their counterparts in networks with tit-for-tat and without any response algorithm implemented, where some nodes carry roughly half of the total traffic in the network (400–500 sessions out of 1000 total). Meanwhile, less cooperative nodes in both Fig. 6 b) and c) are almost unused serving singular sessions at most. The same nodes, in *Carrot and Stick* networks are used relatively more frequently, providing them with more opportunities to improve their reputation and offloading cooperative nodes. Note, a specific g_X distribution in all presented networks where cooperative nodes are more frequent. In networks of more uniform g_X distribution, this results may look different, however general regularities, outlined above, should be present in all cases.

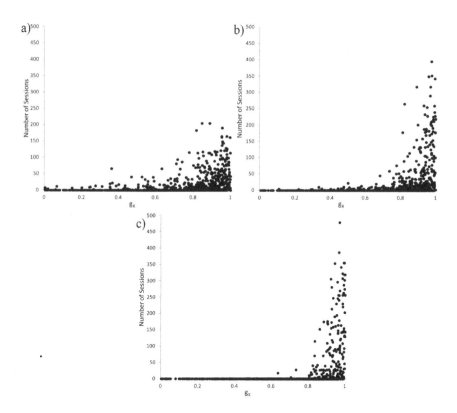

Fig. 6. Plots depict a total number of communication sessions (1000 sessions in a single simulation) for each transit node in the network relatively to its g_X. Chart a) presents results from a network implementing *Carrot and Stick*, b) a network operating accordingly to tit-for-tat approach and c) results from a network without any punishment mechanism.

In addition to the presented setups, Pathrater algorithm was evaluated along with all three reputation reciprocity algorithms, i.e. *enhanced indirect reciprocity*, tit-for-tat and no algorithm at all. Slightly lower average observed PDRs were recorded in all setups, with even more unbalanced traffic distribution, where nodes below Pathrater's threshold[3] were not used at all. In both *enhanced indirect reciprocity* and tit-for-tat, nodes of g_X below the threshold observed virtually no data delivered to their destinations[4].

It is clear that with *Carrot and Stick* approach implemented misbehaving nodes receive results distinctively worse than the cooperative nodes. A node in such a network observes PDR $\leqslant g_X$. In a network where no response mechanism is implemented every node, irrespective of their behavior, has similar chances to achieve the best possible PDR. With any *reputation response subsystem* and any g_X there are situations where the PDR is far from the maximum possible one for a given behavior as its impossible to ensure that there are only "optimally" cooperative transit nodes on the path. Arguably, an uncooperative node experiencing suboptimal network performance will decide to increase their g_X, accordingly to (2). This way every cooperative nodes' performance will improve. The system is successful in discouraging rational nodes, pursuing better performance via misbehavior, from decreasing their g_X and hurting overall network performance.

6   Conclusion

A concept of a novel approach, called *Carrot and Stick*, to using reputation in multihop wireless ad hoc networks was outlined. The main goal of this framework is to incentivize selfish network nodes to cooperate by rewarding cooperation and punishing misbehavior. The core mean of achieving this is a new algorithm, called *enhanced indirect reciprocity*—responding with a service level degraded accordingly to the source and transit nodes' reputations and the difference between them. This approach, via *Reputation-based Balanced Routing* (RBR), influences routing decisions made by rational nodes seeking to optimize their network output, hence contributing to a balanced network traffic and mitigating cooperative nodes' overload, further promoting the cooperative behavior.

Future research includes *Carrot and Stick* evaluation in an error-prone, simulated network environment and working in tandem with an operating *reputation deduction subsystem*. Performance, correctness and ability to incentivize cooperation in rational nodes – dynamically adjusting their behavior – in a real network environment are of primary interest in this upcoming work.

---

[3] The threshold was the same for all nodes in the network.

[4] In case of source routing algorithms this may be unrealistic as nodes would set up their own threshold, corresponding to their g_X and, in this case, both Fig. 5 and 6 above plots would look similar.

References

1. Li, Z., Shen, H.: Analysis the cooperation strategies in mobile ad hoc networks. In: Proceedings MASS 2008, Atlanta, GA (2008)
2. Konorski, J., Rydzewski, K.: Guessing intrinsic forwarding trustworthiness of MANET nodes from end-to-end packet delivery. In: 11th EAI International Conference, ADHOCNETS 2019, Queenstown, New Zealand, 18–21 November 2019
3. Rydzewski, K., Konorski, J.: A reactive algorithm for deducing nodal forwarding behavior in a multihop ad-hoc wireless network in the presence of errors. Int. J. Electron. Telecommun. **6**(1), 193–199 (2020)
4. Szott, S., Natkaniec, M., Banchs, A.: Impact of misbehaviour on QoS in wireless mesh networks. In: Fratta, L., Schulzrinne, H., Takahashi, Y., Spaniol, O. (eds.) NETWORKING 2009. LNCS, vol. 5550, pp. 639–650. Springer, Heidelberg (2009). https://doi.org/10.1007/978-3-642-01399-7_50
5. Konorski, J., Rydzewski, K.: Nodal cooperation equilibrium analysis in multi-hop wireless ad hoc networks with a reputation system. In: Rak, J., Bay, J., Kotenko, I., Popyack, L., Skormin, V., Szczypiorski, K. (eds.) MMM-ACNS 2017. LNCS, vol. 10446, pp. 131–142. Springer, Cham (2017). https://doi.org/10.1007/978-3-319-65127-9_11
6. Buchegger, S., Boudec, J.-Y. L.:Performance analysis of the CONFIDANT protocol. In: Proceedings of 3rd ACM International Symposium on Mobile Ad Hoc Networking. Computing, Lausanne, Switzerland, pp. 226–236 (2002)
7. Marti, S., Giuli, T., Lai, K., Baker, M.: Mitigating routing misbehavior in mobile ad hoc networks. In: Proceedings of MOBICOM 2000, Boston, MA, pp. 255–265, August 2000
8. Hubaux, J.-P., Buttyan, L., Capkun, S.: The quest for security in mobile ad hoc networks. In: MobiHoc 2001 Proceedings of the 2nd ACM International Symposium on Mobile Ad hoc Networking and Computing, pp. 146–155 (2001)
9. Konorski, J., Orlikowski, R.: A reputation system for MANETs and WSNs using traffic shedding. In: Proceedings of International Symposium on Applied Sciences in Biomedical and Communication Technologies, Rome, Italy, November 2010
10. Guaya-Delgado, L., Pallarès-Segarra, E., Mezher, A.M., Forné, J.: A novel dynamic reputation-based source routing protocol for mobile ad hoc networks. EURASIP J. Wirel. Commun. Netw. **2019**(1), 1–16 (2019). https://doi.org/10.1186/s13638-019-1375-7
11. Konorski, J., Rydzewski, K.,: A centralized reputation system for MANETs based on observed path erformance. In: 8th IFIP Wireless and Mobile Networking Conference (WMNC), vol. 2015, pp. 56–63, Munich (2015)
12. Ray Liu, K.J., Wang, B.: Repeated Games and Learning for Packet Forwarding, Cognitive Radio Networking and Security: A Game-Theoretic View, pp. 270–296. Cambridge University Press, Cambridge (2010)
13. Ohtsuki, H., Iwasa, Y.: How should we define goodness? - Reputation dynamics in indirect reciprocity. J. Theor. Biol. **231**(1), 107–120 (2004)
14. Karakostas, G., Kharaud, R., Viglas, A.: Dynamics of a localized reputation-based network protocol. In: 2013 International Conference on Parallel and Distributed Computing, Applications and Technologies, 16–18 December 2013
15. Szott, S., Natkaniec, M., Pach, A.R.: Improving QoS and security in wireless ad hoc networks by mitigating the impact of selfish behaviors: a game theoretic approach. Secur. Commun. Netw. **6**(4), 509–522 (2013)

Cost-Effective Controller Placement Problem for Software Defined Multihop Wireless Networks

Afsane Zahmatkesh[✉], Thomas Kunz, and Chung-Horng Lung

Department of Systems and Computer Engineering, Carleton University,
Ottawa, ON, Canada
afsane.zahmatkesh@carleton.ca, {tkunz,chlung}@sce.carleton.ca

Abstract. In an SDN architecture, solving the controller placement problem (CPP) in a multi-controller environment plays an important role on network performance in terms of delay, reliability, control overhead, etc. In this architecture, control overhead, referred to as the network cost in this paper, consists of controller-device communications to discover the network topology, and exchange configurations and set up flow tables as well as inter-controller communications, if needed, to synchronize different network views and achieve the global view of the network. In software defined multihop wireless networking (SDMWN), because of the capacity limitation and the effect of interference on wireless links, and an in-band architecture in some types of networks to exchange both data and control traffic, it is important to solve the CPP while minimizing control overhead to reduce energy consumption, have lower packet losses and improve reliability. In this paper, the objective is to solve the CPP in SDMWN while minimizing the number of required control packets to be exchanged in the control plane. The novelty of our work is that we consider the characteristics of SDMWN and the capacity of wireless links to solve the CPP and select routes among network devices and controllers in the network. Our results demonstrate the impact of different factors such as the number of controllers, the capacity of wireless links and the arrival rate of new flows in devices on control overhead in SDMWN.

Keywords: Multihop wireless networks (MWNs) · Software defined multihop wireless networking (SDMWN) · Controller placement problem (CPP) · Control overhead

1 Introduction

Multihop wireless networks (MWNs) are self-configuring and self-organizing, in which network devices are able to communicate wirelessly with each other using one or more intermediate devices without the help of any infrastructure such as a base station or an access point. In addition to the common challenges of

© ICST Institute for Computer Sciences, Social Informatics and Telecommunications Engineering 2021
Published by Springer Nature Switzerland AG 2021. All Rights Reserved
L. Foschini and M. El Kamili (Eds.): ADHOCNETS 2020, LNICST 345, pp. 130–146, 2021.
https://doi.org/10.1007/978-3-030-67369-7_10

all wireless networks such as unreliable and shared wireless medium, interference, etc., MWNs face additional challenges, including distributed management, device mobility, energy consumption, quality of service. In MWNs, since network management is distributed among network devices, it is challenging to optimize routing decisions and resource consumption globally, and to adjust to dynamic topology changes efficiently [1–3].

Software defined networking (SDN) [4] is a solution proposed to overcome some existing challenges in configuration and management of the traditional networks by decoupling the control plane and the data plane of the network. In SDN, the removed control plane from network devices is logically centralized in a controller that is responsible for managing the entire network. Although the SDN concept was first proposed for wired networks, applying SDN to MWNs can also be beneficial to overcome the MWN-specific challenges mentioned earlier. In the traditionally distributed management of MWNs, network devices are responsible for establishing the connectivity with each other using local, partial views of the network. While in software defined multihop wireless networking (SDMWN), the controller is able to optimize resource allocation globally and adjust to dynamic topology changes faster.

In SDMWN, a distributed control plane is used as an architecture in which the network is divided into different domains and multiple controllers are responsible for managing the domains separately. A distributed control plane is expected to address the challenges of a centralized control plane, i.e., only one controller manages the entire network, in terms of reliability, scalability, energy depletion issues, etc. However, it raises some new challenges including determining the number of controllers, assigning and placing controllers, referred to as the controller placement problem (CPP) [5], and achieving the global view of the network [6]. We describe these existing challenges using a distributed control plane in more detail in Sect. 2. Addressing these challenges, especially in SDMWN with shared and unreliable communications, has a significant impact on network performance metrics such as latency, cost, reliability and control overhead. To the best of our knowledge, in the related work in solving the CPP, all communications use the shortest paths and the authors have not considered the capacity of wireless links and the effect of interference on the capacity of links, which is crucial in SDMWN.

The objective of this paper is to find the placements of a given number of controllers and their assignments to the network devices in SDMWN with an in-band architecture to minimize the number of required control packets to be exchanged in the network. The control packets are exchanged between network devices and their assigned controllers, and among controllers to discover the network states and topology, exchange configurations and update flow rules in SDN forwarding devices. In an in-band architecture, the control and data traffic share the same band or channel. In SDMWN, minimizing the control packets flowing over links improves scalability and reduces energy consumption and packet losses, which also has an impact on the reliability of the control plane. In addition, to solve the problem, we consider the capacity of links and the effect of interference on controller placements, controller assignment and route selection among network devices and controllers as well as route selection among controllers. We formulate the CPP, which is an NP-hard problem [5], as a nonlinear problem. The formulated CPP is a nonlinear problem because we consider the capacity of links and route selection in the control plane. Therefore, we investigate the CPP with a small network to show the impact of the number of controllers, the arrival rate of new traffic flows, and the capacity of links on the control overhead in the network. In this paper, the terms control overhead and the network cost are used interchangeably.

Similar to the gateway selection in mobile ad hoc network [7], i.e., some devices are selected as gateways in the network, the objective of the CPP in SDMWN is to select network devices in the network to host an SDN controller. The main concern in a gateway selection is to exchange data traffic and provide access to the internet with the aim of different metrics such as load-balancing, throughput and quality of service. While in solving the CPP in SDMWN in this paper, the objective is to minimize control traffic exchanged in the network, considering different characteristics of SDMWN.

The organization of this paper is as follows. Section 2 discusses existing challenges in a distributed control plane architecture and presents an overview of the related work in SDMWN. Section 3 introduces an optimization model to minimize the generated control overhead in the network while considering the characteristics of SDMWN and related constraints. Section 4 shows the evaluation of the proposed model and Sect. 5 is the conclusion.

2 Related Work

As mentioned earlier, SDN has the potential to address the MWN-specific challenges in terms of network management, device mobility, energy consumption, quality of service, etc. Several studies have demonstrated that applying SDN to MWNs can be beneficial [1–3,8–10]. In [1], various studies are reviewed that show the benefits of applying SDN to MWNs, in which the control logic of wireless devices is logically centralized in an SDN controller that programs the whole network.

In most studies on SDMWN, a physically centralized controller manages the network to satisfy the requirements of different types of applications such as routing, scheduling, task allocation, load-balancing, congestion control, etc. In the context of SDMWN, the results show that these approaches, compared to the traditional distributed management, can be beneficial in terms of network performance metrics such as packet delivery ratio, delay, etc. [1].

However, in addition to the existing drawbacks of a centralized control plane such as a single point of failure, scaling limitations [11], applying a physically centralized control plane to SDMWN has some disadvantages. In this case, due to the mobility of network devices and scalability issue, direct connections among network devices and a centralized controller are not reasonable or practical for some scenarios, e.g., constrained resources for network devices. Therefore, network devices need to communicate with a controller in a multihop manner using possibly an unreliable and shared wireless medium to update the general view of the network and receive flow rules. Consequently, network devices may face higher latency, especially devices farther away from the controller, which leads to higher flow setup time [12].

In a distributed control plane environment, controllers are able to control devices that are closer geographically which helps to reduce latency and reacts to topology changes faster. Moreover, in case of a controller failure, other controllers can manage the network. However, using a distributed control plane in an SDN architecture raises several new challenges. Among them are how to determine the number of controllers and their locations, and how to assign controllers to network devices. Heller et al. in [5] refer to those challenges in a distributed control plane as the controller placement problem (CPP) that is a NP-hard problem. The main objective of the CPP is to find the number of controllers and their placements and to assign controllers to network devices while considering different metrics and objectives [13]. In addition, it is challenging to integrate different local views and to achieve the global view of the network to provide inter-domain communications among devices. Most studies in SDMWN with a distributed control plane do not provide any details about inter-controller communications using the wireless medium to achieve the global view of the network in SDMWN [14–17].

Addressing the existing challenges in a distributed control plane has an impact on the generated control overhead in the network [18]. In SDN, in addition to the data packets exchanged among network devices, control packets need to be exchanged periodically among a controller and network devices (controller-device) to discover the network topology, exchange configurations and set up flow tables. Moreover, a number of control packets need to be exchanged periodically among controllers (inter-controller) to synchronize and integrate different network views and obtain a global view of the network to provide inter-domain communications. Some SDMWNs, such as WSNs, because of their characteristics, only have a single interface to forward both control and data messages. Therefore, in such networks, the capacity of links is used to exchange both data and control traffic. Moreover, because of the wireless nature of links, interference can influence the available capacity of links [19]. Therefore, it is important to consider the capacity of links as a constraint in solving the CPP in SDMWN to exchange control traffic.

Although various studies have been reported to solve the CPP in wired networks, only a few studies consider the impact of solving the CPP in wireless networks on network performance. This problem is introduced as the wireless CPP in [20], in which communication links among controllers and network devices are wireless. In this case, in addition to the metrics addressed in the wired CPP, the characteristics of unreliable and shared wireless medium should be considered in solving the wireless CPP, which plays a critical role on connectivity among controllers and network devices. Moreover, most studies do not provide any details about inter-controller communications using the wireless mediums to achieve the global view of the network in SDMWN.

The objective of [20] is to minimize the number of controllers and the total delay, and find optimal controller placements and assignments in a wireless network. The authors formulate the problem as a chance-constrained stochastic program (CCSP) with consideration of wireless communications, in which the total delay consists of the network access delay for the devices, transmission delay, propagation delay and the queuing delay at the controller. Results demonstrate that the proposed model is able to reduce the number of selected controllers and delay in the network. Dvir et al. [21] propose a multi-objective optimization problem to solve the wireless CPP, in which inter-controller communications and communications among controllers and access points are wireless. The authors formulate the problem to minimize propagation delay and link failure probability while considering throughput and a new metric called transparency as constraints. Transparency is defined as the latency in the data plane, which is caused by interference added by the proposed control plane. Then, the authors introduce two heuristic algorithms to solve the problem that are able to find the number of controllers to approximately minimize the objective function and satisfy the constraints. Moreover, the results demonstrate that with increasing the number of devices in the network, link failure probability and delay obtained from both algorithms increase.

The objective of [22] is to solve the wireless CPP in a VANET with a two-layer hierarchical control plane while minimizing the number of controllers and delay in the network, which consists of transmission delay, queuing delay, contention delay, processing and propagation delay. Results show that, compared to a random placement, using the proposed approach, the network experiences lower latency. Moreover, the proposed approach improves network performance in terms of delay and packet delivery ratio. Qin et al. [18], propose an optimization model to find controller placements in wireless edge networks while achieving a tradeoff between minimizing delay among devices and their assigned controllers, and minimizing control overhead (Mbps) in the network. Control overhead in [18] consists of communication among devices and their assigned controllers to set up flow rules, and inter-domain communication to discover the network topology along the shortest paths. To solve for large-scale networks, the authors propose a randomized greedy algorithm to find controller placements. Results show that the proposed algorithm is able to find near-optimal solutions and improve the network performance in terms of minimizing delay and control overhead. However, in [18], the authors do not consider the controller-device communication control overhead to discover the network topology and the characteristics of wireless medium to solve the problem.

The objective of most studies in solving the CPP in both wired and wireless networks is to minimize propagation delay among controllers and devices that is proportional to the distance among them [13]. Minimizing the distance among controllers and devices as well as among controllers has a direct effect on the reliability of the control plane, especially in wireless networks with shared and unreliable communications.

To the best of our knowledge, in the related work of solving the CPP in wireless networks, to minimize propagation delay, the capacity of wireless links and the impact of interference on the capacity of links are not considered when determining the number of controllers and controller placements. Moreover, in the related work, the authors assume that all communications use the shortest paths and they do not consider the capacity of links and the impact of limiting the capacity of links to exchange the control overhead on solving the CPP. Consequently, route selection to provide controller-device and inter-controller communications based on the capacity of links is still an open research area in solving the CPP. Therefore, in this paper, our objective is to solve the CPP to minimize the cost of the network while considering the characteristics of SDMWN and the capacity of wireless links.

3   System Model

We model an SDMWN as a directed graph $G = (V, E)$, where V represents the set of wireless network devices and E is the set of links between each pair of devices such that link (u, v) and link (v, u) are the members of E if and only if device u is within the transmission range of device v (R_T). In this paper, we use the protocol model formulated in [19] to find a set of links in the interference range of link (u, v).

Since in MWNs network devices are responsible for organizing the network, we consider all wireless network devices as SDN forwarding devices, communicating in a multihop manner, controlled by an SDN controller. Moreover, we assume that all network devices are stationary and candidate locations to place a controller. In addition, we have an in-band architecture, i.e., network devices use a single interface to forward data traffic and exchange control traffic with a controller placed on a device and control traffic among controllers.

3.1   Model Outputs

The notations used in the proposed model are listed in Table 1. The outputs of the proposed model are listed as follows while considering the capacity of links as a constraint to place controllers in the network and assign them to network devices.

- Optimal placements of N controllers in an SDMWN
- Controller assignments to network devices
- Route selections among controllers and network devices as well as among controllers
- Optimal cost of placing N controllers in the network

3.2   Objective Function

We formulate the problem as a nonlinear programming (NLP) problem and (1) shows the objective function that aims to minimize the total cost of the network.

$$Min(Cost_{TD} + \sum_{k=1}^{|V|} \sum_{i=1,i\neq k}^{|V|} (R_{Flow\_Rq}\ x_{k,i}[\sum_{\forall(u,v)\in E} f_{u,v}^{k,i}$$

$$+ \sum_{\forall(u,v)\in E} f_{u,v}^{i,k}])) \tag{1}$$

subject to: (3), (4), (5), (6), (7), (9)

Table 1. Notations used in this paper

Notation	Definition
y_k	Output (binary decision variable): The value equals one if and only if there is a controller placed on device k
$x_{k,i}$	Output (binary decision variable): The value equals one if and only if device i is assigned to a controller placed on device k
$f_{u,v}^{a,b}$	Output (binary decision variable): The value equals one if and only if link (u,v) is used to provide communication between device a and device b
$Cost_{TD}$	The total cost of topology discovery (*control packets/second*) running by all controllers on their own assigned network devices and among all controllers in the network calculated using (2)
R_{TD}	The rate of running topology discovery by each controller (*1/second*)
R_{Flow_Rq}	The arrival rate of new flows in each device that triggers a flow request message toward the assigned controller (*1/second*)
N	A given number of controllers
$neighbor[i]$	A set of neighbors of network device i in the network
$neighbor_{i,j}$	The jth neighbor of network device i
$C_{u,v}$	The capacity of link (u,v) to exchange control Packets (*control packets/second*)
$C'_{u,v}$	The required bandwidth of link (u,v) to exchange control Packets (*control packets/second*)
$L_{u,v}^{Int}$	A set of links in the interference range of link (u,v)

The first part of (1) ($Cost_{TD}$) is the total cost of topology discovery in the network calculated using (2). The second part of (1) calculates the cost of controller-device communications using the best routes among controllers and their assigned network devices to exchange configurations and set up flow rules (*control packets/second*). In the case here, we will count control packet transmissions over each hop along their routes.

a) Cost of Topology Discovery: We assume that each device communicates only with its own assigned controller and each controller discovers a partial view of the network including its own assigned devices. Therefore, controllers communicate together to obtain the global view of the network.

$$
\begin{aligned}
Cost_{TD} = R_{TD}(\sum_{k=1}^{|V|} \sum_{i=1,i\neq k}^{|V|} [\sum_{\forall(u,v)\in E} f_{u,v}^{k,i} + (\sum_{m=1}^{|V|} \sum_{j=1,j\neq k,m}^{|neighbor[i]|} \\
\sum_{\forall(u,v)\in E} f_{u,v}^{neighbor_{i,j},m} \ x_{m,neighbor_{i,j}} \ )] \ x_{k,i}) \\
+ R_{TD} [\sum_{k=1}^{|V|} \sum_{p=1,p\neq k}^{|V|} (y_k \ y_p \sum_{\forall(u,v)\in E} f_{u,v}^{k,p})]
\end{aligned}
\tag{2}
$$

The first and the second lines of $Cost_{TD}$ shown in (2) calculate the total number of control packets exchanged among controllers and devices per second to discover the network topology. The third line of (2) calculates the number of control packets exchanged among controllers per second to obtain the global view of the network.

To discover the network topology, each controller constructs and sends probes periodically to its own assigned devices. We calculate the total number of control packets generated by the controllers per second to their own assigned devices and count the number of hops ($\sum_{\forall(u,v)\in E} f_{u,v}^{k,i}$) in the best route while satisfying the constraints in 3.3.

When the assigned devices receive the probes from their controllers, they flood the probes. This cost is inevitable for any controller placement, resulting in a packet being transmitted over a wireless link to discover that link. Therefore, we do not need to model this cost explicitly in solving the CPP. After flooding the probes, their neighbors send the received probes to their own assigned controllers (the second line of (2)). Using these packets, each controller is able to find the links among its own devices and to devices outside of its partial view.

In addition, controllers need to communicate together in an interval of time to achieve the global view of the network while considering the number of hops between each pair of controllers ($\sum_{\forall(u,v)\in E} f_{u,v}^{k,p}$)). With controllers managing only relatively small parts of the network, we assume that the information to be exchanged fits into a single control packet. We consider the same interval of time for both running topology discovery by each controller and inter-controller communications.

b) Cost of Exchanging Configurations and Setting Up Flow Tables: The second part of (1) calculates the total number of control packets exchanged among controllers and their own assigned network devices to exchange configurations and set up flow tables, counting the number of hops in both directions among controllers and devices, and the arrival rate of flow requests in the controllers.

3.3 Constraints

The objective function presented in (1) is subject to the following constraints. The constraint defined in (3) avoids assigning a device to a controller that is not placed in the network.

$$x_{k,i} \leq y_k, \ \forall i, k \in V \tag{3}$$

The constraint defined in (4) ensures that each device is assigned to exactly one controller.

$$\sum_{k=1}^{|V|} x_{k,i} = 1, \ \forall i \in V \tag{4}$$

Equation (5) ensures that there is a given number of controllers in the network.

$$\sum_{k=1}^{|V|} y_k = N \tag{5}$$

Equation (6) defines the control flow conservation constraint, in which the constraint ensures that the total control flow entering each device in the network equals to the total control flow leaving the device except for the source and destination of a flow.

$$\sum_{(u,v)\in E} f_{(u,v)}^{a,b} - \sum_{(v,w)\in E} f_{(v,w)}^{a,b} = \begin{cases} 1, & \text{if } v = b \\ \text{-}1, & \text{if } v = a \\ 0, & \text{otherwise} \end{cases}, \ \forall a, b \in V \tag{6}$$

In this model, we assume that, only a fraction of the link capacity is assigned to exchange control packets. The constraint defined in (7) ensures that each link can handle the total number of control packets flowing over the link per second. In this model, the total number of control packets flowing over link (u, v) in the network consists of the total number of control packets exchanged per second to discover the network topology, and exchange configurations and set up flow tables $(C'_{u,v})$ as well as the total number of control packets flowing over links in the interference range of link (u, v) per second $(C'_{u',v'})$.

$$C'_{u,v} + \sum_{\forall(u',v')\in L_{u,v}^{Int}} C'_{u',v'} \leq C_{(u,v)}, \ \forall(u,v) \in E \tag{7}$$

Equation (8) calculates the total number of control packets flowing over a link per second to discover the network topology (the first, the second and the third lines) and to provide controller-device communications to exchange configurations and set up flow tables (the fourth line).

$$C'_{u,v} = R_{TD}[\sum_{k=1}^{|V|} \sum_{i=1,i\neq k}^{|V|} (f_{u,v}^{k,i}$$

$$+ \sum_{m=1}^{|V|} \sum_{j=1,j\neq k}^{|neighbor[i]|} f_{u,v}^{neighbor_{i,j},m} x_{m,neighbor_{i,j}}) x_{k,i}]$$

$$+ R_{TD}[\sum_{k=1}^{|V|} \sum_{p=1,p\neq k}^{|V|} (y_k \, y_p \, f_{u,v}^{k,p})]+ \qquad (8)$$

$$\sum_{k=1}^{|V|} \sum_{i=1,i\neq k}^{|V|} (R_{Flow\_Rq} \, x_{k,i} \, [f_{u,v}^{k,i} + f_{u,v}^{i,k}]),$$

$$\forall (u,v) \in E$$

Integrality constraints are presented in (9).

$$x_{k,i}, y_k, f_{u,v}^{k,i} \in \{0,1\}, \ \forall i, k \in V, \ \forall (u,v) \in E \qquad (9)$$

4   Model Results and Analysis

We use AMPL (a mathematical programming language) [23] to implement our proposed optimization model running on an Intel Core i7 CPU (3.20 GHz) and 16.0 GB RAM. Moreover, we use the Baron solver 19.7.13 [24] which aims to find the optimal solutions globally for nonlinear optimization problems. We use NEOS server [25–27] to run the proposed model in AMPL running on an Intel Xeon E5- 2698 @ 2.3 GHz, 192 GB RAM and 300G SAS drives setup in RAID5.

Because of the high computational complexity of the proposed model, we consider a small network with 6 wireless network devices as shown in Fig. 1 to illustrate the performance of the proposed optimization model. The links in the interference range of each link in the topology shown in Fig. 1 are not displayed due to the space limit. Here is only an example of the links in the interference range of link $(1,2)$: $L_{1,2}^{Int} = \{(1,3), (2,4), (3,4), (4,2), (4,5), (5,3), (6,4), (2,1), (3,1),$ $(3,5), (4,3), (4,6), (5,4)\}$. Our objective is to place N controllers in this network while minimizing the cost of the control plane defined in (1) and satisfying the defined constraints in 3.3. In this evaluation, we assume that each device receives a new flow every 2 s ($R_{Flow\_Rq} = 0.5$ (*1/second*)) and each controller runs topology discovery every 5 s ($R_{TD} = 0.2$ (*1/second*)) which is adopted from OpenDaylight [28], the most popular open source SDN Controller.

4.1   The Impact of the Number of Controllers on the Cost of the Network

To find the optimal cost of the network when placing different number of controllers, we run our proposed optimization model for different values of N from

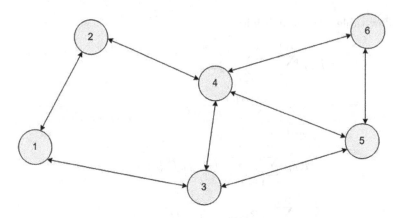

Fig. 1. An SDMWN with 6 wireless network devices

1 (placing a controller in one of the devices) to 6 (placing a controller on each device). As we mentioned earlier, the total cost of the network consists of the total cost of topology discovery and the total cost of controller-device communications to exchange configurations and set up flow tables in devices. Figure 2 demonstrates the optimal total cost of the network when placing different number of controllers in the network. As shown in this figure, when we solve the optimization problem to place three controllers in the network $(N = 3)$, the minimum cost of the network is achieved. In this case, the optimal controller placements are devices 3, 4 and 5. Moreover, as demonstrated in Fig. 2, when we solve the problem to place one or six controllers, the network experiences the highest cost of the control plane defined in (1). Therefore, finding the right number of controllers in a network, depending on the network topology, has a direct effect on the cost of the network.

Figure 3 shows the total cost of topology discovery, which consists of the total cost of controller-device communications to discover the network state and topology, and the total cost of inter-controller communications to integrate views from each domain and obtain the global view of the network. As demonstrated in this figure, as the number of controllers increases in the network, the cost of controller-device communications decreases, while the network faces higher cost of inter-controller communications to integrate different network views. Although placing three controllers in the network results in the minimum total cost of the network as shown in Fig. 2, the optimal cost of topology discovery is obtained when we place two controllers in the network as demonstrated in Fig. 3. Therefore, a solution with the optimal cost of topology discovery does not necessarily result in the overall optimal cost of the network.

Depending on the network topology, placing different numbers of controllers may result in the same network cost. For example, in the topology as shown in Fig. 4a, in case of placing 2 or 3 controllers in the network $(N = 2$ or $N = 3)$, the total network cost is 2.8 (*control packets/second*). Moreover, depending on

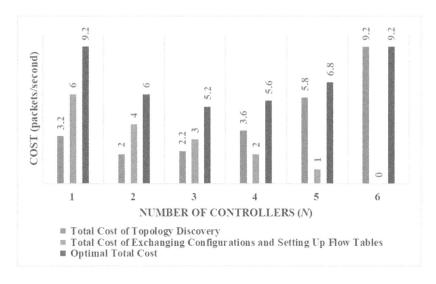

Fig. 2. The total cost of the network (*control packets/second*)

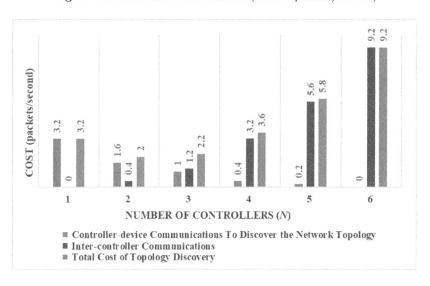

Fig. 3. The cost of topology discovery in the network (*control packets/second*)

the topology, it is possible to have more than one placement to be selected as the optimal placement. For example, in the topology as shown in Fig. 4b, when $N = 1$, both device 3 and device 4 can be selected as the optimal placement by the solver.

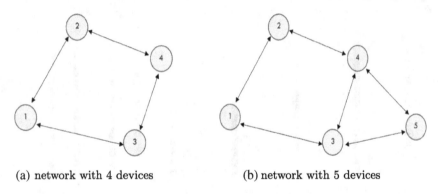

(a) network with 4 devices   (b) network with 5 devices

Fig. 4. Impact of number of controllers and controller placements on the network cost

4.2   The Impact of R_{Flow_Rq} On the Network Cost

Figure 5 demonstrates that if we increase the arrival rate of new flows in each device (R_{Flow_Rq}) in the defined scenario, since the number of control packets exchanged per second to set up new flow rules increases, the optimal solution to minimize the total cost of network is to place one controller on each device ($N = 6$). Therefore, in case of increasing the value of R_{Flow_Rq}, placing more controllers in the network decreases the cost of communications among devices and controllers and the total cost of the network.

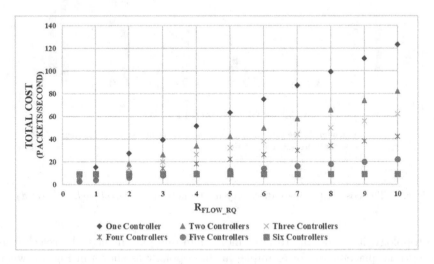

Fig. 5. The impact of increasing the value of R_{Flow_Rq} on the cost of the network

4.3   The Impact of Link Capacity on the Number of Controllers

To show the impact of the capacity of links assigned to exchange control packets on the number of controllers in the network while considering different values of arrival rate of flow requests, first, we limit the assigned capacity of all links to 6 (*control packets/second*). In this case, the solver is not able to solve the problem for $N = 1, 5$ and 6 while satisfying the capacity constraint defined in (7). In this scenario, depending on the network requirements, only two (total cost $= 6$ (*control packets/second*)), three (total cost $= 5.2$ (*control packets/second*)) or four controllers (total cost $= 5.6$ (*control packets/second*)) can be placed on the network while satisfying the capacity constraint.

On the other hand, as shown in Fig. 5, if we assume that $R_{Flow\_Rq} = 4$ (*1/second*), with an increase of the number of controllers in the network, the total cost of the network decreases such that placing six controllers has the minimum cost (10 (*control packets/second*)). In this case, e.g., if we limit the assigned capacity of all links to 10 (*control packets/second*) to exchange control packets, the solver is not able to solve the problem for $N < 6$ while satisfying the capacity constraint defined in (7). In other words, the problem can be solved only for placing six controllers in the network to satisfy the capacity constraint. Therefore, depending on the capacity of links and the value of R_{Flow_Rq}, the number of possible controllers to be placed in the network varies. In addition, in our proposed model, communications among controllers and devices as well as among controllers may not use the shortest paths to ensure the capacity limit of links. Therefore, a solution that would enforce or only consider communication along the shortest path would either violate the capacity constraint or not be a feasible solution.

Finally, results show that when $N = 1$, placing a controller in one of the possible controller placements in the topology shown in Fig. 1 instead of solving the optimization problem does not minimize the cost of the network. We compare the optimal cost of the network when placing one controller in the topology shown in Fig. 1 with the average cost of placing a controller in one of the six possible controller placements each time in the network. Each device k in Fig. 1 can be a candidate to be placed a controller ($y_k = 1$). The optimal cost of placing one controller in the network is 9.2 (*control packets/second*), while the average cost of placing a controller in one of the possible placements is 12.6 (*control packets/second*). The results demonstrate that the proposed model indeed finds a placement that minimizes the cost of the network while considering different factors including the capacity of links to solve the problem.

4.4   The Impact of Increasing the Number of Devices on the Execution Time of the Optimization Problem

The results demonstrate that when we increase the number of devices in the network, it takes a long time to solve the proposed optimization problem and find the minimum number of controllers that aims to minimize the network cost. For example, it takes 0.497515 (*seconds*) to solve the problem in a network with

3 devices, while the solver needs 153.67783 (*minutes*) to solve the problem in a network with 6 devices. Further, as shown in Sect. 4.1, the total cost for different solutions may be close and there may be more than one optimal solution for a specific network topology and a given set of constraint. Therefore, investigating the heuristic algorithms to the proposed optimization model helps to find the near-optimal solutions in large-scale networks.

5   Conclusion and Future Research

In this paper, we proposed an optimization model to find the placement of N controllers in SDMWN and their assignment to network devices while minimizing the total control packets required to be exchanged in the network to discover the network state and topology, and to exchange configurations and set up flow tables in network devices. To solve the CPP in SDMWN, we considered the capacity limits of wireless links and the impact of interference on the capacity of links to select routes among devices and controllers as well as among controllers. The results obtained from the optimization model demonstrate the impact of different factors such as the number of controllers, the capacity of wireless links and the arrival rate of new flows in devices on the generated control overhead in the network. Moreover, our proposed optimization problem is able to minimize the control overhead compared to a random placement.

In this paper, due to the high computational complexity of the optimization model, only a small network was demonstrated for evaluation. Investigating heuristic algorithms to find a near-optimal solution in a large-scale SDMWN in a reasonable time is being conducted. In addition, adjusting the number of controllers and controller placements based on topology changes to minimize the number of required control packets exchanged in the network per second should be addressed in the future.

References

1. Zahmatkesh, A., Kunz, T.: Software defined multihop wireless networks: promises and challenges. J. Commun. Netw. **19**(6), 546–554 (2017)
2. Chahal, M., Harit, S., Mishra, K.K., Sangaiah, A.K., Zheng, Z.: A survey on software-defined networking in vehicular ad hoc networks: challenges, applications and use cases. Sustain. Cities Soc. **35**, 830–840 (2017)
3. Kobo, H.I., Abu-Mahfouz, A.M., Hancke, G.P.: A survey on software-defined wireless sensor networks: challenges and design requirements. IEEE Access **5**, 1872–1899 (2017)
4. Kreutz, D., Ramos, F.M.V., Veríssimo, P.E., Rothenberg, C.E., Azodolmolky, S., Uhlig, S.: Software-defined networking: a comprehensive survey. Proc. IEEE **103**(1), 14–76 (2015)
5. Heller, B., Sherwood, R., McKeown, N.: The controller placement problem. In: Proceedings of the First Workshop on Hot Topics in Software Defined Networks, pp. 7–12 (2012). https://doi.org/10.1145/2342441.2342444

6. Zhang, Y., Cui, L., Wang, W., Zhang, Y.: A survey on software defined networking with multiple controllers. J. Netw. Comput. Appl. **103**, 101–118 (2018)
7. Mahiddin, N.A., Sarkar, N.I., Cusack, B.: An Internet access solution: MANET routing and a gateway selection approach for disaster scenarios. Rev. Socionetw. Strat. **11**, 47–64 (2017). https://doi.org/10.1007/s12626-017-0004-3
8. Haque, I.T., Abu-Ghazaleh, N.: Wireless software defined networking: a survey and taxonomy. IEEE Commun. Surv. Tutorials **18**, 2713–2737 (2016)
9. Rademacher, M., Jonas, K., Siebertz, F., Rzyska, A., Schlebusch, M., Kessel, M.: Software-defined wireless mesh networking: current status and challenges. Comput. J. **60**, 1520–1535 (2017)
10. Jaballah, W. B., Conti, M., Lal, C.: A survey on software-defined VANETs: benefits, challenges, and future directions. CoRR, vol. abs/1904.04577 (2019)
11. Oktian, Y.E., Lee, S., Lee, H., Lam, J.: Distributed SDN controller system: a survey on design choice. Comput. Netw. **121**, 100–111 (2017)
12. Ur Rahman, S., Kim, G., Cho, Y., Khan, A.: Deployment of an SDN-based UAV network: controller placement and tradeoff between control overhead and delay. In: International Conference on Information and Communication Technology Convergence, pp. 1290–1292 (2017). https://doi.org/10.1109/ICTC.2017.8190924
13. Das, T., Sridharan, V., Gurusamy, M.: A survey on controller placement in SDN. IEEE Commun. Surv. Tutor. **22**(1), 472–503 (2020)
14. Alioua, A., Senouci, S.-M., Moussaoui, S.: dSDiVN: a distributed software-defined networking architecture for infrastructure-less vehicular networks. In: International Conference on Innovations for Community Services (2017). https://doi.org/10.1007/978-3-319-60447-3_5
15. Mora, S., Vera, J.: RDSNET: a proposal for control architecture for software defined MANETs. Int. J. Eng. Technol. **10**(3), 816–827 (2018)
16. Kazmi, A., Khan, M. A., Akram, M. U.: DeVANET: decentralized software-defined VANET architecture. In: IEEE International Conference on Cloud Engineering Workshop, pp. 42–47 (2016). https://doi.org/10.1109/IC2EW.2016.12
17. Elzain, H., Yang, W.: Decentralizing software-defined wireless mesh networking (D-SDWMN) control plane. In: Proceedings of the World Congress on Engineering (2018)
18. Qin, Q., Poularakis, K., Iosifidis, G., Kompella, S., Tassiulas, L.: SDN controller placement with delay-overhead balancing in wireless edge networks. IEEE Trans. Netw. Serv. Manage. **15**(4), 1446–1459 (2018)
19. Gupta, P., Kumar, P.R.: The capacity of wireless networks. IEEE Trans. Inf. Theor. **46**, 388–404 (2000)
20. Abdel-Rahman, M.J., et al.: On stochastic controller placement in software-defined wireless networks. In: IEEE Wireless Communications and Networking Conference, WCNC, pp. 1–6 (2017). https://doi.org/10.1109/WCNC.2017.7925942
21. Dvir, A., Haddad, Y., Zilberman, A.: The controller placement problem for wireless SDN. Wirel. Netw. **25**, 4963–4978 (2019)
22. Liyanage, K.S., Ma, M., Joo Chong, P.H.: Controller placement optimization in hierarchical distributed software defined vehicular networks. Comput. Netw. **135**, 226–239 (2018)
23. Fourer, R., Gay, D.M., Kernighan, B.W.: AMPL: A Modeling Language for Mathematical Programming, 2nd edn. Duxbury Press, Scituate (2002)
24. BARON Solver, Version 19.7.13. https://minlp.com/baron-downloads. Accessed Sep 2019

25. Gropp, W., More, J. J.: Optimization environments and the NEOS server. In: Buhman, M.D., Iserles, A. (eds.)Approximation Theory and Optimization, pp. 167–182. Cambridge University Press (1997)
26. Dolan, E. D.: The NEOS server 4.0 administrative guide. Technical Memorandum ANL/MCS-TM-250, Mathematics and Computer Science Division, Argonne National Laboratory (2001)
27. The neos server for baron/ampl. https://neos-server.org/neos/solvers/go: BARON/AMPL.html. . Accessed Sep 2020
28. OpenDaylight (ODL). https://www.opendaylight.org

Efficient Backbone Routing in Hierarchical MANETs

Thomas Kunz$^{(\boxtimes)}$ (ID)

Systems and Computer Engineering, Carleton University, Ottawa, Canada
tkunz@sce.carleton.ca

Abstract. Hierarchical network architectures are widely deployed to reduce routing overheads and increase scalability. In our work, we are interested in large-scale Mobile Ad-Hoc Networks (MANETs) which are formed by interconnecting smaller clusters through a backbone. To support end-to-end routing in such networks, we employ a hierarchical approach as follows. The clusters are MANETs, running OLSR locally. Each cluster has a gateway, and the gateways are interconnected through a backbone. In this paper, we study four different solutions to provide end-to-end connectivity through the backbone: flooding all data packets through the backbone, modifying an ad-hoc routing protocol such as OLSR and AODV, or using a P2P overlay for routing purposes. Running extensive simulations in OMNeT++, our results highlight the strengths and weaknesses of each approach. Flooding, albeit a very simple approach, appears to be quite competitive with more complex routing solutions, with good performance and low overheads.

Keywords: MANETs · P2P overlays · Hierarchical routing

1 Introduction

Mobile Ad hoc Networks (MANETs) are finding applications in a range of areas, including emergency response networks, intelligent transportation systems, outdoor enterprises, small businesses etc. [10,22,23]. One important characteristic is that they are self-organizing and self-configuring wireless multi-hop networks which do not rely on any existing infrastructure to exist; as nodes are by themselves, servers and clients [4,14]. Each node must act as a router to forward traffic unrelated to its own use.

The number of users in MANET applications may vary from just a handful to hundreds of thousands of people and more [2]. As MANETs and mobile devices become increasingly popular and the ensuing networks grow larger, more research effort focuses on devising protocols for route establishment and maintenance in these networks. In a flat network of several interconnected mobile devices, and spanning a large geographical area, for instance, the network will typically incur increasing overheads for route maintenance and establishment

© ICST Institute for Computer Sciences, Social Informatics and Telecommunications Engineering 2021
Published by Springer Nature Switzerland AG 2021. All Rights Reserved
L. Foschini and M. El Kamili (Eds.): ADHOCNETS 2020, LNICST 345, pp. 147–163, 2021.
https://doi.org/10.1007/978-3-030-67369-7_11

and other network functions. This scalability limitation is true for almost any MANET routing protocol proposed for flat networks. Many routing protocols for ad-hoc networks are either proactive (table-driven) or reactive (on-demand) [18,27]. Proactive routing protocols like OLSR or DSDV originate from the traditional distance vector and link state protocols. They continuously maintain routes to all destinations in a network, whereas reactive (on-demand) protocols like AODV or DSR will only seek out routes to a destination when necessary. Both routing protocol approaches scale poorly [18,27]. This is true because of the inherent characteristics of these protocols [26]: on the one hand, the on-demand routing protocols are limited by their route discovery techniques because of the extensive use of flooding. Hop-by-hop flooding usually has a huge negative impact on network performance and often leads to large delays in route discovery [3,22]. On the other hand, proactive routing protocols have these routes readily available, but it comes at a cost of constant route discovery throughout the lifetime of the network. It is evident therefore that both protocols have scalability issues, which get even worse in the case that nodes are mobile and links become generally unpredictable [3,22].

A hierarchical routing architecture, when carefully planned, shows its advantage of simplifying routing tables considerably and lowering the amount of routing information exchanged [8,23], thus increasing search efficiency and increasing scalability. This is best exemplified by the global Internet, which employs a hierarchical architecture and routing structure. The Internet is divided into routing domains. A routing domain typically contains a collection of co-located networks connected by routers (who are nodes) and linked in a common routing domain called the backbone [23].

In this paper, hierarchical routing is adopted to tackle the problem of incurring increasing overheads for route maintenance and establishment and other network functions in large MANETs. The following concerns are also taken into consideration in designing appropriate routing solutions:

- Nodes do not necessarily belong to a single network throughout their lifetime. As nodes are mobile, they may change their cluster membership, clusters may merge or split. So, a more general hierarchical routing architecture that supports various mobility scenarios is desirous. This rules out the hierarchical solutions proposed for the Internet, where nodes belong to IP subnets, and routing information is aggregated to handle routes to specific subnets only.
- In order for hosts within a cluster to route packets destined for hosts in external clusters or domains, there is the need for a protocol or scheme which will be the standard for such applications. OLSR supports a HNA message scheme which is primarily for external access, standardized in RFC 3626 [12]. This scheme is relevant for the designs we explore, as we will use OLSR as intra-domain routing protocol within each cluster.

A simple scheme to provide routing in such a hierarchical network would be for gateways nodes to simply flood all data packets destined for nodes outside a cluster through the backbone. Once a gateway receives a packet, it consults its routing table to determine whether the destination node is in its cluster.

If this is the case, it forwards the packet to the destination, based on the intra-cluster routing protocol (OLSR in our work). While such a scheme is easy to implement and can handle various mobile scenarios, it can easily overburden the backbone, so more efficient routing schemes would be beneficial. We present three additional possible solutions, and compare them using extensive simulations in OMNeT++ [31].

A hierarchical MANET architecture finds application in, for example, a military environment. In such a scenario, there exist platoons which move in groups and each platoon typically consists of soldiers and, probably, a dedicated vehicle (armoured tank/truck). These platoons are MANETs which are then considered as clusters in our study. In such a setting, the number of or size of a cluster is typically not known a-priori, but cluster membership is defined a-priori by the application. Each platoon has a dedicated gateway (this can be the armored vehicle), and, through the gateways, the various platoons are interconnected in a backbone network. The gateways are more powerful devices equipped with capabilities which will enable them effectively support communication between members of their local cluster and the different clusters.

The remainder of this paper is organized as follows. The next section reviews related work. Section 3 introduces our 4 routing solutions. Section 4 discusses the comparative quantitative simulation results we obtained when implementing our schemes in OMNeT++, focusing on the protocol performance when nodes jump from cluster to cluster. Finally, the last section summarizes our work and suggests avenues for future research.

2 Related Work

As discussed earlier, treating the whole MANET as a single, flat routing domain runs into scalability issues, see also [8, 23]. An alternative to flat MANETs is clustering or hierarchical routing. The motivation for exploring hierarchical routing is that it increases scalability, routing efficiency and potentially reduces routing table entries considerably. Typically, rather than assuming that node movement is independent, hierarchical ad-hoc routing protocols group nodes into clusters of nodes that follow the same movement pattern. These protocols are based on the idea that members of a group tend to move together and therefore a node will most likely remain within the same cluster. This allows a node to move freely within its cluster and only inform other cluster members, abstracting node movement within a cluster. Members of other clusters only need to know how to communicate with one of its members. These groups may have some sort of cluster leader, popularly known as gateways or cluster heads. Depending on the algorithm and the clustering technique, there might be gateways providing connectivity with other clusters, and cluster heads who coordinate routing within their clusters and with other clusters. Alternatively a single node acts as both cluster head and gateway, providing connectivity with other clusters through a core/backbone network. Clusters can then be organized into a hierarchy.

In [9,16] the authors present a review of current hierarchical routing protocols and clustering approaches. The authors first introduce fundamental concepts about clustering. Then they classify the proposed clustering schemes into six categories based on their main objectives, which are load balancing clustering, Dominating-Set-based (DS-based) clustering, low maintenance clustering, mobility-aware clustering, combined metrics-based clustering, and energy efficient clustering. They also grouped the clustering cost terms into five categories: the required explicit control message exchange, the ripple effect of re-clustering, the stationary assumption, constant computation round, and communication complexity.

One of the earliest clustering protocols is LCA [7], developed for packet radio networks. The LCA protocol organizes the nodes into clusters according to the proximity of the nodes. Each cluster has a cluster head and all nodes in a cluster are in the direct transmission range of the cluster head. The choice of the cluster head is based on node identifiers, where the node with the largest identifier in a given area becomes the cluster header. The gateways in the overlapping region between clusters are used to connect clusters. LCA specifies that there should only be one designated gateway to interconnect clusters at a given time. A pair of nodes within transmission range of each other can also be used to connect clusters if there are no nodes in the overlap region.

In GPSR [11], packets are routed alternately between the cluster leaders and the gateways. The authors define several extensions that can be added to CGSR, such as priority token scheduling and gateway code programming, to control access to the channel. In addition, they define a LCC (Least Cluster Change) algorithm, designed to reduce the number of changes in the cluster leader, since such changes can generate significant overhead.

The works of [6,15] take a different approach to clustering and present two clustering algorithms. The first of these is DCA, intended for "quasi-static" networks in which nodes are slow moving, if moving at all. The other algorithm is called DMAC, designed for higher mobility. Both algorithms assign different weights to nodes with the assumption that each node is aware of its respective weight. The weights are in turn used to determine the cluster leaders. In the DMAC protocol, if two cluster leaders come into contact, the one with the smaller weight must revoke its leader status.

Another approach is that taken by the CEDAR algorithm [28], which builds a set of nodes (i.e., a core) to perform route computation instead of creating a cluster topology. Using the local state information, a minimum dominating set of the network is approximated to form the core. CEDAR establishes QoS routes that satisfy bandwidth requirements using the directionality of the core path. Link state and bandwidth availability is exchanged to maintain important information for computing QoS routes.

Kleinrock was an early pioneer of hierarchical routing schemes for static networks. In [19], Kleinrock and Kamoun investigated a hierarchical routing scheme with the goal of reducing routing table size. The authors of [25] also adopt a similar approach. The authors determined that the length of the routing table is a strict function of the clustering structure. Clustering generally has the unwanted side-effect of an increase in path length, and so the goal was to find an optimal clustering scheme that optimizes path length. It was determined that the number of entries in a node's forwarding table is minimized when the number of *level-i* clusters in each level $-(i + 1)$ cluster is e, and the number of levels in the clustering hierarchy equals $\ln N$. In this case, the forwarding table contains $e \ln N$ entries.

The Landmark Routing technique [30] is a distinct approach to building a hierarchy as it is based on landmarks, as opposed to transmission ranges. A landmark is a router whose location is known by its neighboring routers up to some radius. All routers within that radius know how to reach the landmark. A hierarchy of such landmarks is built by increasing the radius of some of the routers. Nodes have hierarchical addresses based on the landmarks with which they are associated. A source node routes to a destination by sending the packet to the lowest level landmark with which both nodes are associated. As the packet approaches the destination, the granularity of routing knowledge about that destination improves, and so the packet can be accurately routed to the destination.

Advantages of hierarchical routing, alongside scalability, include the ability to reduce routing table sizes, to shield nodes within a cluster from mobility in other clusters and to use different routing protocols, with possibly different update frequencies, in different clusters. Disadvantages include the difficulty in maintaining the structure of clusters in the face of high mobility (which has a particularly adverse effect if cluster heads change groups), the possible bottleneck presented by gateway nodes (these nodes also suffer greater resource usage) and the use of suboptimal paths. Examples of hierarchical routing protocols can be found in [16].

In our research, scalability is a strong requirement and so, we try to limit routing knowledge and avoid flooding in the backbone. Thus, we apply a hierarchical approach. In the context we are working with, we do not use any special algorithm for cluster formation and maintenance. Rather we assume that clusters are externally given, as is the case when they flow from the application/use of the MANET. For example, we may have different platoons of soldiers (in a military context) or different first responder crews joining in as a group etc. We are focusing in the basic choices of routing through the backbone in this work. The following section outlines 4 quite distinct approaches to routing in the backbone that we are evaluating.

3   Backbone Routing Approaches

Our core network architecture assumes that the MANET is organized into a two-tiered hierarchy. Ordinary nodes are equipped with a single wireless interface and grouped into clusters, given by the nature of the application (or some other means). Each cluster has one (or potentially multiple) gateway nodes that are equipped with two wireless interfaces: one to communicate with other nodes in the same cluster, a second one (with potentially different characteristics such as transmission range or bandwidth) for communication with other gateways. The gateways collectively form the MANET backbone. Nodes in one cluster should be enabled to communicate with nodes in the same cluster, but also with nodes in other clusters.

Routing within a single cluster is done using OLSR, as this allows us to easily explore different alternatives for the backbone interconnecting multiple clusters: each cluster gateway advertises reachability to nodes outside a gateway through OLSR's HNA message by advertising a default route. Regular nodes in the cluster therefore have host-specific routes to all other nodes in the same cluster, and a default route to the gateway for any other destination. This information gets updated locally as nodes join and leave a cluster. It also gets updated periodically to reflect changes in the network topology within a cluster, as nodes are free to move. Due to OLSR's pro-active nature, gateways know which nodes are within their cluster simply by observing their local routing table. To enable routing through the backbone (to enable inter-cluster communication), we designed and implemented a number of different approaches. This section briefly discusses these approaches and provides some quantitative comparison, the next section presents some quantitative results obtained via simulation in OMNeT++.

The 4 solutions differ in the routing approach taken by the gateway nodes to deliver packets to destination nodes in remote clusters. In the discussion below, we will use the term ingress gateway to denote a gateway that receives a packet from a local node in its cluster, destined to a node in a different cluster. Similarly, the egress gateway is the gateway managing the cluster to which the destination node belongs. A key question and differentiating factor for all routing approaches is how much routing information is distributed in the network, and how much effort is required to maintain this information in the presence of node mobility and clusters merging and splitting.

The simplest approach is to broadcast data packets trough the backbone and a simple implementation of that idea would be to flood the data packets through the backbone (i.e., each gateway, when receiving a data packet it has not seen before, rebroadcasts it). No backbone routing protocol is required in this case, and gateways only require knowledge about which nodes are in its local cluster. Once the ingress gateway receives a data packet that is not destined for a node in its cluster, it simply broadcasts that packet over the backbone interface. In case a data packet is received over the backbone interface that is destined to a local node, the egress gateway uses the information in its local routing table to forward the data packet accordingly. While this approach minimizes the amount of routing knowledge in each gateway, it may scale poorly as the backbone grows, as each data packet is transmitted multiple times (in the case of flooding, which we implemented, each data packet is (re-)broadcast by all nodes in the backbone except for the egress gateway).

Another relatively straightforward approach is to exploit the HNA capability in OLSR. In this solution, the backbone runs a second instance of the OLSR routing protocol, this time over the backbone interface. Each gateway advertises reachability to nodes in its cluster via host-specific HNA entries. When an ingress gateway receives a data packet destined to a node outside the local cluster, it will have enough information in its routing table to forward this data packet to the correct egress gateway. As nodes join and leave clusters, gateways learn about the changes in their cluster membership and will propagate this information via the periodic exchange of HNA messages. Compared to the broadcast solution outlined earlier, data packets can be forwarded over a shortest-hop route through the backbone. On the downside, each gateway learns routing information for all nodes in the network: the local OSLR instance propagates routing information to all nodes in the local cluster, the backbone OLSR instance propagates the reachability of all remote nodes via the appropriate gateway. This information is maintained in a pro-active manner, whether needed or not.

A third solution uses a modified version of AODV as backbone routing protocol. Once the ingress gateway receives a data packet from a local node, it will trigger a RREQ through the backbone. Other gateways, upon receiving the RREQ, will check whether the destination node is a member of their local cluster and respond with a proxy RREP. As this information is propagated throughout the backbone, a forward path is set up in intermediate backbone nodes and the data packet can be forwarded over the shortest-hop path, similar to the OLSR-based solution discussed previously. To support node mobility, gateways will have to issue a RERR message when receiving a data packet to a node that has recently left their local cluster, causing the ingress gateway to re-issue a RREQ. To enable a gateway to distinguish a data packet that is meant to be delivered locally from a data packet it simply has to forward through the backbone, we use tunneling: the ingress gateway will tunnel a data packet (using IP in IP encapsulation) to the egress gateway. Unlike the OLSR-based solution, gateways learn (and maintain) much less routing information. Besides the routing information to nodes in the local cluster, a gateway only manages information about destination nodes its local nodes are currently communicating with. This information is than maintained only for the duration of the data flow.

Our final solution is similar to the AODV-based solution, in that ingress gateways learn about the egress gateways on-demand. However, where AODV uses flooding to determine this information (and to re-establish it when the routing path fails), we propose to use a P2P approach, using a Distributed Hash Table (DHT). All gateways join a P2P overlay, storing information about nodes reachable through them under the hash of a node's IP address. Each such entry, if it exists, will list one or multiple gateways through which a destination node is reachable. Once an ingress gateway receives a data packet, it will query the P2P overlay. With the information returned from the overlay, it then tunnels the data packet to the appropriate egress gateway (we are running OLSR as the backbone routing protocol, so an ingress gateway can select the egress gateway that is the closest, for example). The efficiency of this scheme will depend on how easy the P2P overlay resolves lookup requests. As nodes leave and join clusters, the gateways, detecting changes in their local routing tables, update the routing information in the P2P overlay. To support mobility, gateways periodically query the overlay to see whether the routing information has been changed. This solution will store a complete set of routing information, somewhat similar

to the OLSR-based approach. But it will only save a single copy of the routing information (instead of replicating it across each gateway), distributing the
information across all gateways that joined the P2P overlay. The information
is not maintained pro-actively, but updated as the topology changes. The costs
of this approach are that the P2P overlay will have to be maintained, and that
gateways will periodically re-confirm that the (cached) routing information they
are currently using is still accurate/up-to-date.

4   Simulation Results and Discussions

We used OMNeT++ as our simulation platform [31]. The INET Framework, an
open-source library for the OMNeT++ environment [17], provides implementations of MANET routing protocols such as AODV or OLSR, as well as an
IEEE 802.11 MAC layer. OverSim [24] is a flexible framework for overlay network simulation and includes implementations of some structured P2P protocols
(i.e. Chord [29], ... *etc.*). We added an implementation of basic flooding through
the backbone and implemented the modifications discussed above. While these
were quite straightforward in the case of AODV and OLSR, using the DHT as a
backbone routing protocol is more evolved, and the details are discussed in [13].
We selected Chord as the overlay DHT protocol in the results reported here.

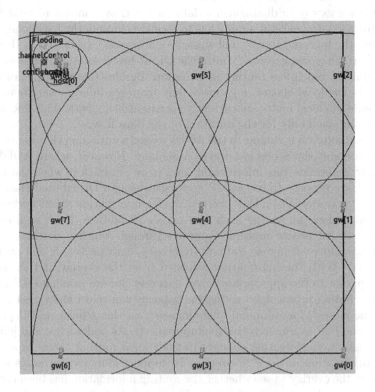

Fig. 1. Basic 3 × 3 grid layout

We focus in our evaluations on how well the proposed backbone routing solutions support nodes switching clusters. We set up a network with 9 clusters in a 3 × 3 grid layout as shown in Fig. 1, which shows a screenshot from the OMNeT++ GUI. We set the radio transmissions range for the backbone radio such that a gateway can only communicate with its direct neighbors in the grid. The local radio's transmission range is set such that nodes can only communicate with one gateway, forming a local cluster. Both local and backbone radios use IEEE 802.11 for the PHY and MAC layers, with a channel rate of 11 Mbps. Two nodes are initially in the same cluster (the top left one), sending 1 kByte UDP packets to each other once every second after an initial delay of 80 s to allow the various routing protocol instances to converge, the Chord ring to form, etc. We then explore two different mobility scenarios. In Scenario A, one node (called the stationary node) stays in the original cluster while the other node (called the mobile node) jumps to a new cluster every 100 s, starting at time 150 s. This continues until the node has visited all other clusters, staying in the last cluster for only 50 s. This results in a total simulation time of 900 s. In a more aggressive Scenario B, the mobile node jumps to a new cluster for 50 s before returning to its home cluster for 50 s. This is repeated until the node again visited all other 8 clusters. Other than the modifications alluded to above, we use all default values that come with the various routing and overlay protocol implementations in OMNet++, for example the Hello and TC message intervals in OLSR, the expanding ring search parameters in AODV, or the finger table maintenance intervals in Chord.

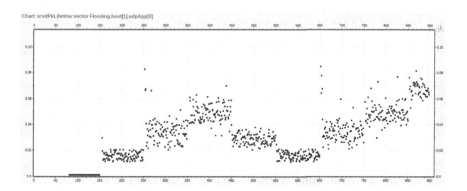

Fig. 2. Flooding: delivering packets to a mobile node

Figures 2 and 3 give an idea of the dynamic nature of packet delivery as time advances. The stationary and the mobile node start sending data packets to each other at time t = 80 s, the mobile node jumps to a new cluster at times 150 s, 250 s, etc. It visits the clusters in the following order, identified by the gateway index in Fig. 1: 5, 2, 1, 4, 7, 6, 3, 0. To reduce collisions in the backbone, packets that are re-broadcast are jittered uniformly random by up

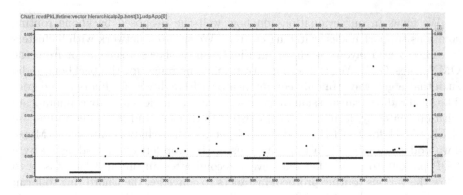

Fig. 3. OLSR: delivering packets from a mobile node

to 10 ms. Consequently, as shown in Fig. 2, the packet latency under flooding is somewhat noisy, but clearly shows a relation with the distance between the two nodes: the latency is lowest when the mobile node is in the same cluster as the stationary node (at the beginning of the simulation, followed by the two cases where the mobile node is in a cluster one hop away: Cluster 5 (from 150 s to 250 s) and Cluster 7 (550 s–650 s). Packet latency is the highest towards the simulation end, when the mobile node is in Cluster 0, 4 hops away from Cluster 8 (which contains the stationary node). It is also worth noticing that packets are almost constantly delivered. The stationary node learns about the default route early on. Once a gateway learns that the mobile node is in its local cluster, it will forward data packets from the backbone, no additional backbone-related routing information needs to be acquired.

When deploying OLSR as routing solution in the backbone, packet latency also shows a strong correlation with the number of hops through the backbone, as shown in Fig. 3, here for packets being sent from the stationary node to the mobile node. Different from the flooding case, packet latency is more uniform and lower, as no jittering is required and packets are delivered as unicast transmissions over a shortest path. Also, there are clear gaps in packet delivery each time the mobile node switches cluster: in addition to updating the intra-cluster routing information, backbone-specific routes need to be learned. Until the new cluster advertises reachability to the mobile node via HNA messages, backbone nodes will route data packets to a previous cluster, where they may be dropped or erroneously forwarded into the local cluster.

To more exhaustively study and compare the performance of our various solutions, Figs. 4 and 5 summarize PDR and average packet latency for 24 runs of Scenario A. For each routing solution, the graphs show the performance when sending packets from the mobile node to the stationary node (first bar), the stationary node to the mobile node (second bar), and the average of the two (third bar). Figure 4 also shows the 95% confidence interval for the average PDR. The results show that Flooding has the best overall PDR performance, in particular when sending data packets to the mobile node, for the reasons explained

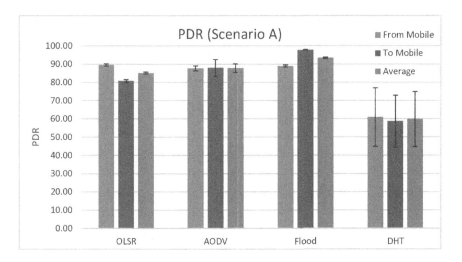

Fig. 4. Average PDR, Scenario A

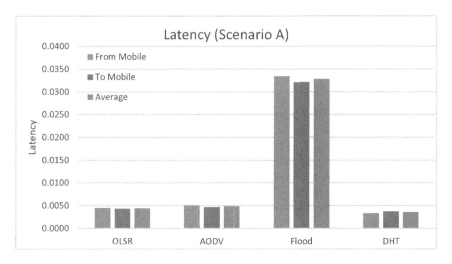

Fig. 5. Average Latency, Scenario A

above. AODV and OLSR have similar average performance, with OLSR somewhat biased towards better delivery of data packets send by the mobile node, while AODV performs similarly in both directions. Our DHT-based solution performs poorest overall, for reasons explained later. In the case of packet latency, the three routing solutions that send data packets via a shortest route perform better (and similar to each other) than Flooding.

In our second scenario, the mobile node only stays in a specific cluster for 50 s. It then returns to its home cluster, Cluster 8, for 50 s, before jumping to another remote cluster. It follows the same order when visiting remote clusters as the mobile node in Scenario A. The next two figures summarize the results we collected in this case for 24 runs for each scenario.

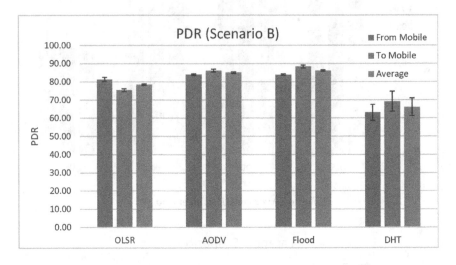

Fig. 6. Average PDR, Scenario B

Comparing the PDR performance of Scenario A (Fig. 4) with the results obtained in Scenario B (Fig. 6), we notice that overall the PDR suffered in the more aggressive Scenario B: as the mobile node changes cluster membership twice as often, more packets get lost due to inaccurate/outdated routing information. This is also true when the mobile node returns to its home cluster: until the stationary node learns that the mobile node has returned home, it will forward data packets to the cluster gateway, to be delivered over the backbone. This also explains why PDR drops in case of Flooding. AODV, on average, performs slightly better than OLSR, as AODV has an explicit route maintenance mechanism: if the incorrect backbone routing information causes data packets to be sent to the wrong cluster gateway, this gateway can at least inform the ingress gateway to stop forwarding data packets to it, triggering a new route request. OLSR, on the other hand, depends on the periodic update of such information, which will not prevent more data packets to be transmitted to the wrong egress gateway in the meantime. Of note here also is the fact that the DHT-based solution, while still performing worse than the other three routing approaches, actually performed better under this more aggressive scenario.

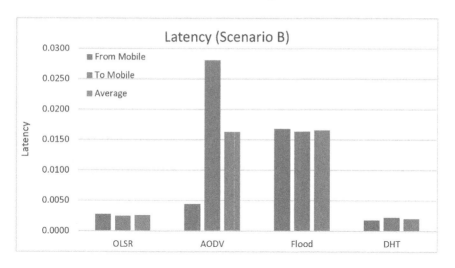

Fig. 7. Average Latency, Scenario B

In terms of latency (see Fig. 7), Flooding cut its end-to-end latency almost in half, as now more data packets (almost 50%) are delivered locally, i.e., when both nodes are in the same cluster. AODV sees its latency increase significantly, in particular for data packets destined to the mobile node. This is a consequence of the need to send more frequent RREQ messages, buffering data packets until a reply is received.

The last two figures focus on the traffic in the backbone network. Since the four routing solutions are very different, and we are interested in a fair comparison, we do not differentiate between control packets and data packets: in the case of Flooding, the protocol should be "penalized" for each unnecessarily retransmitted data packet, for example. And in the case of our DHT-based solution, we have actually two sets of control data packets: the OLSR routing protocol providing connectivity among the backbone nodes, plus the control packets imposed on the backbone by the formation and maintenance of the DHT-overlay, as well as the DHT queries. Figure 8 shows the total number of packet transmissions, averaged over 24 runs, in Scenario A, Fig. 9 similarly shows the average total number of packet transmissions for Scenario B. Flooding imposes the least amount of traffic on the backbone, in particular in the more aggressive Scenario B, where AODV has to issue many more RERR and RREQ messages. OLSR, due to its pro-active nature, causes more backbone traffic than either AODV or Flooding. The DHT-based solution stands out as generating the most backbone traffic. This helps to explain its poor performance overall, as the backbone starts getting congested. We collected the number of packet collisions and packet drops as well, not shown here, and saw that they were particularly high in the case of the DHT-based routing solution.

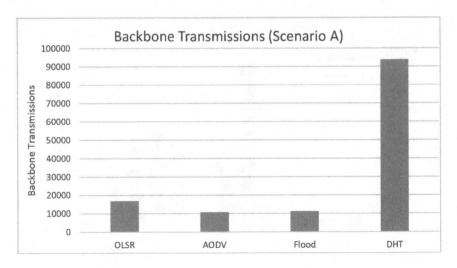

Fig. 8. Backbone packet transmissions, Scenario A

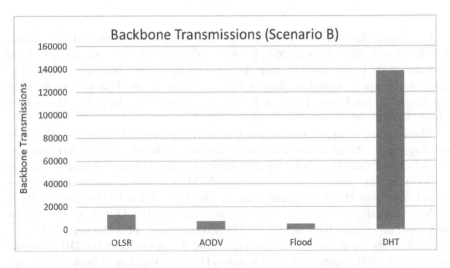

Fig. 9. Backbone packet transmissions, Scenario B

5   Conclusions and Future Work

In this paper we address the problem of routing data packets through a backbone
in the context of a hierarchical MANET. While separating the routing domains is
essential to ensure scalability, a proper solution needs to deal with various levels
of mobility. This makes hierarchical routing protocols developed for the Internet
not suitable. Rather, we proposed 4 quite distinct approaches for a suitable
backbone routing approach, ranging from flooding over modifications to OLSR
and AODV to an innovative proposal based on the use of a DHT. Qualitatively,

the approaches differ in how routing information is propagated among the nodes, in particular the gateway nodes providing connectivity between a cluster and the rest of the network. In flooding, no additional routing information is propagated. The OLSR-based solution has all gateways learn about all nodes in the network, increasing their routing table size considerably as the network scales up. The solutions based on AODV and the DHT learn routing information on-demand, with the AODV-based solution using flooding of RREQ messages while the DHT-based solution looks up the required information based on the P2P mechanism deployed (here, we used Chord, but many other structured P2P systems exist).

We implemented these solutions in OMNeT++ and run extensive simulations to evaluate the performance of these four approaches to support routing between a stationary node and a mobile node that periodically switches clusters. Overall, simply flooding the data through the backbone resulted in the highest PDR, but at the cost of increased packet latency. Flooding also generated the smallest amount of overall traffic in the backbone. Our proposed modification to OLSR worked reasonably well in both scenarios too (high PDR and low latency), whereas the proposed modifications to AODV suffered higher latency under the more aggressive scenario. However, AODV did impose less overall traffic in the backbone, compared to OLSR. The DHT-based solution performed the worst, with relatively low PDR and a high traffic load in the backbone. This is a consequence of our choice of Chord (whose implementation was available) to implement the DHT service. Chord (similar to many other overlay solutions) is agnostic of the underlay network, and a number of cross-layer solutions have been proposed to improve the DHT performance (and to reduce its overhead) particularly in the context of a MANET, such as [1,5], a study to evaluate how well such a cross-layered approach would work is one item of future work.

The results indicate that the flooding-based solution performs best overall: it is simple to implement, reduces the amount of routing information that needs to be propagated in the backbone, and achieves arguably the best performance in terms of PDR and traffic in the backbone. A concern could be the scalability of the protocol as traffic across clusters increases. We plan to explore in more depth at what point such a simple approach would deteriorate. However, we also want to point out that better broadcasting solutions (as opposed to flooding) exist. The broadcast problem has been extensively studied for multi-hop networks. The minimal number of nodes that need to transmit a data packet to ensure that all nodes receive a copy is known as the Minimum Dominating Set. To ensure that packet transmissions can propagate through the network, the nodes in this set should be connected, resulting in the Minimum Connected Dominating Set (MCDS) problem. Optimal solutions to compute a Minimum Connected Dominating Set [21] were obtained for the case when each node knows the topology of the entire network, but these solutions are NP-hard. When implementing an efficient broadcast protocol, many (though not all) solutions employ partial or local neighborhood knowledge, typically acquired through the periodic exchange of HELLO messages (not unlike the OLSR protocol). A good early classification and comparison of a number of proposed protocols is presented in [32].

An efficient broadcast protocol standardized by the IETF is Simplified Multicast Forwarding (SMF) [20], which is based on partial (local) topology information as well. In SMF, for our backbone topology, a subset of three nodes would be selected to re-broadcast data packets while ensuring that all gateways receive it: either gateways 3, 4, and 5, or gateways 1, 4, and 7. This drastically reduces the traffic in the backbone, cutting down the number of packet transmissions from 8 to (at most) 3. In addition, with less contention for access to the media, data packets would need to be jittered less, reducing the latency.

References

1. Abid, S.A., Othman, M., Shah, N.: 3D P2P overlay over MANETs. Comput. Netw. **64**, 89–111 (2014)
2. Abid, S.A., Othman, M., Shah, N.: A survey on DHT-based routing for large-scale mobile ad hoc networks. ACM Comput. Surv. (CSUR) **47**(2), 20 (2015)
3. Ahmad, I., Ashraf, U., Ghafoor, A.: A comparative QoS survey of mobile ad hoc network routing protocols. J. Chin. Inst. Eng. **39**(5), 585–592 (2016)
4. Al Mojamed, M., Kolberg, M.: Structured peer-to-peer overlay deployment on MANET: a survey. Comput. Netw. **96**, 29–47 (2016)
5. Al Mojamed, M., Kolberg, M.: Design and evaluation of a peer-to-peer MANET crosslayer approach: OneHopOverlay4MANET. Peer-to-Peer Netw. Appl. **10**(1), 138–155 (2017). https://doi.org/10.1007/s12083-015-0413-4
6. Basagni, S.: Distributed clustering for ad hoc networks. In: Fourth International Symposium on Parallel Architectures, Algorithms, and Networks, 1999 (I-SPAN 1999) Proceedings, pp. 310–315. IEEE (1999)
7. Bein, D., Datta, A.K., Jagganagari, C.R., Villain, V.: A self-stabilizing link-cluster algorithm in mobile ad hoc networks. In: 8th International Symposium on Parallel Architectures, Algorithms and Networks, 2005. ISPAN 2005. Proceedings, p. 6 IEEE (2005)
8. Belding-Royer, E.M.: Hierarchical routing in ad hoc mobile networks. Wirel. Commun. Mob. Comput. **2**(5), 515–532 (2002)
9. Bentaleb, A., Boubetra, A., Harous, S.: Survey of clustering schemes in mobile ad hoc networks. Commun. Netw. **5**(02), 8 (2013)
10. Caleffi, M., Paura, L.: P2P over MANET: Indirect tree-based routing. In: IEEE International Conference on Pervasive Computing and Communications, 2009. PerCom 2009, pp. 1–5. IEEE (2009)
11. Chiang, C.C., Wu, H.K., Liu, W., Gerla, M.: Routing in clustered multihop, mobile wireless networks with fading channel. In: proceedings of IEEE SICON, vol. 97, pp. 197–211 (1997)
12. Clausen, T., Jacquet, P.: RFC 3626. Optimized link state routing protocol (OLSR) (2003)
13. Echegini, N.: A DHT-based routing solution for hierarchical MANETs. Master's thesis, Carleton University (2018)
14. Furness, J.R.: Optimising structured P2P networks for complex queries. Ph.D. thesis, University of Stirling (2014)
15. Hussein, A., Yousef, S., Al-Khayatt, S., Arabeyyat, O.S.: An efficient weighted distributed clustering algorithm for mobile ad hoc networks. In: 2010 International Conference on Computer Engineering and Systems (ICCES), pp. 221–228. IEEE (2010)

16. Ibrihich, W., Salah-ddine, K., Laassiri, J., El Hajji, S.: Recent advances of hierarchical routing protocols for ad-hoc and wireless sensor networks: a literature survey. Int. J. Inform. Technol. Ijit **9**(2), 71–79 (2016)
17. INET framework user's guide, January 2019. https://inet.omnetpp.org/. Accessed 1 Oct 2019
18. Kaur, H., Sahni, V., Bala, M.: A survey of reactive, proactive and hybrid routing protocols in MANET: a review. Network **4**(3), 498–500 (2013)
19. Kleinrock, L., Kamoun, F.: Hierarchical routing for large networks performance evaluation and optimization. Comput. Netw. **1**(3), 155–174 (1977)
20. Macker, J.P.: Simplified Multicast Forwarding. RFC 6621, May 2012. https://doi.org/10.17487/RFC6621, https://rfc-editor.org/rfc/rfc6621.txt
21. Misra, R., Mandal, C.: Minimum connected dominating set using a collaborative cover heuristic for ad hoc sensor networks. IEEE Trans. Parallel Distrib. Syst. **21**(3), 292–302 (2010)
22. Moussaoui, A., Boukeream, A.: A survey of routing protocols based on link-stability in mobile ad hoc networks. J. Netw. Comput. Appl. **47**, 1–10 (2015)
23. O'Driscoll, A., Rea, S., Pesch, D.: Hierarchical clustering as an approach for supporting P2P SIP sessions in ubiquitous environments. In: 2007 9th IFIP International Conference on Mobile Wireless Communications Networks, pp. 76–80. IEEE (2007)
24. OverSim The Overlay Simulation Framework, January 2019. https://inet.omnetpp.org/. Accessed 1 Oct 2019
25. Özdamar, L., Demir, O.: A hierarchical clustering and routing procedure for large scale disaster relief logistics planning. Transp. Res. Part E Logistics Transp. Rev. **48**(3), 591–602 (2012)
26. Quispe, L.E., Galan, L.M.: Behavior of ad hoc routing protocols, analyzed for emergency and rescue scenarios, on a real urban area. Expert Syst. Appl. **41**(5), 2565–2573 (2014)
27. Sharma, C., Kaur, J.: Literature survey of AODV and DSR reactive routing protocols. In: ICAET, IJCA, pp. 14–17 (2015)
28. Sivakumar, R., Sinha, P., Bharghavan, V.: Core extraction distributed ad hoc routing (cedar). In: Proceedings of INFOCOM 1999 (1999)
29. Stoica, I., et al.: Chord: a scalable peer-to-peer lookup protocol for Internet applications. IEEE/ACM Trans. Netw. (TON) **11**(1), 17–32 (2003)
30. Tsuchiya, P.F.: The landmark hierarchy: a new hierarchy for routing in very large networks. ACM SIGCOMM Comput. Commun. Rev. **18**, 35–42 (1988)
31. Varga, A.: OMNeT++ simulation manual, January 2019. https://doc.omnetpp.org/. Accessed 1 Oct 2019
32. Williams, B., Camp, T.: Comparison of broadcasting techniques for mobile ad hoc networks. In: Proceedings of the 3rd ACM International Symposium on Mobile Ad hoc Networking & Computing, pp. 194–205. ACM (2002)

Transmission Power-Control Certificate Omission in Vehicular Ad Hoc Networks

Emmanuel Charleson Dapaah[(✉)], Parisa Memarmoshrefi, and Dieter Hogrefe

Institute of Computer Science, University of Göttingen, Göttingen, Germany
e.dapaah@stud.uni-goettingen.de,
memarmoshrefi@cs.uni-goettingen.de,
hogrefe@informatik.uni-goettingen.de

Abstract. The frequent dissemination of safety-related beacons among neighboring vehicles in VANET is fundamental for cooperative awareness. Nevertheless, this has over the years raised a major security concern hence the current state-of-the-art requires all safety-related beacons to carry a certificate and a digital signature as a security mechanism to ensure authenticity and integrity. Unfortunately, this security mechanism is characterized by an increase in the size of a beacons payload which as a result, induces an overhead in communication under dense traffic conditions.

Several works have been published in the literature investigating how to reduce this overhead without compromising the level of security achieved, as well as vehicle cooperative awareness. The Neighbor-based Certificate Omission scheme, which conveys the general idea of a vehicle attaching a certificate to its beacon based on changes it observes from its neighboring table was proposed to address this issue. However, on evaluating the scheme under a dense traffic scenario, it was observed that the scheme reduced the level of achieved cooperative awareness among vehicles as it was unable to obtain a fair balance between the number of incurred *cryptographic packet loss* (packets dropped because the vehicle had no corresponding certificate to verify it) and *network packet loss* (packets dropped because of network channel congestion).

In this paper, we propose a Transmission Power-control Certificate Omission scheme, which seeks to achieve a better balance between the number of incurred *cryptographic packet loss (CPL)* and *network packet loss (NPL)* to maximize vehicle cooperative awareness even under dense traffic conditions. Unlike previously proposed schemes, we efficiently control channel load by adopting a congestion detection and congestion control algorithm in our scheme. The simulation results indicate that our proposed scheme can achieve a better balance between the number of incurred CPL and NPL and can maximize vehicle cooperative awareness even under dense traffic conditions.

Keywords: VANET · Security · Certificate omission · Congestion

L. Foschini and M. El Kamili (Eds.): ADHOCNETS 2020, LNICST 345, pp. 164–176, 2021.
https://doi.org/10.1007/978-3-030-67369-7_12

1   Introduction

Critical to the reduction of road accidents is the frequent dissemination of safety-related messages among vehicles. Because, it enables cooperative awareness, which is beneficial for vehicles to make proactive safety decisions. However, in V2V communication, dissemination of safety-related messages is through broadcast. It comprises of two main messages: Periodic Safety Messages (called beacon in this paper) which are broadcasted periodically to announce a vehicles status and Event-Driven Messages which are broadcasted at the detection of an event [1]. In the United States, periodic safety messages are defined as Basic Safety Messages (BSM) according to the SAE J2945/1 standard [2] and as Cooperative Awareness Messages (CAM) by the European Telecommunication Standards Institute (ETSI) [3].

These messages are susceptible to attack as an adversary can inject spoofed messages into the network to mislead vehicles. Therefore to enforce beacon integrity and authenticity, both the IEEE 1609.2 standard and its European counterpart ETSI TS 103 097 mostly rely on the attachment of a digital signature based on Elliptic Curve DSA (ECDSA) and a digital certificate issued by a trusted Certificate Authority (CA) [4].

Despite the benefits of this security mechanism, it increases the beacon payload by approximately 200 bytes [5], which, as a result, induces an overhead in communication and computation. Under high traffic conditions, the periodic broadcast of such a large beacon payload may cause the channel to congest, which in turn increases the number of packet collisions and delay in packet delivery. Therefore, to reduce the overhead and also improve channel efficiency, researchers have proposed several certificate omission schemes and channel congestion control schemes which were described and proven by simulation in [4, 6]. In the omission schemes, if a sending vehicle includes fewer certificates in its subsequent beacons, it increases the number of cryptographic packet loss (CPL) while reducing network packet loss (NPL). Also, if the sending vehicle includes a certificate in all beacons, it eliminates cryptographic packet loss but increases the number of network packet loss.

Therefore, the general drawback of the various omission schemes is how to efficiently achieve a fair balance between NPL and CPL to maximize vehicle cooperative awareness. This we believe is as a result of the schemes inability to efficiently manage channel congestion. With this paper, we propose a Transmission Power-control Certificate Omission which alleviates the general drawback of the previously proposed schemes by combining the advantages of the NbCO scheme discussed in [7] with the advantages of the distributed transmission power control algorithm discussed in [8]. Also, we adopted the concept of channel state transition as described in [9] to cooperatively adjust the transmission power of vehicles taking into consideration their current channel state.

The remainder of this paper is organized as follows: In Sect. 2, we discuss some related works. Next, we present the Transmission Power-control Certificate Omission Scheme (TPCO) in Sect. 3. In Sect. 4, we describe the simulation setup and analyze the simulation results. Finally, we present our conclusion and future work in Sect. 5.

2   Related Work

In this section, we review related works that exploit certificate omission and channel congestion control to improve the efficiency of secured beaconing.

Periodic Omission of Certificates (POoC). In this omission scheme [10], a vehicle attaches a certificate only every nth beacon, therefore omitting its certificate in n–1 beacons sent. Although the approach reduces communication overhead, its performance is dependent on the vehicle's context. For instance, under conditions of high vehicle speed and low beacon frequency, the number of unverified beacons (cryptographic packet loss) increases during the n–1 beacon period (certificate omission period) and this is because a vehicle that has not yet cached the certificate of the sender may have left the senders communication range during the nth beacon period which is the certificate attachment period and as such will have to drop all unverifiable beacons received.

Neighbor-Based Certificate Omission (NbCO). The idea of NbCO [7] is for a vehicle to attach a certificate to its beacon based on the changes observed from its neighboring table. Therefore, every vehicle monitors its neighborhood through beacons received from neighboring vehicles and update its neighboring table as at when it receives a beacon from an unknown vehicle. However, when vehicle density is high, the number of certificate omissions performed by the scheme reduces due to the increase of neighbor changes in the network. Though this may positively reduce the number of incurred CPL, it may also impact the channel load negatively and consequently increase packet collisions which in turn increases the number of NPL.

Congestion-Based Certificate Omission (CbCO). This scheme [6] aims at reducing the overall packet loss incurred by taking into consideration the channel condition before attaching or omitting a certificate. Thus, the scheme attaches a certificate to all beacons if the communication channel is detected to be free and aggressively omits certificates when the channel is congested. Although this trade-off positively impacts the overall packet loss (CPL + NPL), it compromises the individual packet loss (NPL or CPL) based on the current condition. Therefore, the number of CPL is seen to increase when certificates are aggressively omitted during channel congestion and also NPL is seen to increase when the channel is detected to be free.

Channel Congestion Control. Researchers have proposed in literature numerous methods to address the issue of channel congestion and they essentially employ two techniques: beaconing rate control or transmission power control. The concept of beaconing rate control has to do with adapting the transmission rate of a sending node to control its beaconing period. However, several improved beaconing rate control techniques have over the years been proposed in the literature [11, 12]. Sommer [12] proposed an improved approach which considered message utility and channel quality as the baseline for adapting beacon transmission rate to further enhance the adaptation of vehicle transmission rate, for a more effective channel congestion control. Despite the benefits, the general drawback of beacon rate control methods is the lack of sufficient vehicle status information to prevent the degrading of cooperative awareness among vehicles.

Therefore, to better manage channel congestion, a transmission power control scheme [13] was proposed. This scheme controls a vehicles communication range by adapting its beacon transmission power when the channel is congested. Also, Chang [8] in his approach considered the gradual and distributive adjusting of beacon transmission power to achieve an optimal transmission range for maximum awareness.

3   Transmission Power-Control Certificate Omission Scheme

In this paper, we propose an efficient and reliable Transmission Power-control certificate omission (TPCO) scheme which seeks to achieve a better balance between the number of incurred CPL and NPL to maximize vehicle cooperative awareness even under dense traffic conditions and also demonstrate effective control over the communication channel through its ability to adaptively increase or decrease vehicles transmission power based on the observed channel state.

Therefore, to reduce CPL we employed the use of neighboring tables as was proposed by the NbCO scheme [7]. With this concept, each vehicle within the network updates its neighboring table as at when it receives a beacon from an unknown vehicle. And if a vehicle detects such an update, it attaches a certificate to the next beacon it schedules for broadcast. On the other hand, if no such changes are observed, it omits its certificate from all subsequent beacons.

The concept of vehicles maintaining a neighboring table has the advantage of significantly reducing the number of CPL incurred under dense traffic conditions because the frequent update of a neighboring table will force a vehicle to attach a certificate to almost every beacon it sends.

Nevertheless, this will introduce the issue of channel congestion leading to increase in NPL as observed in the NbCO. But peculiar to our Transmission Power-control Certificate Omission scheme is the combination of a congestion detection algorithm and a congestion control algorithm to address the channel congestion drawback introduced by the adopted neighboring table mechanism. Therefore, our TPCO scheme drastically reduces the number of NPL incurred when the channel is congested, causing it to scale very well under dense traffic conditions.

As a congestion detection algorithm, we switch the channel among three states (Relaxed, Active and Restrictive) based on the estimated channel load as was proposed in the ETSI TS 102 687 standards [14]. Each channel state, therefore, determines the transmission power assigned for beacon transmission. In this work, we estimate the channel load using the formula:

$$\text{Estimated\_CL} = \text{N} * \left(\text{beacon\_rate} * M_{length} \right) \tag{1}$$

In Eq. (1), Estimated_CL represents the measured channel load, N represents the number of vehicles within the communication range, beacon_rate represents the number of periodic beacons generated per second and Mlength represents the beacon payload length. The automaton state transition of the congestion detection algorithm is demonstrated in Fig. 1.

Also, to effectively control channel congestion and enhance vehicle cooperative awareness, we employed the concept of a distributed transmission power-control algorithm [8]. Hence, we control channel congestion by adjusting the vehicle transmission power when the estimated channel load exceeds the allowed thresholds. Our maximum

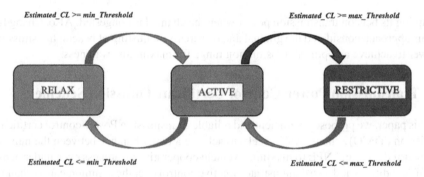

Fig. 1. Channel state transition.

and minimum transmission power assignment were defined in line with the parameter definition Chang et al. [8].

The node state is then switched into a distressed state (Active or Restrictive) and it broadcasts a distress signal to all neighboring vehicles. Vehicles that receive a distress signal gradually adjust their transmission power by a step size (ε) until the estimated channel load of the node in a distressed state gradually converge to a reasonable value below the allowed threshold. The step size is defined to increase or decrease the communication range of the vehicle by 50 m.

Figure 2 describes the operational flow of our channel congestion detection and congestion control algorithm for a sending vehicle. Within a defined time frame of ΔT, the algorithm checks if the estimated channel load (*Estimated_CL*) exceed the allowed thresholds. If the estimated channel load exceeds the allowed thresholds, the vehicle state is changed to a distressed state (Active or Restrictive). It then decreases its transmission power by ε and broadcasts a distress signal to its neighboring nodes and waits for ΔT. This process is continued until the vehicles transmission power reaches the minimum allowed transmission power. However, if the algorithm checks and the estimated channel load has converged to a reasonable value below the allowed threshold, the vehicle state is changed to the non-distressed state (Relax) and its transmission power is increased by ε and waits for ΔT. This process also continues until the vehicles transmission power reaches the maximum allowed transmission power. The pseudocode of the algorithm is illustrated in Table 1.

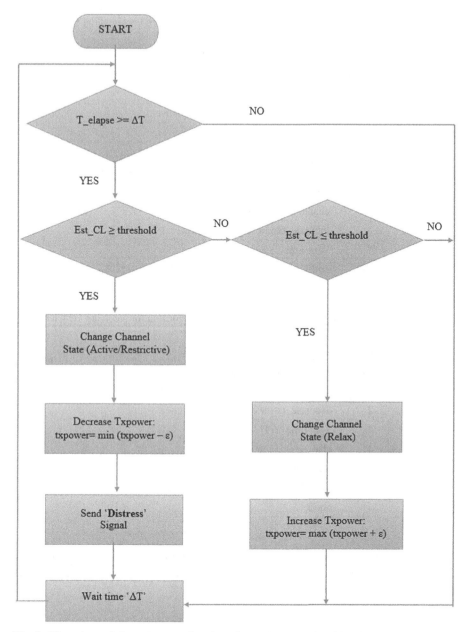

Fig. 2. Flow chart of channel congestion detection and control algorithm for a sending vehicle.

Figure 3 describes the operational flow for receiving vehicles. If a vehicle receives a distress signal, it decreases its transmission power by ε and waits until it receives another distress signal. This process continues until the vehicles transmission power reaches the minimum allowed transmission power. If the vehicle has not received a distress signal and

Table 1. Channel congestion detection and control algorithm for a sending vehicle

Data:	Estimated channel load
Result:	Change in vehicle state and transmission power
1	**If** Est_CL $\geq$ threshold **then**
2	channel_state = Active or Restrictive
3	decrease_txpower = min(txpower-ε)
4	Broadcast 'Distress signal'
5	Wait time 'ΔT'
6	**else**
7	channel_state = Relax
8	increase_txpower = max(txpower + ε)
9	Wait time 'ΔT'
10	**endif**

Table 2. Channel congestion detection and control algorithm for receiving vehicles

Data:	Distress signal (beacon) from neighboring nodes
Result:	Change in vehicle transmission power
1	**If** Distress signal = true **then**
2	decrease_txpower = min(txpower-ε)
3	Wait time 'ΔT'
4	**else**
5	increase_txpower = max(txpower + ε)
6	Wait time 'ΔT'
7	**endif**

its transmission power is below the maximum allowed transmission power, it increases its transmission power by ε until the maximum allowed transmission power is reached. The pseudocode of the algorithm is illustrated in Table 2.

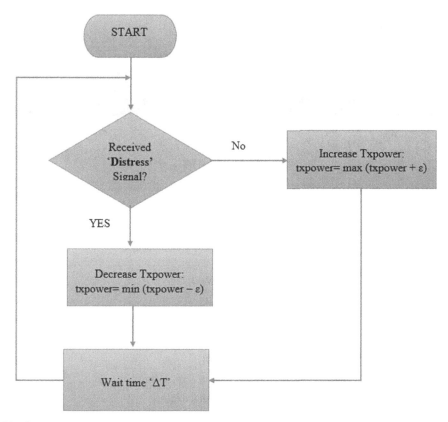

Fig. 3. Flow chart of channel congestion detection and control algorithm for receiving vehicles.

4   Evaluation

To evaluate the performance of our proposed scheme, we focus on a two-directional highway scenario as shown in Fig. 4 and to achieve a dense traffic condition with frequent neighborhood changes we scheduled a total of 100 vehicles where 50 (green vehicles) move on the right lane and the remaining 50 (red vehicles) move on the left lane. Without loss of generality, we focus on the Basic Safety Message (BSM) format as specified in the SAE J2945/1 standard [2].

4.1   Simulation Setup

To conduct our simulation, we used SUMO as the traffic generator, OMNET ++ as the network simulator and VEINS as the VANET simulator. We extended the VEINS simulator by modifying the application layer to implement our beaconing mechanism which encapsulated the neighboring table based certificate omission and attachment strategy. We also modified the mac layer to implement our congestion detection and control algorithm. Table 3 contains a summary of all other relevant simulation parameters which are in line with the previous works by Schoch et al. [7].

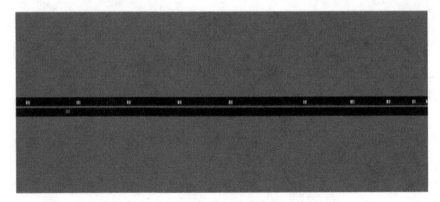

Fig. 4. Two-directional highway scenario.

Table 3. Overview of simulations parameters.

Parameter	Value
Number of nodes	100
Field size	3 km × 3 km
Node density (neigh./node)	1–35
Node velocity (m/s)	40
MAC	802.11p, 3Mbit/s
Transmit power	Adaptive
Beacon frequency	10 Hz
Payload size	50 Bytes
ECC Key type	Nistp256, compressed
Certificate size	125 Bytes
Signature size	56 Bytes
Simulation time (s)	100
Simulation runs	10

4.2 Analysis

To evaluate the performance of our TPCO scheme, we compared it to two previously proposed certificate omission schemes; NbCO [7] and POoC [10] by considering three evaluation metrics. First, we measured the percentage of cryptographic packet loss (CPL) incurred by each scheme and from Fig. 5 we observe that our TPCO scheme performs better than the POoC scheme which recorded a high CPL percentage 7.40%. However, in literature [5], the NbCO scheme is known to outperform other certificate omission schemes in regards to reducing the number of CPL incurred under dense traffic conditions. Yet, our TPCO scheme was able to achieve its goal of not incurring a CPL greater than that of the NbCO scheme and rather went further to slightly outperformed the

NbCO scheme by a margin of 0.30%. Though this performance gap may be considered negligible, we still regard it as an achievement of our scheme and we attribute this slight improvement to the dynamic increasing and decreasing of the communication range of vehicles by adjusting its transmission power.

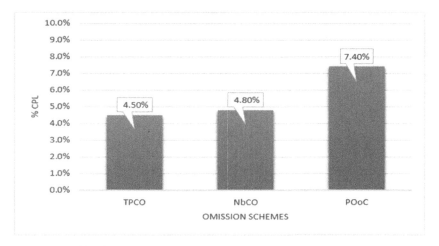

Fig. 5. The average percentage of cryptographic packet loss.

Second, as shown in Fig. 6 we compared each certificate omission scheme by measuring the percentage of network packet loss (NPL) incurred when the channel is congested and in so doing, our TPCO scheme proved to be more efficient than the other schemes as it recorded only 23.10% of NPL. Which was as a result of the channel detection and control algorithm we incorporated into our TPCO scheme to adaptively reduce the communication range of vehicles based on their observed channel state. Hence, justifying our claim that the TPCO scheme increases vehicle cooperative awareness under dense traffic conditions through its ability to effectively control communication channel load to minimize NPL.

Finally, in Fig. 7 we further compared each certificate omission scheme based on the percentage of bandwidth saved as this is directly reflected in the percentage of beacons sent without a certificate attached [7]. We thereby observe that our proposed scheme outperformed the others by saving up to 88.40% of channel bandwidth induced by certificate transfer. In contrast, the POoC is observed to perform worse than the other schemes due to its static certificate transfer which is determined by its predefined n^{th} value.

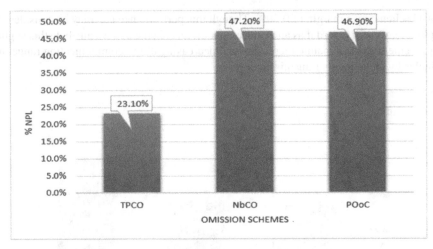

Fig. 6. The average percentage of network packet loss.

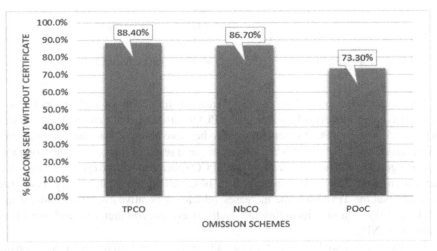

Fig. 7. The average percentage of certificate omissions.

5 Conclusion and Future Work

In this paper, the issue of decreased vehicle cooperative awareness due to an imbalanced trade-off in cryptographic packet loss and network packet loss by certificate omission schemes under dense traffic conditions have been investigated. Based on our analysis we reason that it is as a result of the lack of an efficient congestion detection and control algorithm in previously proposed certificate omission schemes. We addressed this issue by proposing a Transmission Power-control Certificate Omission scheme which performed certificate omissions based on neighbor changes and further control channel load by the cooperative adjustment of the transmission power of vehicles to gradually converge the estimated channel load to a value within a reasonable range. The simulation results show that our scheme increases vehicle cooperative awareness by efficiently controlling the channel load to achieve a reasonable balanced between cryptographic packet loss and network packet loss under dense traffic conditions. Also, in the situation where malicious vehicles decide to ignore distress signals, we believe our scheme will slightly still outperform the NbCO since the distressed node will continue to decrease its communication range until its estimated channel load reaches a value within a reasonable range.

As future work, we aspire to test the performance of our omission scheme in a more realistic scenario by making use of real map scenarios as well as comparing the complexity of our model with already existing models. Also, considering the growth of the number of vehicles in future, secure and privacy-preserving beaconing mechanism need to be optimized with respect to the communication load. Furthermore, centralized authentication mechanisms, which are responsible to issue and prove the authenticity of the certificates may not be efficient and scalable. Therefore, as future work, we also plan to focus on the distributed secure beaconing mechanisms and an investigation of their performance.

References

1. Liu, X., Jaekel, A.: Congestion Control in V2V Safety Communication: Problem, Analysis. Approaches. Electron. **8**(5), 1–24 (2019)
2. Anon: Dedicated Short Range Communications (DSRC) Message Set Dictionary™ (2016)
3. Anon: Intelligent Transport Systems (ITS); Vehicular Communications; Basic Set of Applications; Part 2: Specification of Cooperative Awareness Basic Service.Etsi.org (2019)
4. Feiri, M., Petit, J., Schmidt, R., Kargl, F.: The impact of security on cooperative awareness in VANET. In: 2013 IEEE Vehicular Networking Conference, pp. 127–134 (2013)
5. Feiri, M., Petit, J., Kargl, F.: Evaluation of congestion-based certificate omission in VANETs. In: 2012 IEEE Vehicular Networking Conference (VNC), pp. 101–108 (2012)
6. Feiri, M., Petit, J., Kargl, F.: Congestion-based certificate omission in VANETs. In: Proceedings of the ninth ACM international workshop on Vehicular inter-networking, systems, and applications – VANET'12, pp. 135–138 (2012)
7. Schoch, E., Kargl, F.: On the efficiency of secure beaconing in VANETs. In: Proceedings of the Third ACM Conference on Wireless Network Security – WiSec'10, pp. 111–116 (2010)
8. Chang, H., Song, Y., Kim, H., Jung, H.: Distributed transmission power control for communication congestion control and awareness enhancement in VANETs. PLoS ONE **13**(9), 1–25 (2018)
9. Sommer, C., Dressler, F.: Vehicular Networking, pp. 185–188 (2015)
10. Calandriello, G., Papadimitratos, P., Hubaux, J., Lioy, A.: On the performance of secure vehicular communication systems. IEEE Trans. Dependable Secure Comput. **8**(6), 898–912 (2011)
11. Egea-Lopez, E., Pavon-Marino, P.: Distributed and fair beaconing rate adaptation for congestion control in vehicular networks. IEEE Trans. Mob. Comput. **15**(12), 3028–3041 (2016)
12. Sommer, C., Tonguz, O., Dressler, F.: Traffic information systems: efficient message dissemination via adaptive beaconing. IEEE Commun. Mag. **49**(5), 173–179 (2011)

13. Lu, H., Poellabauer, C.: Balancing broadcast reliability and transmission range in VANETs. ACM SIGMOBILE Mob. Comput. Commun. Rev. **14**(4), 25 (2011)
14. Anon: Intelligent Transport Systems (ITS); Decentralized Congestion Control Mechanisms for Intelligent Transport Systems operating in the 5 GHz range; Access layer part. Etsi.org (2018)

CVNET'2020: The 1st International Workshop on Cooperative Vehicular NETworking

Analyzing Driving Behavior: Towards Dynamic Driver Profiling

Anas Ouardini[1(✉)], Imane El Ouazzany Ech-chahedy[1], Afaf Bouhoute[1], Ismail Berrada[2], and Mohamed El Kamili[3]

[1] Faculty of Science, Sidi Mohamed Ben Abdellah University, Fez, Morocco
anas.ouardini@usmba.ac.ma
[2] Mohammed VI Polytechnic University, SCCS, Ben Guerir, Morocco
[3] Higher School of Technology, Hassan II University of Casablanca,
Casablanca, Morocco

Abstract. This paper aims to use driving data to create a profile of the driver behavior, which can be then added as an additional layer to the Local Dynamic Map of the vehicle. The main contribution of the paper consists of using the *Spherical K Means Clustering*, an unsupervised clustering algorithm for multidimensional datasets, to segment the continuous driving data into multiple segments (*hyperspheres*). Unlike the state of the art, this helps in studying the behavior since all the data will be processed at the same time regardless of the number of features. The generated hyperspheres are an abstract form of the initial numerical values, and can be contribute to a better representation of the driver behavior. We used the UAH Dataset [9] to present the proposed approach, and the cross-validation technique to evaluate the segmentation results.

Keywords: Spherical *K Means* clustering · Driver profiling · Local Dynamic Map

1 Introduction

Connectivity is driving the future of transportation. Thanks to V2X technology, which stands for 'vehicle to everything', cars are becoming increasingly connected to each other, to infrastructure, to pedestrians and to the cloud. V2X relies on different communication technologies to realize the vehicle to vehicle, vehicle to infrastructure and vehicle to person communication and create what is known as Cooperative Intelligent Transportation Systems (C-ITS). CITS are defined as transportation system, where the cooperation between the road components enables and provides an ITS service that offers better quality and an enhanced service level [11]. The communication and cooperation allow drivers to share their car settings and driving profiles with other road users, to have enough knowledge about their surrounding environment. This information about the surrounding environment is maintained by vehicles in a Local Dynamic Map (LDM) [4].

LDM is a conceptual data store that includes different types of data, organized in 4 layers [3,5–7]. The first layer (at the bottom) contains static data such

© ICST Institute for Computer Sciences, Social Informatics and Telecommunications Engineering 2021
Published by Springer Nature Switzerland AG 2021. All Rights Reserved
L. Foschini and M. El Kamili (Eds.): ADHOCNETS 2020, LNICST 345, pp. 179–190, 2021.
https://doi.org/10.1007/978-3-030-67369-7_13

as geographical information, the road network, etc. The second layer includes semi-static data such as information on traffic signs (GPS position, content, etc.). The third layer includes semi-dynamic or precisely temporal data such as information on traffic (accident, traffic jam, etc.), traffic light (its value at a given moment), weather, etc. The forth and upper layer has dynamic or highly dynamic data. Information coming out with a high frequency such as the position, speed and driving information of nearby vehicles, etc.

The main idea of this paper is to use driving data to create a profile of the driver behavior, which can be then added as an additional layer to the LDM. The added layer will provide information about driving behavior, and can open up a whole new level of personalized applications when combined with other LDM data. As a first step towards such implementation, this paper focuses on the problem of driver profile generation. It proposes a dynamic and automatic segmentation of the continuous driving data, essentially needed to build an appropriate model of the driver behavior. Through this work, we intend to build a flexible, multi-use and personnel model. Every driver will have a profile that understand his patterns and behaviors and his preferences. Let's take an older driver with Alzheimer disease as an example [1]. A profile generated from tracking his vehicle data will understand his patterns, can be his mind and help him reduce the risk of crashes [2].

The remainder of the paper is organized as follows. Section 2 presents an overview of the proposed approach. The materials and methods used to deal with the data and to implement the proposed approach are presented in Sect. 3. Section 4 presents the validation approach and discusses the obtained results. Finally, some conclusions are drawn in Sect. 5.

2   Overview

In many behavioral studies, behaviors observed to proceed through a finite number of states may be represented using graphs. Driving is a continuous process, which is generally observed and recorded as continuous trajectories or as discrete sequences of measurable vehicle data. Therefore, driver behavior can be represented by a directed weighted graph, with nodes corresponding to observed driving states and edges to the transitions between them.

Driving behavior is analyzed in terms of changes in measurable properties such as position, direction, and speed, which are acquired using different sensors, either mounted within cars, user devices, or received through V2X communication. As the number of sensors increases, so the amount of data will also increase. This data will need more intelligent and automatic approach to deal with it and transform it into useful, easy to interpret information. The goal of the approach presented in this work is to transform the numerical sensor data into a high level abstracted form that will represent the driver behavior and make easier the extraction of his driving patterns.

Figure 1 shows an overview of the steps involved in the proposed approach. The first step consists of analyzing and studying the different driving variables

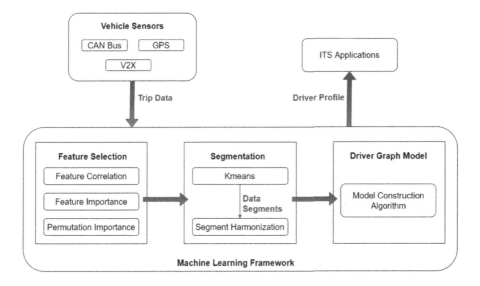

Fig. 1. Overview of the proposed approach

to select important and uncorrelated features. This is mainly performed using three techniques: *Feature Correlation, Feature Importance, Permutation Importance*. Once feature selected, the next step is segmentation. Segmenting the data prior to building appropriate models is important to effectively use data. This considered as the core of our approach: we propose an automatic, unsupervised, clustering based segmentation. Since driving data is generally organized as trip data, Kmeans algorithm [8] is used to generate K clusters per trip. Harmonization is then used to fuse and update the clusters across all trips. These clusters are finally used to construct the graph representing the driver behavior; the clusters will represent the states of the graph. The transitions between states are weighted and updated according to their occurrence, as in [10]. The generated graph is thus a representation of the driver individual driving patterns and can be used by ITS applications to provide more personalized assistance.

3   Materials and Methods

3.1   Dataset

UAH driveset is a public dataset containing naturalistic driving data captured by a smartphone using the driving monitoring app DriveSafe [12]. The dataset contains plenty of information of 6 different drivers on two different routes. A list of the dataset variables used in this paper are presented below:

1. Timestamp (seconds)
2. Speed (km/h)
3. Latitude coordinate (degrees)

4. Longitude coordinate (degrees)
5. Altitude (meters)
6. Acceleration in X (Gs)
7. Acceleration in Y (Gs)
8. Acceleration in Z (Gs)
9. Acceleration in X filtered by KF (Gs)
10. Acceleration in Y filtered by KF (Gs)
11. Acceleration in Z filtered by KF (Gs)
12. Roll (degrees)
13. Pitch (degrees)
14. Yaw (degrees)
15. X: car position relative to lane center (meters)
16. Phi: car angle relative to lane curvature (degrees)
17. W: road width (meters)
18. Distance to ahead vehicle in current lane (meters)
19. Time of impact to ahead vehicle (seconds) [distance related to own speed]
20. GPS speed (km/h) [same as in RAW GPS]
21. Course (degrees)
22. Difcourse: course variation (degrees)

3.2 Feature Selection

Feature selection refers to the process of selecting a reduced subset of the most relevant features in data. Feature selection generally involves studying feature correlation and feature importance.

Feature Correlation. Correlation-based selection is one of the popular techniques used for feature selection. Formally, correlation is a measure among the measure statistics that describes the association between the different random variables. There exist many methods for calculating the correlation coefficient, each measuring different types of strength of association. A strong association between two variables means that they are strongly correlated and only one of them need to be selected. Below are three of the best known methods, which were considered in this work.

– Pearson Correlation Coefficient
– Spearman's Correlation
– Linear Correlation

We studied the correlation between 18 variables instead of 22. The variables Timestamp (seconds), Latitude coordinate (degrees), Longitude coordinate (degrees), and Altitude (meters) are by default selected as they will be needed later to make projection on the map.

The results of correlation using Pearson Correlation Coefficient are presented in Fig. 2. The other two methods provided the same correlation information. Unfortunately, these methods are not enough as they perform well only for linear

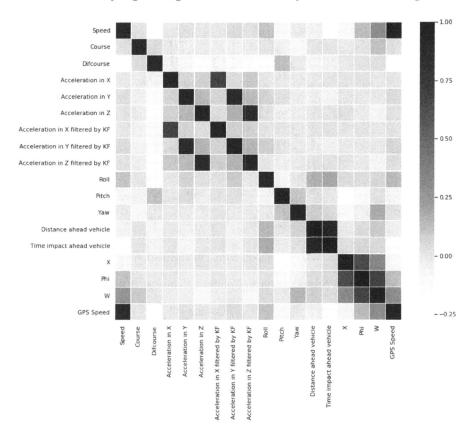

Fig. 2. Pearson correlation

relationships while many other forms of correlation may exist, as illustrated in Fig. 3.

Therefore, we opted for another method to study the correlation. It consists of presenting graphically each feature of data in function of an other one; in our case there are 17^2 combinations resulting in at most 17^2 graphs.

The advantage of the used method is that, in addition to linear correlation, can also detect non-linear relations, i.e. features that have a relation of unknown geometric form, because the graph take a harmonic form. The method results in 6 highly correlated features, which are presented in Table 1.

Feature Importance. According to Table 1, we should either delete the features in column 1 or those in column 2 as the features in both columns are highly correlated. In order to decide which features to keep, we need to study the importance of each feature. Features that are less important will be removed. One common approach is to describe the importance of features relative to a

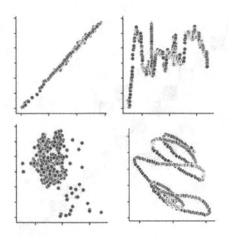

Fig. 3. The different forms of correlation

Table 1. List of correlated features. Columns 1 correlated with columns 2

Columns 1	Columns 2
GPS speed	Speed
Difcourse	Course
Time impact ahead vehicle	Distance ahead vehicle
Acceleration in X	X filtered by KF
Acceleration in Y	Y filtered by KF
Acceleration in Z	Z filtered by KF

model. This can be performed in two ways, using an *Impurity-Based approach* or *Permutation Importance.*

Impurity-Based Feature Importance. Some popular tree-based models provide importance scores computed based on the reduction in the criterion used to select split points. In this work, we used the *XGboost* model to measure importance. The results are presented in Fig. 4a. According to the obtained scores, the features *Yaw, W, Course and Speed* have the higher scores and are thus the most important, while *Acceleration in X filtered by KF, Acceleration in Y filtered by KF, Acceleration in Z filtered by KF, Acceleration in X, Acceleration in Y, Acceleration in Z* have the lowest scores and are thus the least important. Combining these scores with the correlation results in Table 1, we choose to keep the following variables: *Speed, Acceleration in X filtered by KF, Acceleration in Y filtered by KF, X, Phi, Acceleration in Z filtered by KF, W, Course, Time impact ahead vehicle, Roll, Pitch, Yaw.*

Permutation Feature Importance. Permutation importance describes feature importance based on the impact each feature has on the trained model's

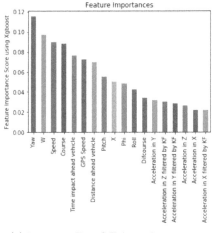

Weight	Feature
0.4538 ± 0.0080	Yaw
0.3023 ± 0.0082	W
0.2151 ± 0.0057	Course
0.0660 ± 0.0061	GPS Speed
0.0632 ± 0.0039	Speed
0.0437 ± 0.0046	X
0.0410 ± 0.0034	Roll
0.0395 ± 0.0052	Pitch
0.0280 ± 0.0043	Time impact ahead vehicle
0.0234 ± 0.0043	Phi
0.0209 ± 0.0026	Distance ahead vehicle
0.0200 ± 0.0023	Difcourse
0.0105 ± 0.0014	Acceleration in Z filtered by KF
0.0092 ± 0.0019	Acceleration in Y filtered by KF
0.0060 ± 0.0034	Acceleration in Y
0.0054 ± 0.0025	Acceleration in Z
0.0048 ± 0.0013	Acceleration in X filtered by KF
0.0046 ± 0.0014	Acceleration in X

(a) Impurity-Based Feature importance   (b) Permutation Feature Importance

Fig. 4. Impurity-based vs permutaion feature importance using XGBoost

predictions. This is done by measuring the increase in the model's prediction error after permuting the feature's values. Here also we used the $XGboost$ model. The results are presented in Fig. 4b. Comparing the results of the both techniques, presented in Fig. 4, we see that there is a small difference in classifying the importance of some variable, e.g. *Speed* has a higher score than *GPS speed* in the impurity based method but a little less importance in case of permutation importance.

The results of feature importance after removing features is presented in Fig. 5. Considering all the resulted obtained so far we decided to only keep the variables *Speed, Course, Roll, Pitch, Yaw, Distance ahead vehicle, X*. Features that have an importance score less than the mean were deleted. Moreover, the variable W corresponding to the road width was deleted as it can be extracted from *GPS* data.

3.3 Data Segmentation

To efficiently deal with the continuous driving data and in order to keep pertinent information enough to be useful in real applications, an unsupervised and automatic segmentation method is needed. In this work, we propose the use of Kmeans clustering to segment driving data.

As shown in Fig. 6, driving data is organized as trip data. Therefore, segmentation will be performed in such way that Kmeans is applied to each trip separately to generate clusters of data which are iteratively merged to form the final clusters. The Kmeans algorithm is applied over the 7 features selected in the previous section. Each trip will then generate K clusters. One of the important things in Kmeans clustering is to use an optimal number of cluster K. Using

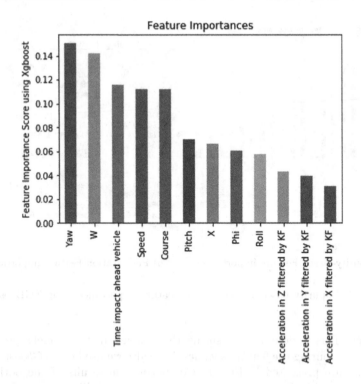

Fig. 5. Feature importance using XGBoost after removing least important features.

a low number could lead to clusters with significant differences while a very large number will generate too many clusters which could lead to overfitting. In order to find the optimal number of clusters, we used the elbow method, a common technique used for this task. Applied over multiple features, Kmeans will generate clusters that can be represented by hyperspheres (n-sphere), i.e. using 7 features will generate 7-dimensional spheres $(\mathcal{E}^7)$. Each hypersphere will be defined by its center and its radius. Thus, we can store a minimum data by storing the radius and the center without losing any information.

3.4   Data Harmonization

Segmenting driving trips allows keeping only relevant information. However, segmentation can produce overlapping clusters, which can lead to grouping different behaviors in the same clusters (same hyperspheres). To deal with issue, the harmonization process is introduced. Harmonization is the process by which the hyperspheres are updated, either by merging or splitting. The update is decided by comparing the distance between the hyperspheres' centers with a predefined threshold. This update is applied iteratively to the hyperspheres generated by each trip (output) as illustrated in Fig. 7. The harmonization method can be briefly described as followed.

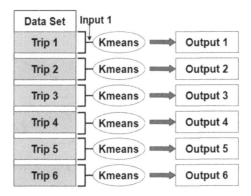

Fig. 6. $KMeans$ applied to data trips

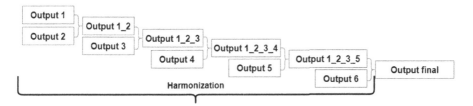

Fig. 7. Data harmonization

Considering two spheres with centers C1 and C2 and radius R1 and R2, respectively. Figure 8a shows an example of two intersecting spheres. Determining whether an intersection exists between the two spheres is similar to the case of circles, as shown in Fig. 8b:

– if $distance(C1, C2) > R1+R2$ then there is an intersection (or a union exists), and an update may be considered
– Others, no update is needed.

To decide whether to update the hyperspheres requires defining a certain threshold D. The update is considered $if\ [R2 - (distance(C1, C2) - R1)] > D$ otherwise the hyperspheres are kept. To illustrate the two cases of intersection and union, we show, for sake of simplicity, figures of circles instead of hyperspheres (Fig. 9).

Considering the case of intersection illustrated in Fig. 9, where x1, x2, x3 and x4 are min(A), min(B), max(B) and max(A), respectively. The update is ruled by the following:

$if\ Distance(x1, x2) \geq D\ then\ create\ an\ hypersphere$
$if\ Distance(x2, x3) \geq D\ then\ create\ an\ hypersphere$
$if\ Distance(x3, x4) \geq D\ then\ create\ an\ hypersphere$

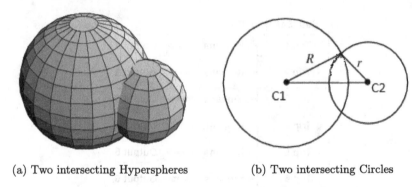

(a) Two intersecting Hyperspheres   (b) Two intersecting Circles

Fig. 8. An example of intersecting spheres and circles

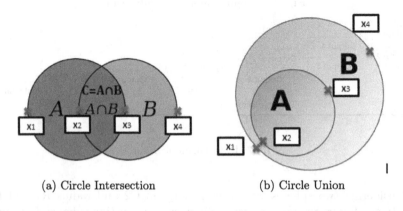

(a) Circle Intersection   (b) Circle Union

Fig. 9. Illustration of union and intersection in case of circles

The update may thus result in creating 3 or 2 new hyperspheres or just a single hypersphere merging the two original ones. The case of union is dealt with in the same way as intersection.

4   Experiments and Results

To validate the proposed segmentation approach, we use the leave one out cross validation method. UAH dataset [9] contains an average of 7 trips per driver. Thus, at each round of the cross validation, one trip is chosen as a test trip and the others are used as training trips. Then, our segmentation method is applied to the training trips and the test trip to get two separate sets of segments, namely, the training segments *train_hyperesphere* and the test segments *test_hyperesphere*. The results are evaluated by comparing the segments in *train_hyperesphere* and *test_hyperesphere*. The error at each round is measured as the number of the test segments not included in any training segments. We define two metrics of errors.

– Metric 1 (E_1): measured as the number of $Test\_hyperspheres$ that can make a modification in the $train\_hyperesphere$, with a given threshold D, divided by the total number of $test\_hyperspheres$. The test segments which can modify the segments from the train are defined as False Positives (FP).

$$E_1 = \frac{FP}{|test\_hyperspheres|} \tag{1}$$

– Metric 2 (E_2): measured s the number of the $hyperspheres$ in the train that can be modified by the $test\_hyperspheres$, divided by the total number of $train\_hyperesphere$.

$$E_2 = \frac{modified\_train\_hyperspheres}{|train\_hyperspheres|} \tag{2}$$

The values of E_1 and E_2 computed using cross validation are 6% and 1%, respectively. This difference in the obtained values is logical since the second error metric depends on the size of the train set, which is large compared to the test set. Moreover, E_2 computes the number of trains that can be modified, however, some $hyperspheres$ can be repeated several times, i.e. they can be modified by several $test_hyperspheres$. This repetition is not taken into account, i.e. the number will not increase.

5   Conclusion

In this paper, we deal with the problem of driver profiling. The aim is to transform the numerical sensor data into a high level abstracted form that will represent the driver behavior and make easier the extraction of his driving patterns. Driving behavior is represented by a directed weighted graph, with nodes corresponding to driving states and edges to the transitions between them. The driving states are considered as an abstraction of continuous numerical values. The paper focused on data segmentation. An unsupervised method (using kmeans) to segment multiple driving features is presented. Since we are dealing with multiple variable, the segments had a form of $hypersphere$. The resulting segments are to be used as driving states to build the driver profile. Since driving is generally recorded as trip data, rules to continuously update the segments were proposed. The proposed approach was applied on the UAH-Dataset and evaluated using cross-validation. In order to evaluate the data segments, two error metrics were defined. Our future work focuses on segmentation of GPS data to create road segments on which driver data will be projected.

References

1. Babulal, G.M., Traub, C.M., Webb, M., et al.: Creating a driving profile for older adults using GPS devices and naturalistic driving methodology. F1000Research 5, 2376 (2016). https://doi.org/10.12688/f1000research.9608.2

2. Divya, G., Sabitha, A., Sudha, D.S., Spandana, K., Swapna, N., Hepsiba, J.:
Advanced vehicle security system with theft control and accident notification using
GSM and GPS module. Int. J. Innov. Res. Electr. Electron. Instrum. Control Eng.
4(3), 64–68 (2016)
3. Andreone, L., Brignolo, R., Damiani, S., Sommariva, F., Vivo, G., Marco, S.:
Safespot final report. Technical report D8.1.1 (2010)
4. SAFESPOT Integrated Project (2012). http://www.safespot-eu.org/
5. Zott, C., Yuen, S.Y., Brown, C.L., Bertels, C., Papp, Z., Netten, B.: Safespot
local dynamic maps: context-dependent view generation of a platform's state and
environment. In: 15th Intelligent Transport Systems World Congress, November
2008
6. Shimada, H., Yamaguchi, A., Takada, H., Sato, K.: Implementation and evaluation
of local dynamic map in safety driving systems. J. Transp. Technol. **5**, 102–112
(2015)
7. ETSI TR 102 863 V1.1.1: Intelligent Transport Systems (ITS); Vehicular Communications; Basic Set of Applications; Local Dynamic Map (LDM); Rationale for
and guidance on standardization (2011)
8. Jain, A.K.: Data clustering: 50 years beyond K-means. Pattern Recogn. Lett. **31**,
651–666 (2010)
9. Romera, E., Bergasa, L.M., Arroyo, R.: Need data for driver behaviour analysis?
presenting the public UAH-DriveSet (Brazil). In: 2016 IEEE 19th International
Conference on Intelligent Transportation Systems (ITSC)
10. Bouhoute, A., Oucheikh, R., Boubouh, K., Berrada, I.: Advanced driving behavior
analytics for an improved safety assessment and driver fingerprinting. IEEE Trans.
Intell. Transp. Syst. **20**(6), 2171–2184 (2019). https://doi.org/10.1109/TITS.2018.
2864637
11. Car-2-car.org. 2020. About   C-ITS.   https://www.car-2-car.org/about-c-its/.
Accessed 14 Oct 2020
12. Bergasa, L.M., Almería, D., Almazán, J., Yebes , J.J., Arroyo, R.: DriveSafe: an app
for alerting inattentive drivers and scoring driving behaviors. In: IEEE Intelligent
Vehicles Symposium (IV), pp. 240–245, Dearborn, Michigan, USA, June 2014

Energy Efficient Adaptive GPS Sampling Using Accelerometer Data

Saad Ezzini[1(✉)] and Ismail Berrada[2]

[1] University of Luxembourg, SnT, Luxembourg, Luxembourg
saad.ezzini@uni.lu
[2] Mohammed VI Polytechnic University, SCCS, Benguérir, Morocco
ismail.berrada@um6p.ma

Abstract. Internet of Things (IoT) is a major component of the connected world. With billions of battery-powered devices connected to the internet, energy and bandwidth consumption become significant issues. Embedding intelligence/cognition in the apparatus is recognized as one of the solutions to mitigate these issues. Global Positioning System (GPS) is recognized as one of the most energy-consuming mobile sensors in smart vehicles/systems. This paper proposes a smart adaptive sampling method for GPS sensors using the accelerometer data. Our approach adapts the sampling frequency of the GPS sensor according to the data stream of the accelerometer, without causing significant distortions to the data. In our experiment, we could reduce the GPS sensing by 78% while preserving an accuracy of 91.4%.

Keywords: Internet of Things · Cognitive IoT · Adaptive sampling · GPS · Accelerometer

1 Introduction

Nowadays, cities worldwide encounter new challenges such as spectacular population growth, massive pressure on city infrastructure (power, water, health-care, transportation), and pollution. The smart city concept came in response to some of those contemporary challenges. Intelligent infrastructure, smart grids, and electric cars provide synergistic advantages for smart cities. One of the principal premises of smart cities is to enhance the quality of life by establishing "smart mobility". With billions of connected devices, the so-called "Internet of Things (IoT)" is quickly becoming a dominant milestone in the next generation of smart communication.

IoT is expected to have enormous economic and social impact. In essence, IoT devices may use internet connection to report, measure, and perform actions autonomously. Many of these devices consist of embedded sensors, actuators, or RFID tags, which are generally low-powered, and require network access, which may not be energy-efficient [8].

With billions of battery-powered devices connected to the internet, data volume, energy efficiency, and bandwidth consumption are believed to be three of

© ICST Institute for Computer Sciences, Social Informatics and Telecommunications Engineering 2021
Published by Springer Nature Switzerland AG 2021. All Rights Reserved
L. Foschini and M. El Kamili (Eds.): ADHOCNETS 2020, LNICST 345, pp. 191–200, 2021.
https://doi.org/10.1007/978-3-030-67369-7_14

the most significant challenges to overcome in IoT. One of the techniques to mitigate these issues is Adaptive Sampling (AS). AS consists of adapting the connected device's sampling frequency to the changes in the measurements, i.e., decrease (increase) the sampling frequency when the changes are small (large), while not exceeding a tolerable distortion to the data. This paper proposes a smart adaptive sampling method for Global Positioning System (GPS) sensors based on accelerometer sensor data. GPS sensor is a receiver that uses a satellite-based navigation system to provide position, timing, and velocity information at a given rate/frequency (ranging from 1 to 10 Hz) and consuming around 30 mA per data record. Compared to other typical motion-related sensors, GPS sensors are very demanding in energy (Fig. 1).

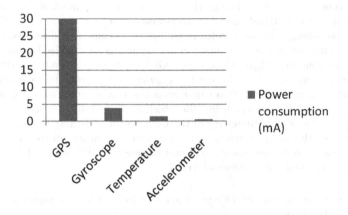

Fig. 1. Power consumption per sample for different sensors

We introduce the SAAF system, which stands for "Sense Acceleration & Adapt Frequency". SAAF is a new approach that senses acceleration data and adapts the frequency of the GPS sensor to reduce the amount of insignificant information, which leads to saving energy and bandwidth consumption and data storage. The proposed approach could form the basis of several IoT GPS-based applications, such as smart-phones, wearable devices, drones, and connected cars [4].

The rest of the paper is organized as follows. The second section summarizes the existing studies on adaptive sampling and filtering techniques. The proposed methodology is outlined in the third section. Section 4 describes the data acquisition process, and the evaluation of the experimental results. The last section concludes this paper and outlines the future work.

2   Related Works

In the literature, there are various approaches to adaptive sampling. Some preliminary work was carried out several years ago. Law et al. [6], proposed to use an adaptive sampling solution based on the Box-Jenkins approach in time series analysis. In [8], the authors focused on developing an energy-efficient adaptive sampling technique that uses temporal correlation among sensor measurements to find the best sampling rate. Kiran and co-workers [13] proposed a healthcare application based on intelligent sparse sensing, which reconstructs the original signal using an on-chip context predictor.

Yurur et al. have used the accelerometer for activity detection to save the energy of human-related sensors [16]. In a similar context, Chan et al. [2] combined the accelerometer and GPS sensors to improve the displacement information accuracy using empirical mode decomposition and adaptive filtering.

As adaptive filtering might save the storage space, it tends to consume more energy when the filtering is performed on the sensor side. Recent approaches use adaptive filtering on GPS data to improve its accuracy [1,7,12].

Several other studies, for instance, [10,14], and [5], have been carried out on adaptive sampling using event detection or penalty functions using the recent records of the same sensor. However, these approaches cannot be generalized. As highlighted by [8], critical applications cannot tolerate the risk of losing data, such as healthcare, and road safety systems. The approach proposed in this paper differs from the existing ones, as it uses low-power sensors to adapt the sampling frequency of greedy power-consuming sensors.

3   Approach

As mentioned in the previous section, adaptive filtering strategies can preserve data storage space and bandwidth but at the cost of higher energy consumption. In this era of big data and connected cities, data storage and bandwidth are not real concerns compared to the energy problem. Thus, we adopted the adaptive sampling strategy over adaptive filtering because of its practicality in solving the aforementioned challenges.

The proposed process design is presented in Fig. 2, which is composed of a four-step loop. The initial step consists of sensing the acceleration record (in time t_i), which allows us to calculate the velocity (v_i) in the next step using the three-dimensional acceleration data. As soon as these steps have been carried out, a new sampling frequency (T_G (t_i)) can be calculated using Eq. (4). The next step is a conditional one, compares the new GPS sampling frequency to the previous one. Finally, based on this comparison, it decides either to update the GPS frequency or to keep the old one. Below, we elaborate on each step of our approach.

3.1   Acceleration Sampling

The constant Accelerometer frequency allows us to sample the acceleration information at a fixed rate. The Accelerometer sensor yields three-axis acceleration information, which is used to calculate the velocity in the next step.

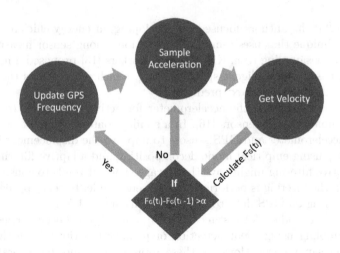

Fig. 2. Process design.

3.2   Velocity Calculation

The proposed algorithm adapts the GPS sampling frequency based on velocity values. Velocity records are calculated by exploiting the three-dimensional accelerometer data, as shown in Eq. (1) for each axis.

$$\begin{cases} v_x(kT_a) = v_x((k-1)T_a) + a_x(kT_a)T_a \\ v_y(kT_a) = v_y((k-1)T_a) + a_y(kT_a)T_a \\ v_z(kT_a) = v_z((k-1)T_a) + a_z(kT_a)T_a \end{cases} \tag{1}$$

Where v_x and a_x stand respectively for the velocity and acceleration according to the x-axis, T_a and k denote respectively the accelerometer sampling period and the sample index.

3.3   New Frequency Calculation

Let pT_a denote the sampling period of the GPS sensor. We would like to adapt the value of p, while making sure that the difference between the actual GPS record and the record at time instant $(k+p)T_a$ does not exceed a predefined threshold ϵ, i.e.,:

$$|u((k+p)T_a) - u(kT_a)| < \epsilon \tag{2}$$

Where $u(kT_a)$ and $u((k+p)T_a)$ stand respectively for the GPS record's value at time kT_a, and at time $(k+p)T_a$. It is worth noting that ϵ can be set to be the uncertainty value associated with the studied GPS sensor.

$$u((k+p)T_a) \approx u(kT_a) + \left[\sum_{i=0}^{p-1} v((k+i)T_a) \right] T_a \tag{3}$$

Considering (3) means

$$\sum_{i=0}^{p-1} v((k+i)T_a) < \frac{\epsilon}{T_a} \tag{4}$$

The objective is to find the optimum value of p that verifies the Eq. (3) and (4).

We use function (5) to adapt GPS sampling frequency, which takes in input the velocity of time t and outputs the new sampling period pT_a.

$$T_G(t) = f(p) = \begin{cases} T_{min} & v(t) > v_{max} \\ T_{max} & v(t) < v_{min} \\ pT_a & Otherwise \end{cases} \tag{5}$$

$T_{max}, T_{min}, v_{max}$ and v_{min} are predefined variables and depend on the use case. This function controls the frequency range (between T_{max} and T_{min}) by setting velocity limits (v_{max} and v_{min}).

3.4   Frequency Update

Once the new GPS frequency $F_G(t_i+1)$ is calculated, compare it to the previous one $F_G(t_i)$. If $F_G(t_i + 1) - F_G(t_i)$ is greater than α then the GPS frequency is updated, else we go back to the first element in the cycle: acceleration sampling. Where α stands for the maximum allowed GPS frequency rate.

4   Experimental Results

In this section, we empirically evaluate our approach.

4.1   Dataset Acquisition

Measurements were taken using purpose-built equipment composed of a Raspberry Pi Model B, Accelerometer, Gyroscope, Thermometer, and two GPS sensors, one with a fixed frequency 1 Hz and the other with adaptive frequency. The data collection was carried out in Rabat, Morocco, using a recent model of Mercedes Benz. The tests were performed on a volunteer's vehicle. One driver participated in the experiment setting, which consisted of three days driving in different paths, including highways, motorways, and local roads. The driver was told to drive as he does in his daily routine.

The complete data set has a size of 412 MB and consists of 3.17 million samples. The content of each column is described below:

- Timestamp (ms)
- Acceleration in X (Gs)
- Acceleration in Y (Gs)
- Acceleration in Z (Gs)
- Latitude coordinates (degrees)

- Longitude coordinates (degrees)
- Altitude (meters)
- Vertical accuracy (degrees)
- Horizontal accuracy (degrees)
- Speed (km/h)
- Roll (degrees)
- Pitch (degrees)
- Yaw (degrees)

The Accelerometer and Gyroscope sensors provide records at 10 Hz frequency.

4.2   Research Questions (RQs)

Our evaluation addresses four research questions:

- **RQ1. What is the optimal ϵ value?** The value of ϵ controls the configuration of our approach. RQ1 identifies the configuration that produces the best overall results.
- **RQ2. How efficient is our approach in a real experiment?** Using the best configuration from RQ1, RQ2 assesses the effectiveness of our approach in energy, storage, and bandwidth reduction versus regular sampling.
- **RQ3. How accurate is our approach to preserving the initial signal information?** After evaluating the effectiveness of our approach, we calculate the distortion error and information loss, providing the accuracy of signal preservation.

4.3   Experiments

RQ1: To answer RQ1, we observed the impact of varying the *epsilon* values as summarized in Table 1. Higher *epsilon* values lead to higher sensing reduction but also higher distortion (higher error). This value is an empirical choice and depends on the use case and the tolerated error. In our case, we assume the intolerance of high distortion, thus taking into account the average GPS error, which is around 5 m, we choose $epsilon = 5.10^{-7}$.

RQ2: The next set of analyses examined the impact of the proposed approach on energy and bandwidth consumption and data storage. Data analysis and comparison were performed on two parallel data issued from two GPS sensors described in the previous section to measure these points. Figure 3 compares the standard GPS signal sampled with default frequency and adaptive GPS signal acquired by applying the proposed approach. It can be seen that the adaptive GPS signal skips noisy/unnecessary values while keeping essential changes.

The concluded results to emerge from the data is that the new signal reduces the data volume and bandwidth consumption of GPS sensor by 78.4% and reduces the energy consumption by 39.2%. Figure 4 shows the reduced power consumption for the used GPS model. These tests also revealed that, in the first ten minutes, our model reduced the data volume of the GPS sensor by at least 1.2 Mb.

Table 1. Comparison between different ϵ values

ϵ	10^{-6}	$7.5.10^{-7}$	5.10^{-7}	10^{-7}	5.10^{-8}
Reduced data (%)	94.29	88.14	78.40	63.45	30.94
Reduced energy (%)	47.14	44.07	39.2	31.72	15.47
Distortion (meter/sample)	7.34	5.76	3.95	1.03	0.57

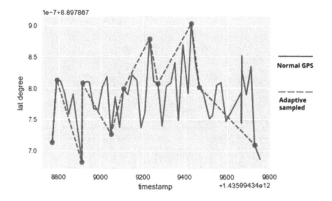

Fig. 3. Normal GPS signal versus adaptive GPS signal

RQ3: To evaluate the accuracy of our method, we measured the distortion between both signals. The average error of the proposed model is around 4 meters/sample. GPS signal is known to be noisy. Thus a preprocessing phase is required to clean and filter the noisy data. In our case, we can deduct the average GPS error from the resulted distortion to have a fair accuracy evaluation. After removing this noise, our model achieves an average accuracy of 91.4%. We believe that those results emphasize the validity of our method.

5   Discussion

As expected, there were some discrepancies in the proposed method due to multiple sensors with different sampling rates. Therefore, this approach will output almost in each use case an irregular time series. Considering the dataset's index is the GPS data, this will require using preprocessing techniques or algorithms for irregular time series.

As an essential step, preprocessing improves the performance and accuracy of the machine learning process by handling topics such as missing data [5], noisy data [15], and data quality [5]. More use cases of preprocessing are investigated by [5,15].

Generally, time series are generated by a regularly spaced interval of time, in which our proposed method fails to guarantee. This violation is caused by the variability of the GPS sampling frequency based on the velocity. In this section,

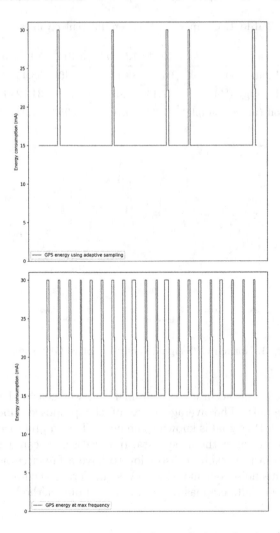

Fig. 4. GPS energy consumption before and after adaptive sampling

The main objective is to discuss the solutions and strategies to deal with this problem.

In the literature, there are few methods for keeping the structure of unevenly time series, such as rolling operators [3], weighted moving averages [9], and exponentially weighted moving averages [9]. The methods that keep working on the non-gaped subsequence of the data are functional for some use cases. Most of the powerful statistical tools for time series could not be applicable theoretically and directly to our data. We propose transforming irregular times series to regular data by using interpolation techniques to apply regularly spaced data methods.

The interval of time should not be highly irregular to transform the data into an equally spaced time series. Such a critical assumption can lead to severe biases in our data [11]. To solve this issue, our method fixes two parameters suggested in Sect. 2, F_{max} and F_{min} reduce the high variability in terms of the time interval.

Some solutions can be disastrous. Using the irregular time series with imputation methods, which can lead to white noise or transform a high irregular time series, can change the initial structure of the series (i.e., in terms of seasonality) completely. Therefore, the transformation cannot be the best solution. Analyzing the series in their unchanged form can be a valid choice [3, 9, 11].

6 Conclusion and Future Work

This paper has proposed a novel approach that applies adaptive sampling to optimize GPS sensing, using Accelerometer's data. Based on the collected dataset, this study's results indicate the capability to reduce energy, data volume, and bandwidth consumption by 78% while preserving a relatively high accuracy: 91.4%. Our work's strength lies in using a second less-energy-consuming sensor (Accelerometer) to produce energy-efficient sensing of a more energy-consuming sensor (GPS). These findings add to a growing body of literature on the adaptive sensing field. The present study has important implications for solving the energy problem of embedded systems and IoT.

Future work should focus on enhancing the performance of this approach. Therefore, we intend to collect a more significant and more varied dataset to verify our work's validity. This will allow us to do more analysis and improve our model's performance.

References

1. Arif, S.W., Coskun, A., Kale, I.: Tracking and mitigation of chirp-type interference in GPS receivers using adaptive notch filters. In: 2020 IEEE 63rd International Midwest Symposium on Circuits and Systems (MWSCAS), pp. 778–781. IEEE (2020)
2. Chan, W.S., Xu, Y.L., Ding, X.L., Dai, W.J.: An integrated GPS-accelerometer data processing technique for structural deformation monitoring. J. Geodesy **80**(12), 705–719 (2006)
3. Eckner, A.: Algorithms for unevenly-spaced time series: moving averages and other rolling operators. In: Working Paper (2012)
4. Ezzini, S., Berrada, I., Ghogho, M.: Who is behind the wheel? driver identification and fingerprinting. J. Big Data **5**(1), 9 (2018)
5. Honaker, J., King, G.: What to do about missing values in time-series cross-section data. Am. J. Polit. Sci. **54**(2), 561–581 (2010)
6. Law, Y.W., Chatterjea, S., Jin, J., Hanselmann, T., Palaniswami, M.: Energy-efficient data acquisition by adaptive sampling for wireless sensor networks. In: Proceedings of the 2009 International Conference on Wireless Communications and Mobile Computing: Connecting the World Wirelessly, pp. 1146–1151. ACM (2009)

7. Linlin, X., Yao, Z., Wenjie, M., Chenxi, S., Fadong, H.: MIMU/GPS information fusion: normal cloud model based fuzzy adaptive filtering. In: 2018 Chinese Control And Decision Conference (CCDC), pp. 4076–4081. IEEE (2018)
8. Masoum, A., Meratnia, N., Havinga, P.J.M.: An energy-efficient adaptive sampling scheme for wireless sensor networks. In: Intelligent Sensors, Sensor Networks and Information Processing, 2013 IEEE Eighth International Conference on, pp. 231–236. IEEE (2013)
9. Müller, U.A.: Specially weighted moving averages with repeated application of the ema operator. In: Internal Document UAM, October 1991. Olsen & Associates, Switzerland (1991)
10. Rachuri, K.K.: Smartphones based social sensing: adaptive sampling, sensing and computation offloading. PhD thesis, University of Cambridge, UK, 2013
11. Rehfeld, K., Marwan, N., Heitzig, J., Kurths, J.: Comparison of correlation analysis techniques for irregularly sampled time series. Nonlinear Process. Geophys. **18**(3), 389–404 (2011)
12. Swathi, N., Dutt, V.B.S.S.I., Sasibhushana Rao, G.: An adaptive filter approach for GPS multipath error estimation and mitigation. In: Satapathy, S.C., Rao, N.B., Kumar, S.S., Raj, C.D., Rao, V.M., Sarma, G.V.K. (eds.) Microelectronics, Electromagnetics and Telecommunications. LNEE, vol. 372, pp. 539–546. Springer, New Delhi (2016). https://doi.org/10.1007/978-81-322-2728-1_50
13. Trihinas, D., Pallis, G., Dikaiakos, M.D.: Adam: an adaptive monitoring framework for sampling and filtering on IoT devices. In: Big Data (Big Data), 2015 IEEE International Conference on, pp. 717–726. IEEE (2015)
14. van der Herten, J., Couckuyt, I., Deschrijver, D., Demeester, P., Dhaene, T.: Adaptive modeling and sampling methodologies for internet of things applications. In: Electrotechnical Conference (MELECON), 2016 18th Mediterranean, pp. 1–5. IEEE (2016)
15. Wiener, N.: Extrapolation, interpolation, and smoothing of stationary time series: with engineering applications. MIT press (1950)
16. Yurur, O., Liu, C.H., Liu, X., Moreno, W.: Adaptive sampling and duty cycling for smartphone accelerometer. In: 2013 IEEE 10th International Conference on Mobile Ad-Hoc and Sensor Systems, pp. 511–518. IEEE (2013)

Deep Anomaly Detector Based on Spatio-Temporal Clustering for Connected Autonomous Vehicles

Rachid Oucheikh[1,2]([✉]) [ID], Mouhsene Fri[3] [ID], Fayçal Fedouaki[2], and Mustapha Hain[2]

[1] National High School for the Arts and Professions, Casablanca, Morocco
[2] School of Engineering, Jönköping University, Jönköping, Sweden
rachid.oucheikh@ju.se
[3] Euro-Med University of Fes, (UEMF), Route de Meknes, Rond-point de Bensouda, 3007 Fès, Morocco
m.fri@ueuromed.org

Abstract. Connected Autonomous Vehicles (CAV) are expected to revolutionize the transportation sector. However, given that CAV are connected to internet, they face a principal challenge to ensure security, safety and confidentiality. It is highly valuable to provide a real-time and proactive anomaly detection approach for Vehicular Ad hoc Network (VANET) exchanged data since such an approach helps to trigger prompt countermeasures to be undertaken allowing the damage avoidance. Recent machine learning methods show great efficiency, especially due to their capacity to handle nonlinear problems. However, an accurate anomaly detection in a space–time series is a challenging problem because of the heterogeneity of space–time data and the spatio-temporal correlations. An anomalous behavior can be seen as normal in different context. Thus, using one deep learning model to classify the observations into normal and abnormal or to identify the type of the anomaly is usually not efficient for large high-dimensional multi-variate time-series datasets. In this paper, we propose a stepwise method in which the time-series data are clustered on spatio-temporal clusters using Long Short Term Memory (LSTM) auto-encoder for dimension reduction and Grey Wolf Optimizer based clustering. Then, the anomaly detection is performed on each cluster apart using a hybrid method consisting of Auto-Encoder for feature extraction and Convolution Neural Network for classification. The results shows an increase in the accuracy by 2% in average and in the precision by approximately 1.5%.

Keywords: Connected autonomous vehicles · Anomaly detection · Vehicular Ad hoc network · Deep learning

1 Introduction

CAV are expected to revolutionize the transportation sector. Equipped with different sensors and Internet of Things (IoT), CAV technology demonstrates

L. Foschini and M. El Kamili (Eds.): ADHOCNETS 2020, LNICST 345, pp. 201–212, 2021.
https://doi.org/10.1007/978-3-030-67369-7_15

the potential to offer high level of safety, reliability and efficiency. In fact, CAV can alleviate road congestion [8], reduce energy consumption [17], accidents and pollution [11,14]. Considering that CAV are connected to internet, they face a principal challenge to ensure security, safety and confidentiality. In fact, communication between Vehicle-to-Infrastructure (V2I) and Vehicle-to-vehicle (V2V) are based on VANET. VANET is composed of three main components: vehicular, road side unit (RSU) and Service. The mentioned challenges motivate several authors to propose frameworks to detect anomalies in the exchanged data. The anomaly detection is defined as a process of identifying outliers or abnormalities which present significantly deviation from normal activities and may indicate suspicious activities.

Anomaly detection consists of three main components **i) Point anomalies** appear randomly as a fluctuation or irregularity at a data point of data without any particular interpretation. **ii) Collective or Group Anomaly** which describes an abnormal behavior of a group of data points. Even if the isolated and individual points can be considered normal, their co-occurrence in a particular way, defined by the problem, can be anomalous. **iii) Contextual anomaly** or conditional anomaly detection refers to the problem of identifying anomalies in specific conditions. A concrete example in CAV data is that the same numbers quantifying speed or flow of vehicles in rush hours are considered anomalous in midnight. To further formalize the notion, we assume that data points are described by contextual features and behaviour features. The contextual features are generally time and space. If the behaviour attributes of a data point are considered anomalous relatively to the behaviour attributes of the data subset having the same or similar contextual attributes, then the corresponding data point is classified as a contextual anomaly.

On the other hand, the network data anomalies can be classified according to their evolution over time into three main types: abrupt, intermittent and gradual. An abrupt anomaly is a abnormal sudden change in the features of the data. This change can be expressed using the step-function which equals $x(t)$ if $t < t_f$ and $x(t) + b$ otherwise. Gradual or incipient sensor anomalies described by the function 1 are usually due to a gradual deterioration of the sensor over a long period of time. Intermittent anomalies are anomalies that appear and disappear periodically.

$$x^f(t) = \begin{cases} x(t) & if\ t < t_f \\ x(t) + s * (t - tf) & if\ t \geq t_f \end{cases} \tag{1}$$

This paper aims to detect in real-time these types of anomalies in the sensor data received by CAV taking into account their context. To achieve this goal, we propose two-phases approach. In the first phase, clustering of data is performed in order to unveil the latent the spatio-temporal features. Then, according to these resulting features, the second phase tries to detect the anomalies using a hybrid framework built upon two deep learning techniques, namely the auto-encoder and convolutional neural network (AE-CNN). The approach is lightweight and can be deployed on vehicles to provide real-time and proactive way for anomaly detection.

The remaining of this paper is organized as follows: the second section provides the background related to time series clustering. The third section introduces our proposed approach for the detection of anomalies in CAV data. Then, in the third section, a performance evaluation of the model is described and its obtained results are discussed. Finally, conclusions are drawn in Sect. 5.

2   Background

Connected autonomous Vehicle is able to connect to wireless networks and can communicate with other vehicles V2V and to infrastructure V2I. Such communication enables CAV to navigate autonomously, avoid collisions and congestion and optimize many constraints such as time and energy. While CAV increase reliability, convenience and safety of both riders and pedestrians, they also present an attack target that could be exploited. Some researches already demonstrate exploitable vulnerabilities in ordinary vehicles [1]. These vulnerabilities become more and more prevalent with the increase of number of connected vehicles. To enhance safety and security of vehicular networks, anomaly detection techniques are used to identify in real-time data points or events which do not follow an expected pattern.

The authors in [10] used machine learning on VeReMi dataset to identify and analyse anomaly behaviours using different features. They demonstrate that machine learning is an efficient method to detect anomalies. The authors in [9] proposed a spatio-temporal framework to detect anomalies in VANET network. The framework is formed by convolutional neural network and trained on dataset from real traffic simulation of a RSU and 12 On-Board Units (OBUs). The authors in [13] propose framework to detect anomaly in alert message comuunicated through VANET, the authors evaluated multiple machine learning algorithms using hyperparameters tuning.

The authors in [6] provide a mechanism, called SHIELDNET, which serves to detect and defend against the vehicular botnets. To provide effective data anomaly detection, [5] combines the characteristics of the vehicular network data and the driver's emotional state extracted using sentiment analysis. The authors design a driver's emotion quantification model to reflect the driving style. Then, output of this model and vehicle driving data are fed to the anomaly detection algorithm designed based on Gaussian mixed model. F. Ghaleb et al. proposed a context-aware data-centric misbehaviour detector which uses sequential analysis of temporal and spatial features of neighbouring vehicles' mobility information [7]. The evaluation of data consistency is performed using jointly the innovation error of the Kalman filter algorithm and Hampel filter.

The main challenge for anomaly detection on VANET is the fact that the data are unlabeled. Various techniques have been developed to draw inferences from this type of data, but they are not effective for complex, high-level structures and functionality such as those dealing with labeled datasets. Standard unsupervised techniques include clustering approaches that are used to group a set of objects together so that objects in the same group, called a cluster, are more similar to each other than to objects in other groups. Such techniques differ in the method for organizing the data as well as the metrics to measure similarity. While clustering techniques have been successfully applied to static data, their extension to time series data remains an challenging problem. Formally, the clustering task is defined as follows:

Definition 1 (Clustering). Consider m data $x_1, x_2, ..., x_m$ set of k clusters $C = \{C_1, C_2, ..., C_k\}$ and a distance measure D. Each cluster C_i is represented by its centroid $\bar{c}_i$. The objective of a clustering algorithm is to partition the data into similar groups such as the optimal clustering minimizing the within-cluster sum of squares, denoted as C^* is expressed in Eq. 2, where C_j is the cluster j and E_c is the space of cluster combinations:

$$C^* = \underset{E_c}{\operatorname{argmin}} \sum_{j=1}^{k} \sum_{x_i \in C_j} \|x_i - \bar{c}_j\|^2 \tag{2}$$

Time series are sequences of data points indexed in time order. Time series data from different domains exhibit considerable variations in important properties and features, temporal scales, and dimensionality. Further, time series data from real world applications often have temporal gaps as well as high frequency noise due to the data acquisition method and/or the inherent nature of the data. They are classified into three categories: hierarchical clustering, pure partitioning space–time series clustering and overlapping partitioning space–time series clustering.

Deep clustering is a family of clustering methods that make use of deep neural networks. It aims usually to optimize a loss function which is typically composed of two components: a) network loss L_n which allow the network to learn the most useful and representative features and avoid trivial solutions and b) clustering loss L_c that plays a discriminative role by driving the feature data extracted from the network to form disjoint groups. The total loss is expressed as: $L = \lambda L_n + (1 - \lambda)L_c$, where $\lambda \in [0, 1]$ is a hyperparameter to balance the two functions.

Recently, clustering algorithms are applied for anomaly detection in different applications including intelligent transportation systems. In [16], N. Peri et al. aim to detect anomalies such as stalled vehicles and collisions using vehicle re-identification and multi-camera vehicle tracking. The bottom up Agglomerative clustering method is used to obtain the multi-camera trajectories. In [18], the authors introduced a vehicle trajectory clustering method that employs a dynamic network representation learning upon a k-Nearest Neighbors (KNN) based internet of vehicles.

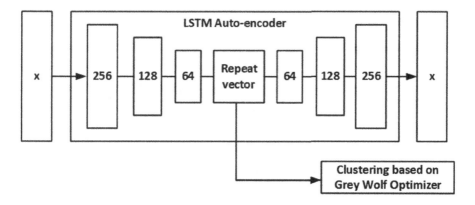

Fig. 1. Spatio-temporal clustering model's

We define the distance between two space–time series x_1 and x_2 as: $d(x_1, x_2) = d_s(x_1, x_2) + d_t(x_1, x_2)$ where d_s is the spatial distance that computes the similarity between feature points of the time-series regarding the spatial component and defines the temporal distance that determines the similarity between the time series components. The time series distance can be euclidean distance L_p or dynamic time warping (DTW).

3   Proposed Approach

The objective of the proposed framework is to provide CAV with a robust tool to detect in real-time anomalies in the networking data and signals received from on-board and external sensors. In our previous work [15], an approach is introduced to identify the type of anomaly: abrupt, intermittent or gradual. The specific aim of this paper is to increase the accuracy of anomalous event detection by considering the contextual information of the event occurrence. To achieve this goal, our proposed approach includes two main parts. First, a spatio-temporal clustering of the raw data is carried out in order to get the context of the events. The result of this phase is the clusters and the space-time subspaces in which the sensor data is similar or has the same features. Then, in the second phase, each anomaly detector is trained on a specific cluster. Regarding the inference process, the cluster of each data sequence received from the CAV is first determined, and then the anomaly detector associated to this cluster is used to classify this sequence as normal or abnormal.

The architecture of the sensor data clustering is illustrated in the Fig. 1 and consists of two main parts:

– **Dimensionality reduction:** Since the data received from the sensors are high-dimensional multivariate time-series, a LSTM auto-encoder is used to reduce their dimension and clean it from noise. The objective of the LSTM

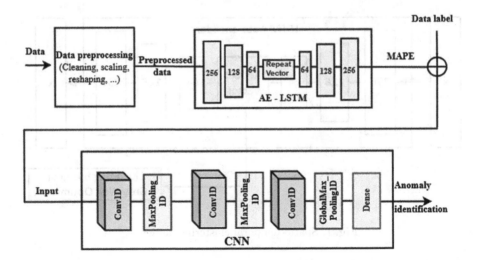

Fig. 2. The proposed model architecture to detect anomaly

auto-encoder which is an unsupervised model is to learn an approximation of the identity function since the target values are equal to those of the input. To learn this mapping, it first compresses the raw data to low dimensional space and then decompresses it to reconstruct the same data as in the input. The idea here is to make use of the compressed version of the data which is less complex, denoised and includes essential features of the original data. The asset of this step is to obtain an informative and efficient latent representation which will afford high quality clustering. As shown in Fig. 2, the network architecture consists of a consecutive LSTM layers with different sizes. This dimensionality reduction is important for further processing to avoid very long sequences which can lead to poor performance.

– **Clustering:** As shown in the Fig. 1, data with reduced dimension which is the compressed version in the decoder output is clustered using Grey Wolf Optimizer (GWO). GWO is a swarm-based metaheuristic developed by Mirjalili et al. [2]. This algorithm is inspired from hunting mechanism of grey wolves. the population of wolves is divided into four groupes, : alpha (α, γ, β and δ, the wolves omega attack the prey. GWO has widely applied in various area, such as, engineering [4], performance measurement system [12], clustering [3].

The first part of our approach provides us with spatio-temporal clusters. The second phase builds the deep models which serve to data training and inference for each cluster. Each model network consists of two components: LSTM autoencoder which builds the data features and CNN classifier which uses the built features to detect anomalous in the corresponding cluster. The overview of the proposed framework is shown in Fig. 2. Each model is trained on specific cluster and will serve for inference of that cluster. The two parts of the network model can be described as follows:

- **Extraction of signal features:** Once we identify the cluster of a data sequence representing the signal data received from the sensors, it will be fed in its raw form to the LSTM auto-encoder shown in Fig. 1. The role of this component is to learn the latent features of the normal data which is free of anomalies. For this reason, only the normal data are used to train the auto-encoder. After a full training of the auto-encoder, it will be able to accurately reconstruct the normal data and get normal outputs approximately similar to that of the original data i.e. input of auto-encoder. This means that the error of the reconstruction will be very small. In contrast, if the data fed to the trained model includes the abnormal data, the predictions will have big margin error. This way, we will be able to build a new relevant feature space. In fact, the problem of anomaly detection is originally a one class classification problem in which only the normal data is known with details. The LSTM will then differentiate the normal data from any other data whatever the anomalies it includes. In real-world the patterns of the anomaly data could be of wide spectrum. In this paper, three anomaly types are used and their error reconstruction features are obtained using the LSTM auto-encoder.

  We build the feature space using distance measure called Mean Absolute Percentage Error (MAPE) described by the Eq. 3 such that $y_{p,x}$ is the xth predicted result, $y_{a,x}$ is actual value, N is the number of predictions. The correspondent error tensor of MAPE is fed to the input of the CNN classifier.

$$MAPE = \frac{100}{N} \sum_{i=0}^{N} \frac{(y_{p,i} - y_{a,i})}{y_{a,i}} \tag{3}$$

- **Anomaly classification:** This component aims to exploit the spatial features of the vector resulting from the previous phase. The CNN model network consists of three One-dimensional convolutional layers with 32 filters and different sized kernels to allow multi-resolution data processing and thus the model can learn from these different levels and granularities. The dropout is used to reduce the overfitting by training the neural network with different architectures in parallel and dropping combination of layers in each iteration. The maxpooling operation is performed after each convolution layer to downsample the feature map representation reducing its dimensionality and allowing for detection of features contained in the sub-regions. A global pooling is applied on the 32 feature maps obtained in the output of the last convolution layer. The reason behind this layer is to downsample and summarize each feature map to a single value ready to feed to the dense layer.

4   Results and Discussion

4.1   Data Collection

To evaluate the proposed approach, we used the dataset collected by Basic Safety Messages (BSM) inside the Wyoming Connected Vehicle (CV) Pilot project [19]. The project aims to reduce incident-related delays and to improve safety in the corridor Wyoming between Canada, United States, and Mexico.

These data are received by other vehicles via Vehicle-to-Vehicle (V2V) communications to help determine immediate threats and alert drivers as necessary. The dataset includes more than 2.5 lines and consists of 69 features such as longitude, latitude and altitude (position), speed, timestamp, acceleration.

4.2   Evaluation and Results

The collected data is first cleaned and then clustering in multi-dimensional space is performed using the deep clustering model based on Grey Wolf. The results of the clustering are depicted in the Figs. 3 and 4, which show the projection in 2-dimensions and each color represents one cluster. The abscissa presents the time converted to real number under format "HHMM" such that "HH" denotes the hour and "MM" denotes the minutes. The ordinates present the scaled latitude in Fig. 3 and the scaled longitude in Fig. 4. The clustering results show that the data having the same features lie in the time intervals $[00:00, 07:00], [07:00, 10:00], [10:00, 15:30], [15:30, 20:00], [20:00, 00:00]$. Regarding the space, the clustering shows that the pieces of road having the same features are delimited by longitude and latitude values that are dynamically changing depending on the time as depicted in the figures. For example, longitude can be divided in two intervals in the early morning and three intervals in between 10 h and 15 h 30.

The data is reshaped into 3D array (samples, timesteps, features) to fit in the LSTM auto-encoder input. Afterwards, four operations are required: normal distribution scaling, window generation, shuffling, and train/test splitting. The obtained preprocessed data is used to train the auto-encoder consisting of 6 layers as described in the Fig. 1. The trained model is then used to build features of normal and anormal data. Before feeding these features to the CNN, two operations have to be performed: dimension shuffling and increase of the sample width. The CNN input is a multi-channel with a single timestep.

Some experiments have been led to evaluate the performance of our proposed model. First, we study the impact of using the contextual information on the classification performance metrics. Table 1 shows the impact of detecting anomalies according to different context. It is clear that the overall performance is increased slightly when using either temporal or spatial context. Spatial context is more informative for the considered data. Using spatio-temporal context gives more improved results with an increase of approximately 1% in the accuracy.

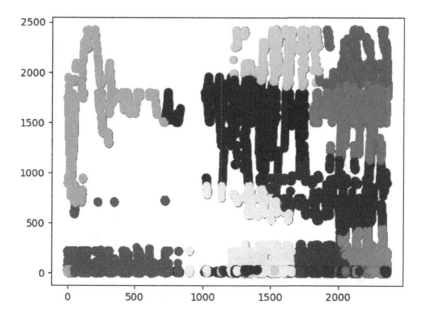

Fig. 3. Clustering results projected on time-latitude plan

The Table 2 shows the classification report of our models and includes more insights of each class. The values shown for the contextual classification represent the average of all the sixteen models for different clusters. In a binary classification scheme, a positive prediction indicates that the designated class is detected, while a negative prediction indicates that the predicted class is different. The accuracy metric allows to measure the total number of predictions a model correctly predict. The accuracies of the models lie in the interval $[92.1, 97.5]$ depending on the anomaly type and cluster.

The efficiency of the model is generally very high, but it varies depending on the anomaly type. The detection of intermittent anomalies is the easiest and the most efficient, then comes the gradual anomalies with difference of 2% in each metric, and finally the abrupt with a drop of 3%. It is worth mentioning that these results are obtained using a window size of $w = 30$.

Table 1. Impact of various contextual information on the overall detection performance

Context	Accuracy	Precision	Recall	Specificity
Temporal	93.4%	92.7%	91.5%	94.6%
Spatial	95.6%	94.5%	93.8%	95.8%
Spatio-temporal	95.7%	94.8%	93.9%	95.4%

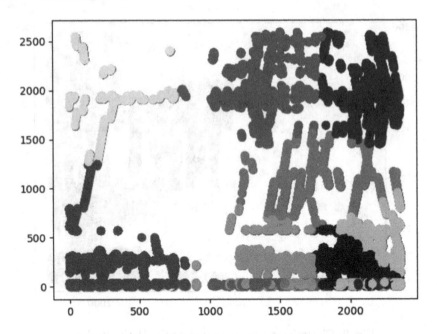

Fig. 4. Clustering results projected on time-longitude plan

The Precision score indicates the percentage of correct positive predictions among all positive predictions, this metric is useful for evaluating that the model makes correct positive predictions and not many false positive predictions. The recall score evaluates how many positive predictions are correct among the correct positive predictions, it is not affected by false-positives and is used to measure positive predictions in isolation. The Specificity score evaluates the rate of correct negative predictions, it is exactly like the Recall, but for negative predictions instead. F1-score is calculated from a balance of precision and recall. The precision increases with an average of 2.6%, the recall with 2.1% and F1-score with 2.3%.

Table 2. Impact of the contextual information on detection performance of different anomalies

Class	Precision		Recall		F1-score	
	Without context	Contextual	Without context	Contextual	Without context	Contextual
Abrupt	90.6	93.4%	89.5	91.7%	89.6	91.5%
Intermittent	94.8	96.2%	93.1	94.4%	92.3	93.8%
Gradual	91.7	94.1%	89.1	92.7%	89.7	92.9%

5   Conclusion

Anomaly detection is a crucial task required to ensure the safety and security of connected autonomous vehicles. The objective of this paper was to provide an approach based on deep learning that enhance the anomaly detector performance using the contextual information of the data received through VANET from the other vehicles. The anomalies are then detected in real-time and their type are identified accurately. The approach uses LSTM auto-encoder to reduce the data dimensions before feeding it to Grey Wolf Optimizer based clustering. To determine if a received data is anomalous, we determine first its cluster then the corresponding model network is used. In fact, each cluster has its own model which consists of LSTM auto-encoder and CNN based classifier. The error quantified by MAPE is obtained by the auto-encoder and plays the role of representative feature to the CNN based classifier which helps to distinguish normal and abnormal data. The results show good improvement comparing to the non-contextual anomaly detection. As perspective of this work, we aim to include more specific contextual events, such as festivals, sporting activities and traffic accidents. By doing this, we can handle the false alarms generated by the anomaly detection system.

References

1. Miller, C., Valasek, C.: Adventures in automotive networks and control units. Def Con **21**, 260–264 (2013)
2. Mirjalili, S., Mirjalili, S.M., Lewis, A.: Grey wolf optimizer. Adv. Eng. Softw. **69**, 46–61 (2014)
3. Kumar, V., Chhabra, J.K., Kumar, D.: Grey wolf algorithm-based clustering technique. J. Intell. Syst. **26**(1), 153–168 (2017)
4. Alahmed, A., Taiwo, S., Abido, M.: Implementation and evaluation of grey wolf optimization algorithm on power system stability enhancement. In: 2019 IEEE 10th GCC Conference and Exhibition (GCC). IEEE, April 2019
5. Ding, N., Ma, H., Zhao, C., Ma, Y., Ge, H.: Driver's emotional state-based data anomaly detection for vehicular ad hoc networks. In: 2019 IEEE International Conference on Smart Internet of Things (SmartIoT). IEEE, August 2019
6. Garip, M.T., Lin, J., Reiher, P., Gerla, M.: SHIELDNET: n adaptive detection mechanism against vehicular botnets in VANETs. In: 2019 IEEE Vehicular Networking Conference (VNC). IEEE, December 2019
7. Ghaleb, F.A., Aizaini Maarof, M., Zainal, A., Rassam, M.A., Saeed, F., Alsaedi, M.: Context-aware data-centric misbehaviour detection scheme for vehicular ad hoc networks using sequential analysis of the temporal and spatial correlation of the consistency between the cooperative awareness messages. Veh. Commun. **20**, 100186 (2019). https://doi.org/10.1016/j.vehcom.2019.100186
8. Ma, K., Wang, H.: Influence of exclusive lanes for connected and autonomous vehicles on freeway traffic flow. IEEE Access **7**, 50168–50178 (2019)
9. Nie, L., Wang, H., Gong, S., Ning, Z., Obaidat, M.S., Hsiao, K.F.: Anomaly detection based on spatio-temporal and sparse features of network traffic in VANETs. In: 2019 IEEE Global Communications Conference (GLOBECOM). IEEE, December 2019

10. Singh, P.K., Gupta, S., Vashistha, R., Nandi, S.K., Nandi, S.: Machine Learning Based Approach to Detect Position Falsification Attack in VANETs. In: Nandi, S., Jinwala, D., Singh, V., Laxmi, V., Gaur, M.S., Faruki, P. (eds.) ISEA-ISAP 2019. CCIS, vol. 939, pp. 166–178. Springer, Singapore (2019). https://doi.org/10.1007/978-981-13-7561-3_13

11. Coelho, M.C., Guarnaccia, C.: Driving information in a transition to a connected and autonomous vehicle environment: Impacts on pollutants, noise and safety. Transp. Res. Procedia **45**, 740–746 (2020)

12. Fri, M., Douaioui, K., Tetouani, S., Mabrouki, C., Semma, E.A.: A DEA-ANN framework based in improved grey wolf algorithm to evaluate the performance of container terminal. In: IOP Conference Series: Materials Science and Engineering, vol. 827, p. 012040, June 2020

13. Khot, A., Dave, M.: Position Falsification Misbehavior Detection in VANETs. In: Marriwala, N., Tripathi, C.C., Kumar, D., Jain, S. (eds.) Mobile Radio Communications and 5G Networks. LNNS, vol. 140, pp. 487–499. Springer, Singapore (2021). https://doi.org/10.1007/978-981-15-7130-5_39

14. Kopelias, P., Demiridi, E., Vogiatzis, K., Skabardonis, A., Zafiropoulou, V.: Connected and autonomous vehicles - environmental impacts - a review. Sci. Total Environ. **712**, 135237 (2020)

15. Oucheikh, R., Fri, M., Fedouaki, F., Hain, M.: Deep real-time anomaly detection for connected autonomous vehicles. Procedia Comput. Sci. **177**, 456–461 (2020). https://doi.org/10.1016/j.procs.2020.10.062

16. Peri, N., et a l.: Towards real-time systems for vehicle re-identification, multi-camera tracking, and anomaly detection. In: 2020 IEEE/CVF Conference on Computer Vision and Pattern Recognition Workshops (CVPRW). IEEE, June 2020. https://doi.org/10.1109/cvprw50498.2020.00319

17. Qu, X., Yu, Y., Zhou, M., Lin, C.T., Wang, X.: Jointly dampening traffic oscillations and improving energy consumption with electric, connected and automated vehicles: A reinforcement learning based approach. Appl. Energy **257**, 114030 (2020)

18. Wang, W., et al.: Vehicle trajectory clustering based on dynamic representation learning of internet of vehicles. IEEE Trans. Intell. Transp. Syst. **21**, 1–10 (2020). https://doi.org/10.1109/TITS.2020.2995856

19. WY Department, of Transportation: WY DOT Connected Vehicle Pilot: Improving Safety and Travel Reliability on 1–80 in W (2020). https://wydotcvp.wyoroad.info

Cacao, a CAN-Bus Simulation Platform for Secured Vehicular Communication

Olivier Cros[(✉)], Alexandre Thiroux, and Gabriel Chênevert

JUNIA, Department of Computer Science and Mathematics, 41 Boulevard Vauban, 59000 Lille, France
{olivier.cros,gabriel.chenevert}@yncrea.fr, athiroux@ssl247.fr

Abstract. In its native version, the Controller Area Network (CAN) bus protocol used in most personal vehicles does not use any encryption nor message authentication mechanism. In order to test solutions dedicated to signing messages and protecting CAN infrastructures from external attacks, we built CAn enCryption simulAtion mOdule (Cacao). It is a CAN bus simulation platform dedicated to simulate a real CAN network. The following work presents this tool and the signature solution we did integrate in it to implement various vulnerabilities protection among the CAN bus.

Keywords: CAN bus · Simulation · Signature · Framework

1 Introduction

1.1 About CAN Bus

Embedded networks are concerned by cybersecurity and protection issues. In industrial domains such as automotive or spacecraft, the CAN bus is a well-known network backbone for all internal communications. It interconnects critical and less critical subsystems, sensors and actuators in order to perform the in-vehicle communication.

Recently, the CAN bus was built in a completely closed approach, relying on the fact that a vehicle was not meant to be connect to the outside. Thus, it was built considering that each node in the CAN bus was reliable in terms of security. The CAN bus, in its standard version, does not integrate any encryption nor signature functions. Some solutions, for spacecraft for example, were to avoid these problems by defining additional specific upper layers. But that leaves the CAN standard version (used in most cars) unprotected.

But, with the emergence of Vehicle to Infrastructure (V2I), Vehicle to Everything (V2X) and similar infrastructures, cars have become more and more connected: to other cars, to tolls, to grid management, etc. These interconnections represent a wide set of potential attack vectors from the outside, targetting the vehicle critical functions through CAN bus misuse or corruption. This can imply erroneous commands, data leaks and even unwanted remote control of the vehicle, all vulnerabilities which should be corrected.

© ICST Institute for Computer Sciences, Social Informatics and Telecommunications Engineering 2021
Published by Springer Nature Switzerland AG 2021. All Rights Reserved
L. Foschini and M. El Kamili (Eds.): ADHOCNETS 2020, LNICST 345, pp. 213–224, 2021.
https://doi.org/10.1007/978-3-030-67369-7_16

1.2   Related Work

The CAN bus protocol was designed in 1983 (and 1991 for the second version [8]) as a common network backbone for embedded networks, particularly in the context of automotive and spacecraft [15]. At this time, the purpose of such a bus was to offer a common network standard for all internal communications inside a vehicle, no matter the type or number of sensors and actuators it has.

Authentication solutions for embedded networks and Cyber Physical Systems (CPS) are not new. Moreover, integrating cryptography in embedded network architectures is not an issue specific to CAN. Various approaches based on elliptic curves were already proposed for networks such as Zigbee [11] but appeared costful in terms of energy consumption and computation time. Concerning the CAN bus, both solutions MaCAN [9] and CaCAN [12] propose to encrypt data transmission inside CAN and provide key rotation solutions. Such solutions rely on CAN additional abstraction layers or extensions of the CAN protocol like CAN+ [18,21], CANAerospace [16] or either CAN-FD [10]. These solutions are fully reliable but are based on CAN additional layers, making them impossible to integrate in a simple CAN architecture without any further support for additional protocol.

Moreover, CANAuth [19] proposed a solution of frame hash inside strict CAN, based on tiny encryption [13]. This solution proposes a solution to compute a hash based on a private key (MAC algorithm). In a similar work [5] another signature protocol for CAN bus based on CANAuth was proposed. We show here its integration in Cacao.

The market of CAN bus simulation is pretty mature, and several libraries already exists such as Python-CAN [3] or CaringCaribou [2]. However, these libraries are built upon direct CAN communication whereas Cacao is architectured as a standalone CAN bus simulator which can perform virtual, real or hybrid simulation of CAN traffic. The Cacao framework is built as an additional abstraction layer of the cantools [4] library. In the following work, we intend to show and test its additional functionalities on a real CAN bus implementation.

2   The Cacao Simulator

2.1   Introduction

Cacao is the combination of a physical CAN bus simulation platform and a development framework dedicated to CAN bus analysis. The purpose of the Cacao platform is to be able to test and analyse various cryptographic and signature algorithms through CAN protocol. It is dedicated to network simulation where each sensor or actuator from an actual vehicle is represented as an independent node generating random (or configurable) data and sending it on the CAN bus. Each node is represented by a set of software modules, and all nodes in a networks are linked among them by a common CAN bus. Cacao is basically oriented for vehicle internal communications but can be extended to all contexts of use of the CAN bus protocol.

2.2   Hardware

Fig. 1. Cacao simulation tool

Physically, Cacao consists in a Raspberry Pi (RPi) based backbone with additional CAN Shields. These shields are interconnected through two CAN interfaces (high rate and low rate). The whole rack is connected to a monitoring computer through Ethernet. Cacao is built on a modular approach. We can easily interconnect any additional RPi to the structure just by connecting it to the CAN bus and ethernet monitoring network. In its native version, Cacao is composed of 5 different RPi, which was considered sufficient for our simulation purposes.

Each RPi is shielded by a PiCAN 2 shield [7] which offers a high and a low rate bus connection (compliant to CAN standards [15]). All shields are linked among themselves through both buses (high rate and low rate). The complete tool bus is pictured on Fig. 1. As we can see, each Raspberry Pi is connected by Ethernet (through a dedicated switch) to a monitoring computer (see Fig. 3).

Each RPi emulates a dedicated set of nodes, all independantly connected to the CAN bus. Each subnetwork is connected to the CAN bus through the corresponding PiCAN 2 shield. We performed various experimentations on Raspberry Pi computation power (see Subsect. 4.1) to determine that we can, in its default configuration and considering the computation potential of the RPi, further simulate 30 nodes per RPi. It means that, in the regular 5-cards configuration of Cacao, we can emulate up to 150 different nodes, which corresponds to the number of nodes found in small vehicles [17, 20].

2.3 Architecture

Cacao modelling is based on the concept of nodes. A node is a network end-point, able to send and receive messages. Each node behaves as an emission and reception entity, able to generate, send, receive and analyze its own messages. Nodes in Cacao are based on a structure of independant threads. As a result, each node is represented as a duo of threads, one for transmission and one for reception. Then, each individual node is connected to a common CAN bus.

The software part of Cacao is based on a CAN-dedicated library written in Python [1] and based on an open-source library named cantools [4]. Whereas cantools provides the basic interfaces to interconnect and send messages to the CAN bus, the threading and monitoring layer is integrated in Cacao framework directly. The software architecture of Cacao is detailed in Fig. 2.

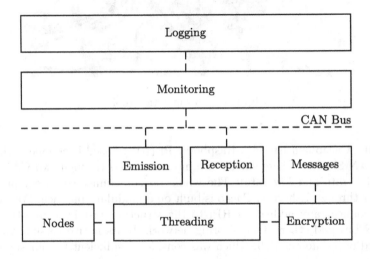

Fig. 2. Cacao framework modules

The framework is built around an object-oriented structure split into 4 different modules:

- The node module, dedicated transmission and reception (node simulation).
- The message module made for message and data management.
- The threading module allowing nodes to connect send and receive messages to and from the bus independantly.
- The monitoring module, dedicated to logging and data analysis.

This module-oriented structure integrates genericity in the tool, permitting to define additional tools as complementary functions for each module. For example, the encryption and signature functions such as the ones presented in [5] are defined as an upper layer of the message module.

In the bus, the Ethernet network is dedicated to maintenance and monitoring purposes. All the logs are centralized and managed by an administrating computer (connected to each RPi through Ethernet). All the nodes configuration and management are performed through a set of JSON configuration files (network and subnetwork size, traffic, etc.). This network architecture is detailed in Fig. 3.

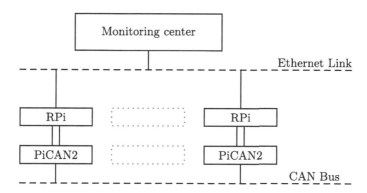

Fig. 3. Cacao architecture

2.4 Attack Model

When Cacao was designed, the primary goal was to test and improve signature solutions in the CAN bus. We detail below the attack model we target with these solutions.

Error management in the CAN bus is detailed in Fig. 4. It is based on 2 internal error counters integrated in each node. Each node has its own counters, one for transmission errors $(t_{c,n})$ and one for reception errors $(r_{c,n})$. Given a node n, when there is a difference between a message sent by n and what is on the bus (due to a message with higher priority), n will increase its internal transmission counter $t_{c,n}$ by 8 and send on the bus a message to warn that it got an error.

Once its transmission counter $t_{c,n}$ went beyond a threshold of 128, a node n is put on passive error state, meaning that it cannot warn all the other nodes anymore by sending error messages. This mechanism is further detailed in the litterature [5,8,14].

When targetting a given node for an attack, it is possible for an attacker to listen to the bus and send messages at the exact same time that the targetted node. Following this approach, the transmission error counter of the target will tend to increase. According to Fig. 4, once the transmission error counter goes beyond 255, a node will put itself in bus off mode, rendering it unable to send nor receive any message from the bus. In this situation, the node is considered,

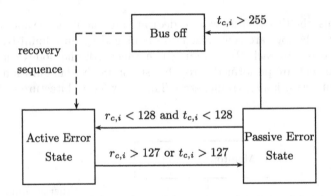

Fig. 4. Error management in CAN bus

from the point of view of the network, as dysfunctional. No further command can be sent nor received from this node, which makes it out of order for the vehicle. We can imagine attack scenarios targetting mechanics or safety-related sensors with this attack, putting the brakes or the airbag out of order in emergency situations.

3   Signature Modules

3.1   Signature Among CAN Bus

In [5], a signature solution for CAN bus was proposed, allowing to sign all messages in the network by reusing part of the CAN frames data and header to store the signature data. We summarize this process below, mostly the parts related to its integration in Cacao.

A CAN frame is composed of two different parts (see Fig. 5): a header to store the message identifier, and a payload to store the message content itself. In the CAN 2.0B version of, the number of bits (29) used to store the message identifier is higher than the number of different required ID in a regular CAN bus vehicle (around 1000) [17,20]. As a result, part of these bits (16) can be used to store signature data instead of message ID.

Algorithmically speaking, the signature of each message is computed with the SHA-256 algorithm. Each node stores local keys (see below, Sect. 3.2) and uses one specific local key (depending on the nature of the message) to compute a signature. The signature S of a given message will then depend on the local key K, the message data D and a random value r (unique for each message). The obtained signature is then truncated on 3 bytes to be integrated in the CAN frame (2 bytes in the headers, 1 byte in the payload). We keep the first three bytes of it [6]. The signature is then computed as follows:

$$S = SHA256(K \parallel D \parallel r)[0:3] \tag{1}$$

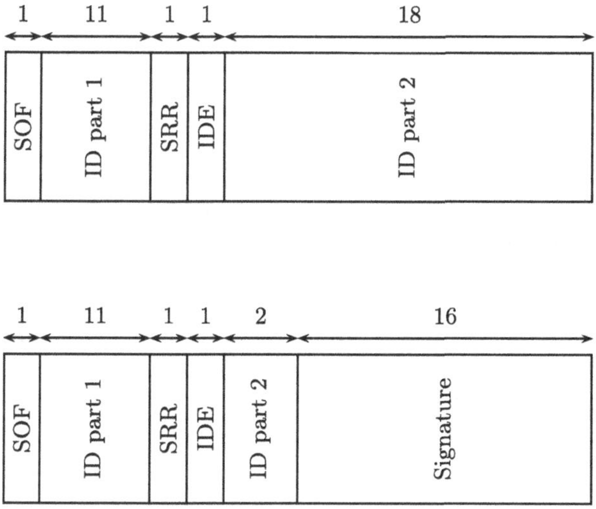

Fig. 5. CAN 2.0B protocol frames (without signature/with signature)

3.2 Group Keys

In a regular vehicle, each set of functions is associated to a given message id in the bus. For example, we have a dedicated ID for wipers speed increase, one for the decrease, one id for each steering wheel direction, a set of ids for gps tracking, etc. Each id concerns a group of sensors: each message from the steering wheel is only dedicated to be processed by specific nodes in the network. As a result, each message m_i concerns a static group of nodes determined by the network designer.

Each message can be sent to a specific set of nodes, which can be the entire bus or any subset of nodes. For example, the message corresponding to brake command will tend to concern mainly the brake pedal and the brake mechanism in the wheels. We reuse this to define groups. Each subset of nodes having, at least, one message in common is a group. If there is different messages identifiers for the same subset, then these messages will be in the same group.

In order to centralize and clarify the key management inside the simulator, a dedicated key management Application Programmable Interface (API) is integrated in the framework. The API integrates a mapping of every node in the network and its corresponding groups. Whenever a node or a message requires a specific key either to hash a message or to verify a hash, it makes a direct call.

In the section below, we call a message any data frame with a specified ID and a dedicated function. For example, hitting the brake will tend to emit a given message m_i, and hitting it several times will tend to send the same message m_i several times. Inside the CAN, there is no identification of the nodes. Only the messages are identified, and their id is transmitted in each message [8]. Each node is then configured with a set of masks and filters in order for the node to receive only the messages it is supposed to manage. Each node can be configured to receive a specific set of messages corresponding to some ids. We propose to reuse this configuration to define message groups. This mechanism filter is further detailed in [8].

Given that each message m_i is associated with a group of nodes $\mathcal{G}_i$, we propose to define an encryption key K_i for each group of nodes. This way, each node from group $\mathcal{G}_i$ will be able to sign all messages concerning specifically $\mathcal{G}_i$. Each set of messages in the same group will be associated with the same key K_i, and only the nodes concerned by a group $\mathcal{G}_i$ will get to know and be able to sign all messages with ID m_i.

For each group $\mathcal{G}_i$, we define a group key $K_{\mathcal{G}_i}$. Using this approach, we can guarantee that, even if a node is corrupted, it will be likely to corrupt only the subsets of nodes which share a common group with it instead of all of the network like it is the case in standard CAN protocol.

3.3   Generating Keys and Keymapping

Each group key $K_{\mathcal{G}_i}$ is stored locally in each node of $\mathcal{G}_i$ and is never meant to be shared among the CAN bus. Each key is pontentially unique and is generated as follows: As we can see in Fig. 6, each key is an ASCII string. This is based on the approach that the keys in the network should be manipulated by potential external operators like passwords, for maintenance purposes. In a future version of Cacao, we can imagine group keys generation by *AES* key generation algorithms.

```
i = randomint(8, 12)
key = ""
for j in range(0,i):
    key = key + randomchar()
return key
```

Fig. 6. Group key generation algorithm in Cacao

Moreover, based on a key rotation mechanism detailed in [5], the group keys are frequently changed and randomized. Doing this prevents a potential attacker to corrupt a node just by copying its internal memory. It also prevents the network designer to have to manually generate keys for each group of nodes when performing maintenance tasks. Basically, the keys are randomly generated at start.

4   Experimentations

During the simulations, we generated CAN bus traffic over 150 independant nodes. The attackers were represented by a various set of external nodes (between

1 and 5) to perform a more efficient bruteforce. Each attacking node is in charge of forging random signatures with a constant set of data. We then compute the number of triggered errors dued to these messages.

4.1   Subnetwork Size Computation

In the Cacao platform, the nodes are grouped under different RPi cards. Each card represents a subset of nodes of a given size, all the cards among themselves representing the global CAN bus network. Following this approach, we operated a benchmarking process to test which number of nodes was adequate for each card. Considering the number of cores and the scheduling of all threads linked to the nodes, if the number of nodes goes beyond a certain limit, the nodes will not be fully independant because all the threads will tend to block each other due to scheduling and performance constraints. The results of this benchmark are shown in Fig. 7.

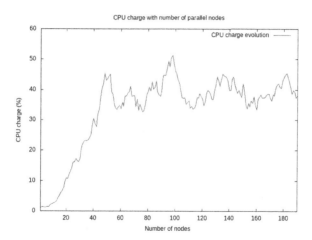

Fig. 7. CPU charge with the number of nodes

The Fig. 7 shows that, starting around 50 nodes per card, the CPU load represented by the Cacao framework will tend to converge. It means that, starting around 50 nodes per RPi, there is no more independance between the nodes and the different threads tend to block each other. In order to lower the risk and to anticipate an error margin, the default configuration of Cacao operates with 30 nodes per card.

4.2   Signature

Considering the signature solutions we integrated in the bus, performing an attack to put a node in bus-off state will now require enough messages to forge a corrupted signature, i.e. to bruteforce the signature. We developed a tool which acts as an additional set of nodes connected to the CAN, but designed to send corrupted messages in it. Through the monitoring of the bus, we counter the number of corrupted signatures which were not detected by the nodes as false. The results are shown in Fig. 8.

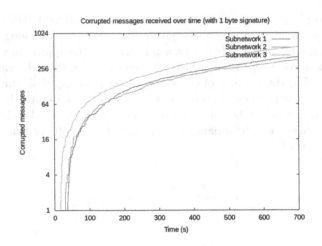

Fig. 8. Simulation of bruteforce on CACAO

In Fig. 8, we performed a simulation on 90 nodes splitted in 3 subnetworks of 30 nodes. We performed a random bruteforce attack, massively forging corrupted messages and sending them through the bus. We monitored the number of messages forged by the bruteforce tool (split on 10 threads). During the simulation, we observed the number of messages who had a valid 1-byte signature. During this duration, we also observed the number of corrupted messages who had a valid 3-bytes signature but did not observe any. This is due to the key rotation mechanism, which allowed to perform a sufficiently frequent rotation to avoid bruteforce in reasonable time (a few hours) of our signature model.

4.3   Attack Detection

In order to be able to detect a bruteforce attack on the CAN bus, we monitored the global bandwidth of the bus. These are the results shown in Fig. 9. We observed during a window of time of 80 s, with an attack during 20 s. As we can see, there is a strong increase of the used bandwidth between 50 and 70 s, which corresponds to the period during which we launched the bruteforce attack. As a conclusion, a solution to monitor the bandwidth of the CAN bus (coupled with signature implementation) could provide a potential solution to detect bruteforce attacks. Moreover, the needed time to detect an attack through bandwidth monitoring is far smaller than the needed time to forge a valid 3-bytes signature for a corrupted message. As a conclusion, our solution (tested on Cacao) can provide a sufficiently reliable signature solution to represent an interesting potential of CAN bus communication protection.

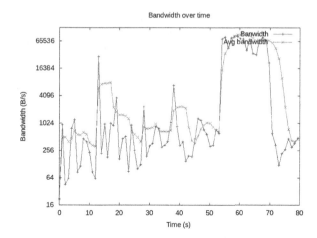

Fig. 9. Bandwidth monitoring

5   Conclusion and Perspectives

The Cacao project allows us to test various signature solutions among CAN and particularly the one developed in [5]. We conclude with the results of the benchmark that the signature protocol we provide implements a protection against the presented attacks in CAN bus. This way, we can prevent nodes to be put off the network by external attackers. It is a first step towards encryption in vehicular networks based on standard CAN and Cacao allowed us to test our solution on a real CAN infrastructure;

Thus, the perspectives of this work includes improvements to Cacao,mainly by increasing the degree of configuration available to the user but also by proposing a more advanced solution of data managing and monitoring, for example through visualization tools.

References

1. Can bus simulation framework. https://github.com/DoctorSauerkraut/canbus. Accessed 29 Sept 2020
2. Caring caribou security exploration tool. https://github.com/CaringCaribou/caringcaribou. Accessed 29 Sept 020
3. Python can bus simulation library. https://github.com/hardbyte/python-can. Accessed 29 Sept 2020
4. Python cantools. https://github.com/eerimoq/cantools. Accessed 29 Sept 2020

5. Cros, O., Chênevert, G.: Hashing-based authentication for can bus and application to denial-of-service protection. In: Cyber Security in Networking Conference CSNet 2019. IEEE (2019)
6. Dang, Q.: Recommendation for applications using approved hash algorithms. Technical report (2012)
7. Electronics, S.P.: Pican 2 datasheet. Technical report (2016)
8. GmbH, R.B.: Can specification version 2.0. Technical report (1991)
9. Hartkopp, O., Schilling, R.M.: Message authenticated can. In: Escar Conference, Berlin, Germany (2012)
10. Hartwich, F., et al.: Can with flexible data-rate. In: Proceedings of the ICC, pp. 1–9, Citeseer (2012)
11. Hoceini, O., Afifi, H., Aoudjit, R.: Authentication based elliptic curves digital signature for ZigBee networks. In: Bouzefrane, S., Banerjee, S., Sailhan, F., Boumerdassi, S., Renault, E. (eds.) MSPN 2017. LNCS, vol. 10566, pp. 63–73. Springer, Cham (2017). https://doi.org/10.1007/978-3-319-67807-8_5
12. Kurachi, R., Matsubara, Y., Takada, H., Adachi, N., Miyashita, Y., Horihata, S.: CaCAN-centralized authentication system in can (controller area network). In: 14th International Conference on Embedded Security in Cars (ESCAR 2014) (2014)
13. Jukl, M., Čupera, J.: Using of tiny encryption algorithm in can-bus communication. Res. Agric. Eng. **62**(2), 50–55 (2016)
14. Microchip: Dspic30f family reference manual, section 23. Technical report (2003)
15. Plummer, C., Roos, P., Stagnaro, L.: Can bus as a spacecraft onboard bus. In: DASIA 2003-Data Systems in Aerospace, vol. 532 (2003)
16. Ren, L.P., Zhou, J.: Canaerospace-upper layer protocol for can and its design application. Measur. Control Technol. **2**, 59–61 (2008)
17. Stence, R.W.: Digital by-wire replaces mechanical systems in cars. Technical report, SAE Technical Paper (2004)
18. Stock, M.: Interface specification for airborn can applications v1.7. Technical report (2006)
19. Van Herrewege, A., Singelee, D., Verbauwhede, I.: Canauth-a simple, backward compatible broadcast authentication protocol for can bus. In: ECRYPT Workshop on Lightweight Cryptography, vol. 2011 (2011)
20. Wang, Q., Sawhney, S.: Vecure: a practical security framework to protect the can bus of vehicles. In: 2014 International Conference on the Internet of Things (IOT), pp. 13–18. IEEE (2014)
21. Ziermann, T., Wildermann, S., Teich, J.: Can+: a new backward-compatible controller area network (CAN) protocol with up to 16× higher data rates. In: Proceedings of the Conference on Design, Automation and Test in Europe, pp. 1088–1093. European Design and Automation Association (2009)

Author Index

AbdAllah, Eslam G.   44
Alfandi, Omar   3
Aloqaily, Osama I.   100
Andrieux, Guillaume   29
Azer, Marianne A.   44

Badawy, Wael   44
Baras, John S.   55
Berrada, Ismail   179, 191
Bitaillou, Alexis   29
Bouhoute, Afaf   179
Brown, J. David   70

Chênevert, Gabriel   213
Cros, Olivier   213

Dapaah, Emmanuel Charleson   164

El Kamili, Mohamed   179
El Ouazzany Ech-chahedy, Imane   179
Elgammal, Ali   44
Ezzini, Saad   191

Fedouaki, Fayçal   201
Fri, Mouhsene   201

Gholami, Anousheh   55

Hain, Mustapha   201
Hogrefe, Dieter   164
Huang, Changcheng   44

Jalel, Ben Othman   87

Kulkarni, Adita   16
Kunz, Thomas   130, 147

Lung, Chung-Horng   130

Memarmoshrefi, Parisa   164

Otoum, Safa   3
Ouardini, Anas   179
Oucheikh, Rachid   201
Oumaima, El Joubari   87

Papagianni, Chrysa   55
Parrein, Benoît   29

Rydzewski, Karol   116

Safwat, Mena   44
Salmanian, Mazda   70
Seetharam, Anand   16

Thiroux, Alexandre   213
Torkzaban, Nariman   55

Véronique, Vèque   87

Willink, Tricia J.   70

Yehdego, Hermon   3

Zahmatkesh, Afsane   130

Printed in the United States
By Bookmasters